*This book is dedicated
to the memory of*

MARTIN LUTHER KING, JR.

*a Black American whose life
was so beautiful as to be unbearable.*

BOOKS BY C. ERIC LINCOLN

My Face Is Black
The Black Muslims in America
The Negro Pilgrimage in America
Sounds of the Struggle

IN SYMPOSIA (Selected)

The Outlook for Youth
Assuring Freedom to the Free
Die Herausforderung des Islam
Sermons to Men of Other Faiths and Traditions
Minority Problems
The American Negro Reference Book
Poverty, Education and Race Relations

Is Anybody Listening

to Black America?

Edited, with an Introduction

by C. ERIC LINCOLN

 THE SEABURY PRESS • NEW YORK

A Word of Thanks . . .

Without the cooperation of the persons named below and the publishers, radio and television stations, journals, magazines, and newspapers quoted and acknowledged throughout the text, this work, humble as it is, could not have been accomplished. I am grateful for their cooperation, and I absolve them from the responsibility, which I alone must bear.

My thanks to Rae Pace Alexander, James Cone, Sally Dennison, Sally Jelinek, Lawrence Jones, Lucy Cook Lincoln, Joan Nichols, Catherine O'Reilly, Charles Sutton, Leon Watts, and Juanita Wright.

C. Eric Lincoln

Second Printing

Every attempt has been made to trace the ownership of all copyrighted selections included in this book and to make proper acknowledgment thereof. If error has inadvertently occurred, the Seabury Press will make the necessary correction in subsequent editions provided notification is received. In selections quoted at some length, where there were no subheadings in the original text, the Editor has inserted, as subheadings, phrases or statements from the text that identify the subject matter for the convenience of the readers.

Copyright © 1968 by The Seabury Press, Incorporated
Library of Congress Catalog Card Number: 68–29829
610–868–C–10–5
Printed in the United States of America

Introduction

This is a book about contemporary America. It is a book about how Americans perceive themselves and their place in society, and how they perceive each other across the barrier of *color*. Color is important in America. Perhaps it is the most important value Americans know about. We behave as though it is. When Americans talk about people, it is very important to know whether the discussion is about *white* people or *black* people. If the color of the subject is in doubt, the validity and the meaning of what is said is left in jeopardy.

In this book, Americans themselves are speaking—by color, about *race*. In our country, color is made to function as an (unsophisticated and frequently unreliable) index to racial identity. Race is really what our problem is all about. Color provides the chief visual data of racial identification. The life chances of every American are affected by these data.

For the most part, "white people" and "black people" occupy different ends of the socioeconomic scale, with black people at the least favored extremity. The access Black Americans have to political, social, or economic status is limited and controlled by Americans who are white. How Black Americans view this arrangement, and how white Americans react to their views, is what I have tried to capture in this brief volume. This is not intended to be a "balanced presentation" of the issues, nor of their merits. I have not consciously weighted the arguments of one race against the other. Nor have I sought necessarily to provide "equal space" for contending ideologies *within* one group or the other. My basic intent has been to present a *spectrum* of black opinion and a *spectrum* of white response. Judgments as to the reasonableness of one position in contrast to another are left to the reader. If some opinions seem underrepresented, this may be charged to the fact that since my chief sources have been the news media, some data were more plentiful and more readily available than others.

Neither black America nor white America speaks with a single voice. Nor do the "spokesmen" for the black community always say what is representative of black opinion any more than is true of their white counterparts. Part Two represents an effort to provide a forum in which Black Americans express themselves as individuals, apart from any leadership function they may have. Obviously there are problems in attempting this: who is a leader, and when is he expressing a leadership function? Are sociologists, novelists, ministers, leaders—merely because they write or speak? Does a black militant who is interviewed on TV become a "spokesman" for the black ghetto?

Because of the impossibility of resolving these and similar problems, there is much overlap in Part One, where "spokesmen" are "speaking for the people" and Part Two, where "the people speak for themselves." Some individuals appear in both sections. Part Three, "Is Anybody Listening," is treated as a unit, not because white "spokesmen" are necessarily representative or because white opinion is monolithic, but only because the section is concerned with white response as a total category.

The murder of Martin Luther King, Jr., coincided with the conclusions of my research for this book. With all my heart I regret the occasion to honor him by dedicating this paltry offering to his memory. Our perspectives were not always in agreement, but there was never a time when his courage, his nobility, and his love for humankind did not excite my admiration and support. I can only hope that as he speaks again from these pages, someone will be listening.

C. ERIC LINCOLN

Union Theological Seminary
New York City
April, 1968

CONTENTS

PART ONE

Speaking for the People

I Just Want to Do God's Will

"A great revolution is taking place in our world, a social revolution in the minds and souls of men. And it has been transformed into a unified voice, crying out, 'We want to be free.' "—*1960*

"It may get me crucified. I may even die. But I want it said even if I die in the struggle that 'He died to make men free.' "—*1962*

"So listen to me, children: Put on your marching shoes; don'cha get weary; though the path ahead may be dark and dreary; we're walking for freedom, children."—*1962*

"In the spirit of the darkness of this hour, we must not despair, we must not become bitter —we must not lose faith in our white brothers."—*1963*

"I have a dream that my four little children will one day live in a nation where they will not be judged by the color of their skin but by the content of their character. I have a dream. . . ." —*1963*

"The question is not whether we will be extremist but what kind of extremist we will be. Will we be extremists for hate or will we be extremists for love? Will we be extremists for the preservation of injustice—or will we be extremists for the cause of justice?"—*1963*

"Some of you have knives, and I ask you to put them up. Some of you have arms, and I ask you to put them up. Get the weapon of nonviolence, the breastplate of righteousness, the armor of truth and just keep marching."—*1964*

"I believe that unarmed truth and unconditional love will have the final word in reality. That is why right, temporarily defeated, is stronger than evil triumphant." —*1964*

"What good does it do to be able to eat at a lunch counter if you can't buy a hamburger?" —*1965*

"The Negro needs the white man to free him from his fears. The white man needs the Negro to free him from his guilt."— *1966*

"Like anybody, I would like to live a long life. Longevity has its place. But I'm not concerned about that now. I just want to do God's will. . . ."—*Memphis, April 3, 1968*

"I want you to sing for me tonight. I want you to do that song for me, 'Precious Lord, Take My Hand.' Sing it real pretty." —*Memphis, April 4, 1968*

MARTIN LUTHER KING, JR.,
Southern Christian Leadership Conference

"This thing is becoming two armed camps, but it's a risk black people arc willing to take. Look, we started the whole civil-rights business with two Presidents who both told Martin Luther King we can't get a civil-rights bill—it's impossible. But the pressure of events made it possible. Confrontation is both inevitable and creative. There's nobody who can call in anybody and turn it off."

JOHN CONNERS, Detroit, U.S. Representative
(*Newsweek,* Nov. 20, 1967)

Christianity and Black Power

by James H. Cone

My purpose is to examine the concept of Black Power and its relationship to Christianity and the Church. Some religionists would consider Black Power the work of the Antichrist. Others would suggest that such a concept should be tolerated as an expression of Christian love to the misguided black brother. It is my thesis, however, that Black Power, even in its most radical expression, is not an antithesis of Christianity, nor is it a heretical idea to be tolerated with painful forbearance. It is rather Christ's central message to 20th Century America. And unless the empirical denominational Church makes a determined effort to recapture the Man Jesus through a total identification with the suffering poor as expressed in Black Power, that Church will become exactly what Christ is not.

The Church Must Be Prophetic

That most churches see an irreconcilable conflict between Christianity and Black Power is evidenced not only by the structure of their community (the 11:00 a.m. hour on Sunday is still the most segregated hour of any weekday), but by their typical response to riots: "I deplore the violence but sympathize with the reasons for the violence." What churchmen, laymen and ministers alike, apparently fail to recognize is their contribution to the ghetto-condition through permissive silence—except for a few resolutions which they usually pass once a year or immediately following a riot—and through their cotenancy with a dehumanizing social structure whose existence depends on the enslavement of black people. If the Church is to remain faithful to its Lord, it must make a decisive break with the structure of this society by launching a vehement attack on the evils of racism in all forms. It must become *prophetic,* demanding a radical change in the interlocking structures of this society.

Of course the Church must realize, in view of the Christian doctrine of man, that this is a dangerous task. But obedience to Christ is always costly. The time has come for the Church to challenge the power-structure with the power of the *Gospel,* knowing that nothing less than *immediate* and *total* emancipation of all people is consistent with the message and style of Jesus Christ. The Church cannot afford to deplore the means which oppressed people use to break the chains of slavery because such language not only clouds the issue but also gives comfort and assistance to the oppressor. Therefore, I hope to be able to show that embracing Black Power is not only possible but necessary if the Church wants to remain faithful to the traditions of Christianity as disclosed in the person of Jesus Christ.

Definition of Black Power

What does Black Power mean? It means nothing other than full emancipation of black people from white oppression by whatever means black people deem necessary. The methods may include selective buying, boycotting, marching, or even rebellion. Black Power, therefore, means black freedom, black self-determination, wherein black people no longer view themselves as animals devoid of human dignity but as men, human beings with the ability to carve out their own destiny. In short, as Stokely Carmichael would say, Black Power means T. C. B., Taking Care of Business—black folk taking care of black folk's business not on the terms of the oppressor, but those of the oppressed.

Black Power is analogous to Albert Camus' understanding of the rebel. The rebel is the man who says no and yes; he says no to conditions considered intolerable, and yes to that "something within him which 'is worth while . . .' and which must be taken into consideration." (*The Rebel* [New York: Random House, 1956], p. 13.) He says no to "the humiliating orders of his master," and by so doing testifies to that something which is placed above everything else, including life itself. To say no means that death is preferable to life, if the latter is devoid of freedom. In the words of the Black Spiritual, "before I be a slave I'll be buried in my grave." This is what Black Power means.

Blacks Should Keep Their "Cool"

Unfortunately, many well-intentioned persons have insisted that there must be another approach, one which will not cause so much hostility, not to mention rebellion. Therefore, appeal is made to the patience of black people to keep their "cool" and not to get carried away by their feelings. These men argue that if any progress is to be made, it will be through a careful, *rational* approach to the subject. These people are deeply offended when black people refuse to listen and place such liberals in the same category as the most adamant segregationists. They simply do not see that such reasoned appeals merely support the perpetuation of the ravaging of the black community. Black Power, in this respect, is by nature *"irrational,"* i.e., not denying the role of rational reflection, but insisting that human existence cannot be mechanized or put into neat boxes according to reason. Human reason, though valuable, is not absolute, because moral decisions—those decisions which deal with human dignity—cannot be made by using the *abstract* methods of science. Human emotions must be reckoned with. Consequently, black people must say "No!" to all do-gooders who insist that they need more time. If such persons really knew oppression—knew it existentially in their guts—they would not be confused or disturbed by black rebellion, but would join black people in their fight for freedom and dignity. It is interesting that most people do understand why Jews can hate Germans. Why can they not also understand why black people, who have been deliberately and systematically murdered by the structure of this society, hate white people? The general failure of Americans to make this connection suggests that the primary difficulty is their inability to see black men as men.

The Source of Hatred

This leads us to another reason why the concept of Black Power is rejected. Some persons would have us believe that advocating Black Power creates too much resentment or hate among black people and this makes significant personal relationship between black and white impossible. It should be obvious that the hate which black people feel toward white is not due to the creation of the phrase "Black Power." Rather it is a result of the deliberate and systematic ordering of society on the basis of racism, making black alienation not only possible but inevitable. For three hundred years black people have been enslaved by white power. For three hundred years they have cried, waited, voted, marched, picketed, and boycotted, but whites still refuse to recognize their humanity. In light of this, attributing black resentment to the creation of Black Power is ridiculous, if not obscene.

Furthermore while it is true that black people do hate whites, it is misleading to suggest that hatred is essential to the definition of Black Power. Carmichael denies the "black supremacy" charge: "There is no analogy—by any stretch of definition or imagination —between the advocates of Black Power and white racists. . . . The goal of the racists is to keep black people on the bottom, arbitrarily and dictatorially, as they have done in this country for over three hundred years. The goal of black self-determination and black self-identity—Black Power—is full participation in the decision-making processes affecting the lives of black people." (Stokely Carmichael and Charles Hamilton, *Black Power: The Politics of Liberation in America* [New York: Random House, 1967], p. 47.) In hate, one desires something which is not his; but the black man's intention is to claim what *is* his—freedom. It is not the purpose of the black man to repudiate his enslaver's dignity, but only his presumption as an enslaver. The rebellion in the cities should not be interpreted as the work of a few blacks who want something for nothing, but as an assertion of the dignity of black people who have been deprived of everything. The black man is assuming that there is something of value common to all men, something that is implied in being human. In his rebellion, he is testifying to his determination to have that "something" recognized. He is expressing his sense of solidarity with the human race.

The Options

In reality, then, *accommodation* or *protest* seem to be the only options opened to the black man. For three hundred years he accommodated, thereby giving credence to his own enslavement. Black Power means that he will no longer accommodate; that he will no longer tolerate white excuses for enslavement; that he will no longer be guided by the oppressor's distortion of justice. He recognizes the difference between theoretical equality and factual inequality. He will not sit by any longer waiting for the white man's love to bridge the chasm the white man needs for his psychic security. He will protest, violently if need be, in the interest of absolute emancipation. Now! Whenever one group breaks the human covenant of mutual respect for human freedom, the seeds of rebellion are implicit in that act.

Many concerned persons have pointed out the futility of black rebellion by contrasting the present conditions of the black man in the ghetto and other revolutionaries of the past. They say that successful revolution depends on cohesion, discipline, stability and the sense of a stake in society. The ghetto, by contrast, is relatively incohesive, unorganized, unstable and the number of potential revolutionaries is too small to be effective. Therefore, it is argued, rebellion for the black man can only mean his extermination.

The rebellion in the cities is not an effort to take over; it is the Black American's attempt to say *yes* to his own dignity even in death. Nor is the question whether black people are prepared to die. The rebellions testify to their willingness. The crucial question is whether whites are prepared to kill them. Perhaps that answer is also implicit in the death tolls we tabulate at the end of every American summer. This willingness of black people to die is not novel. It is a part of the heritage of Christianity. Christians know how to suffer and die for what is right.

The Message of Black Power Is the Message of Christ

It is ironic that America prides itself as a Christian nation when it has never learned either love or contrition. It is even more ironic that the typical member of the Christian establishment has neither the strength of will to do justice, nor the courage to suffer for what is just. The Christian man knows that while God's ultimate kingdom is in the future, God's present concern is ever with the oppressed and the persecuted.

When we make Jesus' message contemporaneous with our life situation, his message is clear enough. The message of Black Power is the message of Christ Himself. To be sure, that statement is both politically and religiously dangerous. It is so politically because Black Power threatens the very structure of the American way of life. It is theologically dangerous because it may appear to overlook what Karl Barth has called "the infinite qualitative distinction between God and man." But if Luther's statement, "we are Christ to the neighbor" is to be taken seriously, and, if we can believe the New Testament witness which proclaims Jesus as resurrected and thus active even now in the midst of human misery, then he must be alive in men who are where the action is. If the Gospel is a gospel of liberation for the oppressed, then Jesus is where the oppressed are—proclaiming release to the captives and looking askance at those Christians who silently consent to their discomfiture. If Jesus is *not* in the ghetto, if he is not where men are living at the edge of existence, if he is somehow ensconced in the split-level hypocrisy of suburbia, then the Gospel is a prevarication and Christianity is a mistake. Christianity cannot be alien to Black Power; it *is* Black Power!

The Church and Black Power

What is the Church and its relationship to Christ and Black Power? According to the New Testament, the Church is the *laos theou,* the "people of God." It is a community of people who have encountered God's action in history and thus desire to participate in Christ's continued work of liberation. As Bonhoeffer puts it: the Church is "Christ existing as community" or Christ's "presence in history." This means that the Church's work and message is nothing other than a continuation of the message and work of Christ. It is, as Barth puts it, "God's provisional demonstration of his intention for all humanity."

If the real Church is the *laos theou* whose primary task is that of being Christ to the world by proclaiming the message of the gospel (*kerygma*), by rendering services of liberation (*diakonia*), and by being itself a manifestation of the nature of the new society (*koinonia*), then the empirical Church has failed on all counts. It certainly has not rendered service of reconciliation to the poor. Rather it illustrates the values of a sick society which oppresses the poor. The chief mistake of the contemporary theologians who have announced the death of God lies in their apparent identification of God's reality with the signed-up Christians. If we were to identify the work of God with the denominational Church, then, like Altizer, we must "will the death of God with a passion of faith." Or as Camus would say, "If God *did* exist, we should have to abolish Him!"

The Church has not only failed to render service to the poor, but also failed miserably at being a visible manifestation of God's intention for humanity. It seems that the Church is not God's redemptive agent but rather an agent of secular society. It fails to create an atmosphere for radical obedience to Christ. Some Church fellowships are more concerned about smoking or temperance than about children who die of rat bites or men who are killed because they want to be treated like men. The society is falling apart for want of moral leadership and moral example, but the Christian Church passes innocuously pious resolutions and waits to be congratulated.

The Church does not appear to be a community willing to pay up personally. It is not a community which views every command of Jesus as a call to the cross. Rather it sits in hypocritical judgment on the results of its own complicity in a conspiracy of evil. And it intimidates those clergymen who confuse popularity with integrity. When a minister blesses by silence the conditions which produce riots and condemns the rioters, he forfeits the right to his credentials as a Christian minister and becomes inhuman. He is an animal—just like any other racist. The Church needs men who can themselves refuse to be animals in order that the whole society may be uplifted. Perhaps Black Power is the key to the spirit that is lacking.

James H. Cone is Professor of Philosophy at Adrian College, Adrian, Michigan.

The Sevenfold Path of Blackness

US doctrine is a shield to protect you, a weapon to attack with and a pillow of peace to rest your head on.

The Seven-fold path of Blackness is to Think Black, Talk Black, Act Black, Create Black, Buy Black, Vote Black, and Live Black.

To go back to tradition is the first step forward.

Nationalism in its primitive stage uproots people without giving them an alternative. We never take away what we can't replace and improve.

We must institute holidays which speak directly to the needs of Black people.

Nationalism is a belief that Black people in this country make up a cultural nation.

A cultural nation is a people with a common past, a common present and, hopefully, a common future.

Our society may be American, but our values must be Afro-American.

Yesterday we thought we were Negroes. Today we know we are Black men but we still have some Negro hang-ups.

We stress culture because it gives identity, purpose and direction. It tells us who we are, what we must do, and how we can do it.

If we can wear a French beret, a Russian hat and Italian shoes and not feel funny, we should be able to wear an Afro-American Buba.

Man is only man in a philosophy class or a biology lab. In the world he is African, Asian or South American. He is a Chinese making a cultural revolution, or an Afro-American with soul. He lives by bread and butter, enjoys red beans and rice, or watermelon and ice-cream.

No man is any more than the context to which he owes his existence.

Maulana Ron Karenga, in *Black Power Revolt*, ed. by Floyd B. Barbour (Boston: Porter Sargent, 1968) pp. 165-168. Reprinted by permission of Ronald Hobbs Literary Agency, New York City.

Culture is the basis of all ideas, images and actions. To move is to move culturally, i.e., by a set of values given to you by your culture.

The seven criteria for culture are:

1. Mythology
2. History
3. Social Organization
4. Political Organization
5. Economic Organization
6. Creative Motif
7. Ethos

Negroes have been copying white culture so long and are so mixed-up from doing so, they think it's theirs.

Culture provides the bases for revolution and recovery.

To talk Black is to start talking "we" instead of "me."

Revolution

The revolution being fought now is a revolution to win the minds of our people. If we fail to win this we cannot wage the violent one.

A revolt is an attempt to overthrow the system; while the revolution is the complete overthrow of that system.

A lot of brothers play revolutionary; they read a little Fanon, a little Mao and some Marx. Although this information is necessary it is not sufficient for we must develop a new plan of revolution for Black people here in America.

You can't fight a revolution on a local level. It has to be fought through a national struggle.

We must fight for the right of self-determination, race pride and the pursuit of Blackness.

The only thing that will make us invincible is for us to fight— to fight for our freedom and not our personal selves—to fight to get back the freedom we lost in 1565.

Negroes who envy leaders who have an education don't understand revolution. Mao had an education; Nkrumah had an education; all people who have waged revolution have had an education. But the thing that keeps them revolutionary is that they are tired of the ways of the white man.

The more you learn, the more resentful you are of this white man. Then you see how he's tricking your people, emasculating your men, raping your women and using his power to keep you down.

The white boy has been waging a race war ever since he has been here. Now that we plan to retaliate he calls us racists.

Blacks live right in the heart of America. That is why we are best able to cripple this man. And once we understand our role we won't talk revolution, we'll make it.

The white boy knows if he moves against us he moves against himself. If he drops an A-bomb it's got to get some of them. If he drops poison gas the wind might change and it will go to his neighborhood.

When the word is given we'll see how tough you are. When it's "burn", let's see how much you burn. When it's "kill", let's see how much you kill. When it's "blow up", let's see how much you blow up. And when it's "take that white girl's head too", we'll really see how tough you are.

Whenever Blacks revolt, white people use every issue but racism as the cause.

The sad thing about revolution is that the strong brothers will be moved on first. It will be the dead brother who wakes up who will continue the revolution.

We are revolutionists. We believe in change. We believe in being realistic, but as for reality, we have come to change it.

We cannot have a revolution without direction, and that direction can only come through an ideology developed for our own situation.

To play revolution is to get put down.

We are the last revolutionaries in America. If we fail to leave a legacy of revolution for our children we have failed our mission and should be dismissed as unimportant.

Revolution to us is the creation of an alternative.

There must be a cultural revolution before the violent revolution. The cultural revolution gives identity, purpose and direction.

We must gear the money going from the church to the support of the revolution. Revolution cannot succeed without finance.

No revolt is isolated. When Blacks revolt in any section of the country it is an expression of the entire nation of Afro-America.

The American revolution is sacred to whites, and Black revolts are sacred to us.

If we fight we might be killed. But it is better to die as a man than live like a slave.

Black people must understand history and from historical knowledge we can evolve our own theory of revolution.

There are two kinds of violent movements. The first is defensive violence and the second is pre-emptive violence which means moving against the enemy if you know the enemy is going to move against you.

We say with Touré that for *US* there are no intellectuals, no students, no workers, no teachers; there are only supporters of the organization.

I remember my mother used to tell me—if you're bad the devil will get you. I didn't know that until the cops came.

MAULANA RON KARENGA,
Founder, US Organization

"To attempt to merge the civil rights movement with the peace movement, or to assume that one is dependent upon the other, is in our judgment a serious tactical mistake. It will serve the cause neither of civil rights nor of peace.

"We are not a peace organization nor a foreign policy association. We are a civil rights organization. The N.A.A.C.P. remains committed to its primary goal of eliminating all forms of racial discrimination and achieving equal rights and equal opportunities for all Americans."

ROY WILKINS, NAACP

On Love and Power

by The Reverend Lawrence N. Jones

In the black ghettoes the Gospel is more and more suspect as being antithetical if not in downright opposition to the legitimate aspirations of the persons to whom it is proclaimed. The attacks here are on the political grounds that the Gospel, in substance, is conservative, in collusion with the status quo, and an instrument of the privileged to solidify their exploitation of the disprivileged.

The attack directed at the black churches is both from within and from without. From without, black churches are criticized as bastions of institutionalized passivity. They are considered, in some instances with devastating accuracy, as having such a vested interest in the status quo as to stand in veritable opposition to change. Moreover, the clergy in these churches are portrayed as being pastoral entrepreneurs whose security and privileges are so linked to life as it is as to force them to be in opposition to any significant altering of things as they are. The predominantly white churches in America do not escape the criticism of the ghetto dweller either. The white churches are objects of scorn because they have sold out, many of them, to a racist culture.

Hard Questions for Black Ministers

Black clergymen bear the brunt of the attack. Challenged as "Uncle Toms" by persons outside the church and confronted by congregations that are increasingly sensitized to the injustices of the society, black ministers are hard pressed to answer their critics. Among these questions are some on this order: "Is it possible to be a Christian and fight for social change if you are black?" "Can one defend the doctrine of the unity of the body of Christ, when in fact it is segmented along historic lines reaching back into slavery times, and when it appears that the majority of white Christians apparently see no contradiction of the gospel in this segregated church?"

Some black clergymen, such as Detroit's Albert Cleage have

wrestled with these questions and have come up with unorthodox solutions. Mr. Cleage's solution is to remythologize the Scriptures in such a way as to emphasize their essential compatibility with black nationalism and revolution. This "transformed" racialized Gospel upon which radical surgery has been performed, is heavily laced with words of judgment directed at the white Christian community for its complicity in the racism of the Church and American society. We should not write the Reverend Mr. Cleage off, he is not kidding, he is deadly serious—he is trying to find a way to remain within the Christian faith and to find that faith in the service of the legitimate aspirations of the community he serves.

I heard one clergyman in the ghetto say that he was going to amend the New Testament passage which says, "If your enemy smites you on one cheek turn the other," by adding, "but if he smites you on the other cheek knock hell out of him." In an unambiguous way and with almost unanimous agreement, the enemy, as the ghetto dweller sees him, is anyone who has white skin. In more colloquial terms, he is "whitey." Now for white persons whose self-conception does not fit this image, this is unjust and irrational if not paranoid. But in large measure it conforms to the experience which too many black men have known. Not to see whitey as the enemy, not to be suspicious of him would seem to them to be irrational, because their uninterrupted experience of the white man has been that of being victimized by him. All around are concrete evidence of exploitation: poor housing, inferior schools, lack of job opportunity, coercive, often brutal police presence, injustice in the courts—all the ways in which social power is exerted against him are ultimately in the hands of white men. Insofar as black men feel themselves to be victimized by the establishment which is clearly within the control of white men, whitey is the victimizer and hence the enemy. For the typical ghetto dweller the identity of the ultimate enemy is clear. The question that confronts the black Christian is clear, too: How do you love this man without acquiescing in the injustice that is visited upon you?

Take the World, But Give Me Jesus

Part of the reason why the principle of love, as the Christian community has understood it, is a problem is that the conventional and to some extent the historical understanding of love does seem to counsel passivity in the face of massive social injustice. An old spiritual, often sung in black churches, has this refrain, "you take the world and give me Jesus." The orientation of the preaching emphasized negative piety in this world in the hope of reward in a world to be. The principal characteristics of Christian love as conventionally preached were self-effacement, submissiveness, and uncritical acceptance of what life brought to one. To love was to have consistent unambiguous feelings of good will towards everyone. Love was conceptualized primarily as an emotion or feeling and as an ethical norm governing one's relations with the neighbor immediately at hand. The posture towards the enemy was one of acceptance and deference and self-effacement. The consequences of this understanding of love cut the nerve of any significant movement to social reform because it was felt that such activities were at root incompatible with love.

This dominant understanding of love and its rejection have to be seen against the backdrop of life within the community. Throughout the areas of concentrated racial community there has been an intensification of indignation and resentment growing out of an increased awareness of the injustice of discrimination, heightened expectations of change which have not been realized, and increasing lack of confidence in the capacity of the establishment and of individual white men really to deliver on the "promissory" note given in the Constitution and promised by those in power. How love the enemy, as love has been customarily understood, when he dehumanizes and degrades, and exploits you?

An additional dimension of this understanding of love was that love only prevails when there are peace and harmony. Suffering was to be absorbed into oneself, internalized—long-suffering in the face of evil, conspicuous evil was extolled as a virtue. Heaven was pictured as the place where all injustice would be redressed— where deferred dreams would come true. Place this understanding of love as the reign of peace and harmony over against the legitimate aspirations of black men for full equality and dignity in the society, and hear the way in which it strikes a discordant note in the midst of the ferment for change.

Just now the black community is severely agitated by the riot reports from Newark which show the police as expressing rabid racism under cover of law enforcement, but more particularly the community is outraged at the events in Orangeburg, South Carolina, where with three students dead, nearly fifty students injured, all the elements that describe a massacre are present. The students had no weapons. It is evident that what you had here was the catharsis of hate and racist feeling under the guise of law enforcement. The covert power of the state is always present, but in recent times the overt power of the state as an instrument of institutionalized injustice has become increasingly clear. The tragedy is compounded in the Orangeburg instance that there is no recourse in the courts. What then is the response of a community to this kind of activity? Must it forgive? In her powerful play, "Raisin in the Sun," Lorraine Hansberry asked poignant questions to this effect: Why must black men always forgive; why must they stand still in the face of injustice? It appears to be the case to many persons in our society that the only way to combat injustice is by directing violence against those who perpetrate violence against you. How love the enemy who brutalizes you, who robs you of your manhood, and who can do it all under the flag and in support of a system of law and order that you experience as being antithetical to your best interests? This is the dilemma of the black Christian.

No Power, No Voice

Not only has love been delineated as signifying the absence of conflict and acquiescence in an unjust status quo, but it has also been associated with powerlessness. In this view, in order truly to love, one had to resign power, since power was seen as a denial of love. To use Professor Tillich's fine phrase, what we had here was "powerless love and loveless power." Love defined as being empty of power goes against the facts of reality as well as against an even superficial understanding of what it means to be human. As Silberman has so well emphasized, one of the primary areas of self-awareness that has come to black men has been their recognition of and their frustration in connection with their powerlessness. These men have come to see that in our society as in human relationships of more intimate scope, one has no voice if one has no power; one has no initiative with regard to one's destiny if one has no power; one cannot command respect in a society which gears

itself so exclusively to power considerations, if one has no power
—economic, social, political, or power of individual personhood.
The black community clearly has learned that in quite concrete
terms the power interests in the society are coterminal with the
white community. How love the enemy when his overwhelming
power institutionalizes an unjust status quo?

This understanding of love which is so much in debate in the
black churches and so much rejected outside of them certainly has
roots in the Christian history, but it is not the only understanding
of love that the community has affirmed. No one can doubt that if
love is understood exclusively in terms of emotional and ethical
norms, and if its legitimate, if not exclusive sphere of application
is the area of interpersonal relations, then it is incompatible with
and a barrier to the fulfillment of the legitimate aspirations of the
disprivileged folk of this world. However, there is an equally valid
and honored understanding of love in the Christian tradition which
modifies and qualifies the former. This understanding recognizes
and takes seriously the inevitability and the possible redemptive
function of conflict and the interplay of power in interpersonal as
well as in corporate relationships which do not of necessity indicate the absence of love. Some element of power is present in any
relationship. I am a father, I have two children, I love them, I
have power over them, and oftentimes I am in conflict with them.
I exercise physical power over my son. I exercise that power,
hopefully in awareness of the meaning of responsible parenthood,
guided by genuine considerations of love. Sometimes because of my
loving concern, for them, or theirs for themselves, or sometimes because of my loving concern for myself we are in conflict and power
lurks in the background of the conflict and we are aware of it.
Precisely because we love we are in conflict—hopefully out of the
conflict we are all enhanced, enlarged, and more mature and
responsible.

This parent-child analogy is not unproductive for an understanding of what is taking place in terms of intergroup relationships today. For three hundred years the experience of the majority of black people has been that they have been "children" in the
view of the white majority. They have been treated as children
surviving and dependent upon the largess of a paternalistic and

benevolent white majority, while, as in actual family relationships, below the surface in the child there has been a veritable volcano of repressed feelings of aggression and hate, of anger and resentment. The present black revolution may be understood as the growing maturity of the community where it feels empowered to verbalize and act out its feelings and frustrations. And as in family relationships, the family itself will not be healthy until the character of the relationship truly takes into account the legitimate dignity and rights of the other. One of the reasons why the word "man" has so much meaning among black people is that the reality of their experience is that they are treated as children, and participate in the essential powerlessness of children vis-à-vis the larger society.

The Images of Power

There is no word in our vocabulary that is freighted with more ominous overtones than the word "power." This is because often the reality of power and the images its use invokes are surrounded by negative connotations which are quite at variance with what it denotes. The word "power" evokes images of force, coercion, compulsion, even violence, and the powerful image of the capacity for imposing one's will upon another. This definition is concretized in the life of many individuals, particularly in the lives of the poor and the black in America. Moreover, when one speaks of changing the power relations in a society, the status quo is in jeopardy and all those who have an interest in the way things are, are threatened and made anxious. Professor Daniel Williams, in his book *God's Grace and Man's Hope,* noted that one of the premises upon which any good society rests is "that every man shall be able to participate with power in the making of decisions which affect his life; and every group shall be able to participate with power in the decisions which affect its interests as a group."

Here there is no eschewing of power, but an affirmation of its indispensability as an element in the interrelationships of the society. Moreover, there is recognition that there must be a redistribution of power if the society is to survive. This is a lesson that black men have only learned recently. Says Professor Williams: "The importance of the power problem for Christian ethics derives from the fact that power, whether economic, political, military or spiritual means capacity to determine life for good or ill, and from the fact that some fundamental redistribution of power is necessary as a condition of the freedom and dignity of men in their social relations." In our time it is precisely the recognition that there can be no stable society until there is a redistribution of power that is the source of so much fear and accounts for the fact that efforts in that direction elicit such violent responses as in Orangeburg. Those who have power, who have a vested interest in the status quo, rarely solicit change. Moreover, because power linked primarily to considerations of privilege always has guilt attached to it, men fear changes in power relations because they fear that power may be used against them as they are using it.

Power Is the Condition of Love

But power is neither good nor evil; it is, rather, the capacity to accomplish purpose or purposes. For example, a 95-pound woman dusting china in a china shop is infinitely more powerful in that context than is a 10,000-pound elephant. The goodness or evil of power is determined by the purposes in whose achievement it is invoked. In the Christian view, power expended for the purposes of love is good, power expended to perpetrate injustice or to perpetuate injustice is evil. Power is the condition of and the energy that delivers love from vapid sentimentality; it is also the judgment that delivers those who use power from falling victim to its inherent capacity to corrupt. Some such understanding of the Christian meaning of love and some appropriation of the essential uses and possibility of power linked to and judged by love, seem appropriate to the Gospel in the ghetto. The most loving service a citizen may perform for his society, for his neighbor, or that groups of citizens may perform on behalf of their nation, would be to confront them with the ways in which both the overt power of the state and the covert power are used to undermine the ends of justice and are found in preserving an unjust status quo. The highest, most loving service black men and concerned Christians of whatever racial group in America may perform for themselves and their nation is to shatter its comfortable image and force it to see itself as its minorities see and experience it.

Which Neighbor?

Christians will be forced to make difficult choices in the days ahead. Not black Christians alone. Many may make the grave choice of joining in with violence. But whatever course one chooses, one must labor to see that the violence is channeled to good purposes, and that it be brought to an end as speedily as possible. Christians must learn that the choice of whose claim one will acknowledge will be crucial. If being Christian means to accept unlimited liability for the neighbor, which neighbor will you in the first instance accept liability for? Will the choice be made on the basis of race considerations or on the basis of a more rational concern? What is clear here is that the Christian seeks no rationalization of violence, nor of legitimate hate, nor to provide a catharsis for hate in the invocation of "lex talionis." Rather, he seeks creative ways of channeling power so that it will express love in ways that are redemptive, edifying, liberating and humanizing.

Lawrence N. Jones is Dean of Students at Union Theological Seminary, New York City.

Ballots or Bullets

If we don't do something real soon, I think you'll have to agree that we're going to be forced either to use the ballot or the bullet. It's one or the other in 1964. It isn't that time is running out— time has run out! 1964 threatens to be the most explosive year America has ever witnessed. The most explosive year. Why? It's also a political year. It's the year when all of the white politicians will be back in the so-called Negro community jiving you and me for some votes. The year when all of the white political crooks will be right back in your and my community with their false promises, building up our hopes for a letdown, with their trickery and their

Malcolm X, in *The Burden of Race*, ed. by G. Osofsky (New York: Harper & Row, 1967), pp. 596–597. Reprinted by permission.

treachery, with their false promises which they don't intend to keep. As they nourish these dissatisfactions, it can only lead to one thing, an explosion; and now we have the type of black man on the scene in America today—I'm sorry, Brother Lomax—who just doesn't intend to turn the other cheek any longer.

Don't let anybody tell you anything about the odds are against you. If they draft you, they send you to Korea and make you face 800 million Chinese. If you can be brave over there, you can be brave right here. These odds aren't as great as those odds. And if you fight here, you will at least know what you're fighting for.

I'm not a politician, not even a student of politics; in fact, I'm not a student of much of anything. I'm not a Democrat, I'm not a Republican, and I don't even consider myself an American. If you and I were Americans, there'd be no problem. Those Hunkies that just got off the boat, they're already Americans; Polacks are already Americans; the Italian refugees are already Americans. Everything that came out of Europe, every blue-eyed thing, is already an American. And as long as you and I have been over here, we aren't Americans yet.

Well, I am one who doesn't believe in deluding myself. I'm not going to sit at your table and watch you eat, with nothing on my plate, and call myself a diner. Sitting at the table doesn't make you a diner, unless you eat some of what's on that plate. Being here in America doesn't make you an American. Being born here in America doesn't make you an American. Why, if birth made you American, you wouldn't need any legislation, you wouldn't need any amendments to the Constitution, you wouldn't be faced with civil-rights filibustering in Washington, D.C., right now. They don't have to pass civil-rights legislation to make a Polack an American.

No, I'm not an American. I'm one of the 22 million black people who are the victims of Americanism. One of the 22 million black people who are the victims of democracy, nothing but disguised hypocrisy. So, I'm not standing here speaking to you as an American, or a patriot, or a flag-saluter, or a flag-waver—no, not I. I'm speaking as a victim of this American system. And I see America through the eyes of the victim. I don't see any American dream; I see an American nightmare.

MALCOLM X

Black People Must Run the Black Ghetto

"Ownership of businesses in the ghetto must be transferred to black people—either individually or collectively.

"All government facilities in the ghetto must be run and operated by black people. For example, the post office, the judiciary system, Police Department, Welfare Department, Board of Education and all other such agencies."

FLOYD McKISSICK, CORE

What Fools?

They keep telling us, over and over again, that Dr. King believed in non-violence, as if we didn't know it. Dr. King believed in non-violence, they say, and therefore any violence that black people might engage in, in retaliation for his violent murder, would be a disgrace to his memory.

A white man murdered Dr. King because he was a black leader and because he demanded justice and equality for black people. He murdered him violently and brutally and in the presence of over 150 policemen and other witnesses. Yet white people are now trying to make us believe that Dr. King's death proves that non-violence really works.

What fools do they think black folks are? If Dr. King's murder proves anything, it proves that non-violence does not work in this violent white American society. Dr. King hoped and prayed that his non-violence would redeem white people. And what did white people do to him? They killed him.

They keep telling us that Dr. King believed in America and in the goodness of white people. We know that he believed these things, but we also know what white people did to him. He is dead. Nothing can change that fact, and that is why 40 American cities were in flames.

Every black man, woman and child knew that something had to be done to express our indignation. Is it conceivable that we could have let the murder of Dr. King pass without any kind of retaliation? Would prayer services, memorial services and a national singing of "We Shall Overcome" have been enough?

If there had been no general uprising in black ghettos across the nation, the life of any black leader could have been snuffed out by any white racist bigot without a second thought, and we would have been back in slavery before the first fall frost.

Rev. Albert B. Cleage, Jr.

A Negro Psychiatrist on the Black Psyche

Self-hatred

In recent years social scientists have come to attribute many of the Negro's social and psychological ills to his self-hatred and resultant self-destructive impulses. Slums, high crime rates, alcoholism, drug addiction, illegitimacy and other social deviations have all been attributed in part to the Negroes' acting out of their feelings of inferiority. Many behavioral scientists have suggested that the recent urban Negro riots are a manifestation of subconscious self-destructive forces in black people stemming from this chronic feeling of self-denigration. . . .

The self-hatred thesis appeals on the one hand to racists, who reason that if Negroes develop enough "self-love" they might wish to remain complacently segregated and stop trying to "mongrelize" the white society, and on the other to Negro militants, including the Black Muslims and Black Power advocates, who scream from soapboxes, "We must undo the centuries-old brainwashing by the white man that has made us hate ourselves. We must stop being ashamed of being black and stop wanting to be white!" . . .

No one denies that many Negroes have feelings of self-hatred.

Alvin F. Poussaint, in *The New York Times Magazine,* August 20, 1967. © 1967 by The New York Times Company. Reprinted by permission.

But the limitations of the thesis become apparent when one realizes that a Negro with all the self-love and self-confidence in the world could not express it in a system that is so brutally and unstintingly suppressive of self-assertion. Through systematic oppression aimed at extinguishing his aggressive drive, the black American has been effectively castrated and rendered abjectly compliant by white America. Since appropriate rage at such emasculation could be expressed directly only at great risk, the Negro repressed and suppressed it, but only at great cost to his psychic development. Today this "aggression-rage" constellation, rather than self-hatred, appears to be at the core of the Negro's social and psychological difficulties. . . .

How It Began

Let us briefly look at the genesis and initial consequences of this oppressive behavior and the Negroes' responses to it. The castration of Negroes, and the resulting problems of self-image and inner rage, started more than 350 years ago when black men, women and children were wrenched from their native Africa, stripped bare both psychologically and physically, and placed in an alien white land. They thus came to occupy the most degraded of human conditions: that of a slave, a piece of property, a nonperson. Families were broken up, the Negro male was completely emasculated, and the Negro woman was systematically sexually exploited and vilely degraded.

Whites, to escape the resultant retaliatory rage of black men and women, acted to block its expression. The plantation system implanted a subservience and dependency in the psyche of the Negro that made him dependent upon the goodwill and paternalism of the white man. . . .

It became a virtue within this system for the black man to be docile and nonassertive. "Uncle Toms" are exemplars of these conditioned virtues. . . .

"Miss Joan"

For reinforcement, as if any was needed, white supremacists constructed an entire "racial etiquette" to remind Negroes constantly that they are only castrated humans. In their daily lives, Negroes are called "girl" and "boy." . . . Negroes are also addressed by their first names by whites no matter how lowly, but are in turn expected to use courtesy titles when addressing whites. It was sickening for me to hear a Southern white dime-store clerk address a Negro minister with a doctoral degree as "Jimmy," while he obsequiously called her "Miss Joan." . . .

Adam Powell—an Example of Prejudice

Nonassertiveness was a learned adaptation to insure survival. For example, the whole system of Southern legal justice has been designed—and still functions—to inflict severe and inequitable penalties on Negroes showing even minor aggression toward whites. In both the North and the South, Negroes who dare show their anger toward whites are usually punished out of proportion. . . . The recent unseating of Congressman Adam Clayton Powell and the use of guns and bullets by police and National Guardsmen on rioting Negro college students (white college-age rioters are seldom even tear-gassed) are examples of this inequitable white retaliation. . . .

Similarly, various forms of religious worship in the Negro community have fostered passivity in blacks and encouraged them to look to an afterlife for eventual salvation and happiness. Negroes have even been taught that they must love their oppressor and it is "sinful" to hate or show appropriate anger. It is significant that the civil-rights movement had to adopt passive-resistance and non-violence in order to win the acceptance of white America. But, alas, even in nonviolent demonstrations there was too much "aggression" shown by Negroes. Whites recoiled and accused civil-rights groups of "provoking violence" by peaceful protest.

The lack of self-assertion has had devastating consequences in terms of Negro social behavior and psychic responses. It has been found for instance that Negroes are less likely to go into business than are members of other ethnic groups. The most obvious explanation for this (and one missed by Glazer and Moynihan in their "Beyond the Melting Pot") is that central to the entrepreneurial spirit is assertiveness, self-confidence and the willingness to risk failure in an innovative venture. A castrated human being is not likely to be inclined in any of these ways.

A trained incapacity to be aggressive would also account in large part for Negroes' below-par achievement in school. Negro girls, who are not as threatening to whites and therefore not as systematically crushed as are Negro boys, have been found to exceed boys in achievement in elementary schools. The pattern of behavior set for the young Negro, especially the male, is directly opposed to that upheld as masculine for the rest of American youth. . . .

Of course, this is also conveniently protective for the white racist, because Negroes who are nonassertive will be afraid to compete with him for education, jobs and status. . . .

The Negro's Rage

What happens then to the accumulated rage in the depths of each Negro psyche? What does the black man do with his aggression?

The simplest method for dealing with rage is to suppress it and substitute an opposing emotional attitude—compliance, docility or a "loving attitude." . . .

The greater the repressed rage, the more abject the pretense of love and compliance. Thus feet-shuffling, scraping and bowing, obsequiousness and Uncle Tomism may actually indicate inner rage and deep hatred.

Sometimes rage can be denied completely and replaced by a compensatory happy-go-lucky attitude, flippancy or—a mechanism extremely popular among Negroes—"being cool."

Or the aggression may be channeled into competitive sports, music, dance. Witness the numbers of Negroes who flock to these activities, among the few traditionally open to them by white society. Negro males in particular gravitate to sports as a means for sublimating their rage and aggression.

Another legitimate means of channeling rage is to identify with the oppressor and put all one's energy into striving to be like him. The most obvious example of this is the Negro who feels that the most flattering compliment his white friends can pay him is, "You don't act like all the other Negroes," or "You don't seem Negro to me." Such blacks usually harbor strong, angry anti-Negro feelings similar to the white racists. They may project their own self-hatred onto other Negroes. . . .

Another technique for dealing with rage is to replace it with a type of chronic resentment and stubbornness toward white people

—a chip on the shoulder. Trying to control deep anger in this way frequently shows itself in a general irritability and it always has the potential of becoming explosive. Thus the spreading wave of riots in Negro ghettos may be seen as outbursts of rage. Although these riots are contained in the ghetto, the hatred is usually directed at those whom the rioter sees as controlling and oppressing him economically, psychologically and physically—store owners and policemen.

The same hostility which is expressed in a disorganized way by a collection of people in a riot can be expressed in an organized way in a political movement. In this connection the Black Power movement is relevant. . . .

Rage is also directed inward in such deviations as alcoholism, drug addiction and excessive gambling. These escapist expressions are very prevalent among poorer Negroes and often represent an attempt to shut out a hostile world. . . .

It appears that more and more Negroes are freeing themselves of suppressed rage through greater outspoken release of pent-up emotions. Perhaps this is an indication that self-love is beginning to outbalance self-hate in the black man's soul. . . .

The old passivity is fading and being replaced by a drive to undo centuries of powerlessness, helplessness and dependency under American racism. . . .

The implication of all this seems to be that black people can obtain dignity only through continued assertive social and political action against racism until all of their just demands are met. It also appears that old-style attempts to destroy the natural aggression of the black man and to fail to give him his full rights can only provoke further outbreaks of violence and inspire a revolutionary zeal among Negro Americans. . . .

Since this assertive response appears to be growing more common among Negroes, the implications for American society are clear: stop oppressing the black man, or be prepared to meet his expressed rage.

ALVIN F. POUSSAINT, M.D.,
Tufts University Medical School

How Now, America?

Futility is what I feel. Sadness and futility. America is rocketing to perdition, and nobody seems to give a damn.

We are all worried about the war in Viet Nam. And well we might be, for that war is part of what is wrong with America. It is one of the symptoms of the dreadful malaise that drains and debilitates us, that reduces the extraordinary moral and social potential of this nation to a confused and truculent impotence.

However, my worries are deeper than Viet Nam, for I know that the Vietnamese issue is fundamentally a military expression of the same ideological presuppositions that are illustrated in other ways at home. We can, if we wish, disengage ourselves in Viet Nam, but we cannot, in the same sense, disengage ourselves at home. We are one people and—barring some absolute madness—we are likely to remain so.

It is with this recognition that the prior urgency of the racial situation at home becomes apparent. When our unhappy adventure in South East Asia has been concluded, we will still have the black ghetto—with all its implications for the escalation of tragedy and the enlargement of scandal—to face.

What is crucial to the protection of our moral integrity, no less than to the preservation of peace and order here at home, is the recognition of urgency: *we have got the black ghetto—with all its implications*—RIGHT NOW! It is our own American Frankenstein. We created it; and, tortured monster that it is, it is unimpressed by an order of priorities that does not begin with it.

The Racial "Fix" Against Reality

We await the sanguinary summer implicit in the prelude already performed at Orangeburg. There is something titillating about the prospect of blood. In the frenzied rhetoric symptomatic of their neurosis, some flagellated blacks have verbalized their frustrations with promises of vengeance and retaliation. We are not impressed

---

C. Eric Lincoln, in *Christianity and Crisis*, April 1, 1968, pp. 56–59. Reprinted by permission.

by their threats *or* their logic. But we shall see. We do not understand their madness, but there is comfort in knowing that it is too late to do anything about it. Anything except to arm ourselves and see that the Officers of the Law are properly equipped and rededicated to the suppression of crime in the streets. We must, of course, have order and, above all, property must be protected. If there is blood, if people are killed, how can we possibly be blamed? After all, it is *their* madness.

It is their madness and ours. It is our common madness. If we persist in it, there *will* be blood. More blood. And people will be killed. *More* people. The blood will be uniformly red. The people will be uniformly black. The killers and the killed will be 100 percent American. Their brothers are fighting together and dying together in Viet Nam—allegedly for some principles we do not seem to understand in America. We wait for the agony and the blood, but we have washed our hands of it in advance. Somewhere, there is a precedent for this.

We have watched the black moderates abandon nonviolence one by one, because we exploited their nonviolence with cynicism and deceit. The placebos we gave them for their people did little for their conditions and left a bitter aftertaste.

Now comes Martin Luther King in a final effort to redeem nonviolence as a reasonable and effective technique of social change. He is asking for bread. Will you give him a stone? He is perhaps the last bridge of moderation between the black masses and an indifferent society. There is danger and desperation in his Washington venture.

If he fails, his present portfolio will be exhausted so far as the black masses are concerned. This is the last chance for nonviolence. The greater tragedy is the possibility that his presence in Washington with thousands of poor and hungry blacks may initiate violence. Either possibility, should it occur, represents the cruel entrapment of a man dedicated to peace and motivated by love. But then, if there is a premium on love and peace in this society, it has been carefully obscured by our misalliance with lesser values.

It is our unwillingness—perhaps our *inability*—to confront the reality of our deep complicity and to make the hard choices implicit that saddens me. Again, Viet Nam is illustrative of our national myopia. We seem totally incapable of recognizing in our involvement there the fundamental inconsistencies that seem obvious to everyone else. This extraordinary predisposition to be deliberately oblivious of any reality in conflict with our popular ideological preferments suggests a very dangerous paranoia.

Here in America, the distressingly facile and cynical techniques of obliviousness we have developed to avoid confronting our racial prejudices work like super-potent narcotics: they insulate the mind against a perception of what is real and from what is unpleasant about oneself or one's behavior. With a periodic "fix," the bigoted individual never finds it necessary to confront his bigotry. We get our fixes from institutions we create or support, and from selected others in whose views we find consensus with our own. The tragedy is that problems do not go away merely because we choose to delude ourselves about their origin or the fact of their existence.

One of the common techniques of obliviousness avoids the confrontation of white racism by making *prior* objections to the generalized inadequacy of all black people. If the "unreadiness" of blacks can be inferred from the behavior of some of them, one need not be concerned with the question of the rejection of those blacks who *are* ready, or the more fundamental issue of why some are "not ready," and who it is that creates the circumstances of their unreadiness.

It was predictable that the explicit indictments of the President's Commission on Civil Disorders would hardly penetrate the consciousness (much less prick the conscience) of white America, because it took one look at the headlines and ran out to get the customary fix. Presidential-aspirant Richard Nixon, who wants to lead the country, succeeded in leading an inevitable corps of racial junkies by complaining loudly and publicly that the report blamed everyone except those responsible for the riots. Nixon is dead wrong. The report did, in fact, place the blame where it belonged —unequivocally and for the first time ever.

But it must be obvious that its conclusions can neither be appreciated nor accepted if they are never entertained. Mr. Nixon's uncamouflaged appeal for emotional involvement in the peripheral issue of riots was intended as a deliberate derailment of the central message of the Kerner Report. It was a fix—an insulation against a more fundamental reality and the need for honest introspection regarding it.

The Crippling Covenant-in-Bigotry

Ever since the report's publication anybody who is black and articulate, and who is "willing to speak objectively" or "write dispassionately" on the subject of "Negro Crime," or "Black Militancy," or "How Rap Brown Hurts the Negro Cause" is in demand at you-name-it fees. In fact, one doesn't even have to be articulate, if only he can make the proper sounds or gestures. But one does have to be *black*—for authenticity.

One is reminded of the pathetic little American drama that occurred a number of years ago when a Black American announced that he would refuse to fight for this country. With frantic haste, the most prominent black athlete who could be found was snatched from the playing fields, flown to New York and hauled before the cameras to testify on behalf of all black folk that he would fight for America, and that that other Negro spoke only for himself. Thus reassured, America could rest easy again. The black revolution was not yet, and we had the *authentic* word of "one of them" to prove it.

Well, the black revolution *is now,* and authentic words about "Negro crime" or "H. Rap Anybody" do not diminish the requirement that this society recognize the validity of the revolution and make a responsible response to it. *Now.*

If crime is what we need to talk about before we can get down to substantive issues, let us begin with that fundamental criminal consensus which defiles the whole spectrum of our social institutions with the most feculent racism. It is that pervasive, pernicious, consensual covenant-in-bigotry that qualifies so severely the life chances of anyone who is black and sets the conditions that make inevitable a predisposition to crime by untold numbers of youth. America is the loser, for if these young Americans had a realistic opportunity to exploit their genius in approved channels of personal development that investment could only redound to the common social interest.

I have called the black ghetto an American Frankenstein. It is more than that. It is a repository for all of the evils of society. Its decaying, rat infested tenements are impacted with wasted human bodies, and the ghetto itself is serviced with all of the negatives of human existence—poverty, misery, unemployment, crime, hunger, disease, futility and hatred. The Black Americans who live there have few of the satisfactions normally available to other Americans—a fact increasingly difficult to rationalize in or out of the ghetto. Nevertheless, they experience all of the pressures, direct and indirect, that demand conformity with norms established beyond the pale that separates them from a society that holds them to strict account. There is no expectation that their patterns of behavior will be different or that their approach to consumption, display and personal success will be in any sense unique. It seems clear that "crime" in the black ghetto represents, at least in part, the alternative efforts of people who are deprived of normal access to satisfactions and status to acquire those values under pressure of the expectations of the society that has predetermined their failure through a vicious racial consensus. The rate and the order of crimes reflect the quantity and the quality of satisfactions available at a given time, and the degree of rage and frustration will derive from the inability to rationalize obvious disparity and make it acceptable.

All this would seem to be elementary. What may be more difficult to conceptualize is the fundamental crime: the covert racist conspiracy that programs, with accuracy and proficiency, the life chances of successive generations of Black Americans. This is the crime implicit in every page of the Kerner Report. This is the mother of crimes and criminals. It is the source of human tragedy far beyond the obvious.

For if racism operates to limit the social development of people who are black, so must it limit the moral development of people who are white. In trying to preserve intact the white prerogative for white youth (who may not need it or want it), racism consigns to recidivism and atrophy the integrity, the courage, the capacity to love *and to be loved* of all who accept shelter under its grotesque and sinister mantle. No one can hate and, except for his hatred, be a whole person. The racist (of whatever color) is drenched in a malignity that colors his perceptions and pervades all his judgments.

Leadership, Where Art Thou?

The Kerner Report has asked America to accept the fact of her racism and to do something about it. It is a constructive request, based on an honest and competent appraisal. It deserves something more than evasion. Had not President Johnson sensed the need to know more about the causes of, and the possible remedies for, the racial unrest that characterizes the black ghetto? And it was he who appointed the commission with the charge: "Let your search be free . . . find the truth and express it in your report." The commission executed his mandate with consummate skill and integrity, and with a determined thoroughness that ranged far beyond the riots to the attitudinal catacombs from which the riots emerge to trouble us.

It is depressing to note that Mr. Johnson has not seen fit to give it his endorsement. His personal aims and accomplishments in bringing Black Americans into the mainstream of American life have been—by comparison to any of his predecessors—unimpeachable. But he has been strangely silent on the Kerner Report, and he has offered no leadership in a critical moment of history when Americans are once again facing a moral challenge in conflict with established patterns of thought and behavior. Once more the country is deserted by leadership and left without guidelines for facing up to an unsettling moment of truth.

The last such occasion—at an equally critical moment in our history—started us on the road to this ultimate encounter with the basic assumptions that structure our society. It was the 1954 Supreme Court decision that abolished segregation in the public schools. At that time, it was President Eisenhower who offered no leadership. He gave no hint of the proper response Americans should make to so profound a challenge to their sense of fairness, and the need to rethink their racial traditions. As a direct result we had Little Rock and Clinton, Tenn., and countless other tragic confrontations as the people sought to test the degree of support the President was prepared to give to the Court's decision.

It seems that we are always appointing commissions; we are always obtaining decisions. And yet the problem never seems to be resolved. The job never seems to get done. So now we are in the streets.

Must we go into the streets? I am sick of the sight of blood and nauseated by the promise of more to come. I am not frightened by the threats and the promises of vengeance that come from some black militants. I do not condone their invective, but I do understand the anxiety and frustration from which it derives. But I do not think America is frightened by their threats, either. The willingness to be "scared" is not an effective camouflage for the determination to be vindictive. America has the means. . . . America has the will. . . . Perhaps America has the intent to destroy what frightens her. This is what frightens *me*. Perhaps it should frighten *you*.

It is the promise of blood implied in the frantic stockpiling of Stoner guns, machine guns, sawed-off shot guns, gas masks and immobilizing chemicals by police departments across the country. It is the vast expenditures for command cars, half-tracks and other sophisticated weaponry that appalls me. It is the tacit unleashing of enforcement personnel, already overcommitted to the containment of the black ghetto. It is the organization of vigilantes. . . .

Who is the enemy about to invade America? If we are about to engage in the slaughter of *citizens* on a scale suggested by our public and private armaments, we are a long way down the road. This is madness. I *know* it can't happen here. But there is a worrisome uneasiness that gnaws at my gut-strings and refuses to be quieted. A feeling that it *is* happening. After all, there *are* precedents—in Germany and South Africa. And in America.

Doesn't anybody care? Are we really resigned to having Americans slaughter Americans like so many hogs? Is the crutch of race so indispensable? Is the racial advantage so crucial that it must be maintained in blood? Do our children want the package of privilege and prerogative—which we protect with such ferocity—if it comes wrapped in duplicity and tied with suspicion and guilt? Perhaps we ought to ask them. Is it worth being hated with such intensity by so many of our people whose tradition is one of love and respect, and pride in being "American" and in sharing America?

Can't we let black people be Americans? Can't we let black Americans share America? Black people *are* Americans; America *is* theirs to share. The recognition of this fact beats killing; and it reduces crime—in the streets and in the board rooms, in the ghetto and in suburbia. Their crime. And yours.

How now, America? How now?

C. ERIC LINCOLN

"You must realize that we as the most exploited group in the United States, must assume leadership of our own struggle. And anyone who doesn't like it can go to hell.

"We're going to liberate you whether you like it or not."

JAMES FORMAN, SNCC
(quoted in *The Progressive,* October, 1967)

White Liberals and Black Liberations

Several months ago I received a telephone call from a stranger. The caller identified himself as a Negro and said that he was confused. He felt he was damned if he did and damned if he didn't.

"Just a few years ago," he said, "civil rights leaders were saying that the creative and radical thing to do was to break down Jim Crow by integrating white neighborhoods." So he and his bride met the challenge and battled their way into a lily white suburb. They overcame the vandalism and survived the physical threats and the isolation. They made it. "Now," he went on, "Negroes call us Uncle Toms and ex-colored folk for living out here with all these white people."

Soon the Los Angeles City School Board, after years of prodding by militant civil rights leaders, is expected to come up with plans for total desegregation of the city's schools. If these plans take shape, they will not now be hailed as a victory by the black community. The scattered applause which may greet the change will be smothered by the relentless opposition of those who demand local community control of ghetto schools instead of dispersal of their children.

The agenda of the black ghetto is changing rapidly. Last week's cliches have a hollow ring. Yesterday's answers have lost their relevance. If white America is bewildered by the swirl of shifting demands, it is not alone. There is lack of comprehension among many black folk, too.

James Farmer, in *The Progressive* (January, 1968), pp. 13–16. Reprinted by permission.

Behind the rhetoric and posturing of today, a fundamental debate is rending the black community. The shallow newspaper headlines have done nothing to clarify the controversy, and the news accounts have oversimplified and distorted it. The issue is not militancy versus moderation. There are militants indeed and there are moderates, too, in both camps. Nor is "integration versus separation" the definitive division. Which is it—integration or separation—when a black student joins a campus Afro-American association after choosing freely to enter an integrated university? Then, is it youth against age? The young, it is true, carry the burden of the argument on one side, while many of their elders form the bulwark on the other. But chronology must not be confused with ideology.

Is the question, then, "black power" ? How does one debate a slogan without a precise statement of its meaning?

There is an issue, however, and it is frighteningly real. The question stripped bare is this: What is the way for black Americans to find a meaning for their existence and to achieve dignity in the American context? Is it through assimilation? Or is it through racial cohesiveness?

This is not an unfamiliar debate on American soil. All immigrant groups have wrestled with it, and it has torn many asunder. In each case there have been voices speaking for group cohesion, for maintaining cultural identity, for a kind of sub-nationalism within this nation. There have also been voices urging dispersal, and assimilation, and pressing the smaller group to enter the larger group of their new national home. Invariably, in the first generation, internal insecurity of the group and external hostility toward it gave ascendancy to the voices favoring group cohesion. The greater the external pressure, the greater the cohesion. Immigrants and their descendants remained Irish-Americans, Italian-Americans, Polish-Americans, Jewish-Americans, with the accent on their original identity. As the external pressure was reduced, the voices of assimilation became more compelling. The ethnic hyphens faded, but they have never completely disappeared.

Two Souls, Two Thoughts

Among black people, the ideological division has been of longer duration, because of their high visibility and the background of slavery. After emancipation the debate began, but in a low key. Many Negroes wanted then to return to Africa, and some did. But most sought somehow to make their way here—some as a separate people, and some as an assimilated group. What was the American Negro—or the Negro American? A black man who happened, through historical accident, to live in America, or an American who, by genetic accident, happened to be black? In 1903, W.E.B. Du Bois put the dilemma thus:

"One feels his two-ness—an American Negro, two souls, two thoughts, two unreconciled strivings, two warring ideals, in one dark body. . . .

"The history of the American Negro is the history of this strife—this longing to attain self-conscious manhood, to merge his double self into a better and truer self. . . . He would not Africanize America, for America has too much to teach the world and Africa. He would not bleach the Negro soul in a flood of white American-ism, for he knows that Negro blood has a message for the world. He simply wishes to make it possible for a man to be both a Negro and an American without being cursed and spit upon. . . ."

The ferocious quality of the debate in black America is of recent vintage, and was triggered by three failures—the failure of newly won legal and constitutional civil rights prerogatives to effect any meaningful change in the life situation of black people; the failure of the assault on segregation to halt the trend toward increasing segregation in housing and schools; and the failure of all efforts to have any discernible impact on racism in the nation's society. "Everything has changed, but everything remains the same," one hears constantly in the South. *De facto* segregation throughout the nation continues to rise. The income gap is still widening. Racism, like a miasma, is still breathed with the air.

Be Black to Be American

Throughout this century the ascendancy among the contending Negroes has been held by those who sought dispersal and assimila-tion. With the Supreme Court school desegregation decision of 1954 this ascendancy rode on a wave of euphoria. Two years ago, however, optimism receded to leave the bitter taste of hollow vic-tories in the mouths of the black masses.

What has been said to the black man throughout this century, by his leaders and by white liberals, is that he must think of himself as an individual and not as a member of a group, and that if, as an individual, he gained education and money he would first be acculturated and then assimilated into a racially integrated society. He would become, in reality, a white man with an invisible black skin in a color-blind community. Men of good will, black and white, bowed to the myth that proximity would, in itself, produce color-blindness. If assimilation were achieved, the black man would have no ethnic or racial identity; he would be an American distributed through every phase of the nation's life. The black ghetto would disappear; the Harlems would become nightmares of the past.

For many years no responsible leader would have suggested that improvement of educational or housing conditions in the ghetto could possibly serve any useful purpose. The ghettos were seen as an anachronism; to improve them would be to perpetuate the evil of segregation. Privately supported Negro colleges almost went bankrupt. A. Philip Randolph was castigated in the late 1950s for urging formation of a "Negro American Labor Council." White students in integrated colleges complained that black students were not yet truly emancipated, for when two Negroes entered the dining hall they frequently sat together and talked with each other, rather than distributing themselves in the best integrated fashion. The cry was "segregation in reverse."

Efforts to implement this dispersion concept of integration obviously have failed, though some still argue for it—naively, I think. It no longer enjoys the widespread acceptance in the black community which it once had. Indeed, it is today under fierce attack. What the dispersion concept required of the black man was a kind of abnegation, a losing of himself as a black man to find himself as an American.

Its opponents argue for an ethnic cohesiveness, a finding of himself as a black man, as the urgent goal. They advocate group self-assertion. They foster pride in pigmentation, rather than white mimicry. Rather than disperse the ghetto and reject self, they would preserve, cherish, and develop the ghetto, and love the black self.

Some of the ethnic unity advocates are separationists and view the ghetto, which they seek to upgrade, as a separate community preferably to remain alienated from the body politic. Others see it as an ethnic community among many ethnic communities in our cities, and as a power fulcrum to propel the black man into the political and economic mainstream, thereby changing the mainstream significantly. So, there are debates within debates. The debates are creative and good. The truth, I am sure, will emerge somewhere between the extremes.

The black man must find himself as a black man before he can find himself as an American. He must now become a hyphenated American, discovering the hyphen so that he can eventually lose it. This involves accepting the stark reality that the black ghettos of our cities are not going to disappear in the foreseeable future. Nor is racism.

The Afro-American cannot skip the hyphenated phase in his development, and the losing of his hyphen will be more difficult for him, as I have suggested, because of his high visibility, because of the experience of slavery, and because of a racial mystique, deeply rooted in both white and Negro, which holds the Negro inferior. Paradoxically, the black man must, I think, strengthen his ghetto on the one hand, and continue to provide an exit on the other. He must build the economic and political power of the ghetto as he simultaneously fights for open-occupancy housing, which eventually will destroy the ghetto, but will provide the Negro with a new potency as a full American.

This is bound to be a long and agonizing process, encompassing a series of progressive and regressive steps—some dramatic, some prosaic, some violent, some passive. A thin line separates group self-pride and self-hate. To expect that all will walk that line without crossing it is naive. To ask that it not be walked because some will step over it is to ask the impossible. If the rhetoric of proponents of black consciousness is sometimes excessive, it is because they are trying to "de-program" themselves. They, too, are creatures of a national culture which has held them worthless. "Black is beautiful and it is so great to be black." If they shout too loudly, it is because they are shouting down the echoes of 400 years of contrary conditioning.

The Shattered White Liberal

Those least capable of understanding what is happening in the ghetto today are, I hear, the white liberals. Their reaction is more than a matter of unrequited love. The new formulations of black unity fly in the face of their liberal dogmas and challenge every cliche they hold dear. Such a cliche is "breaking up the ghetto." Another is the "color-blindness" mystique. Still another is the shibboleth of inter-racialism, which requires, for instance, that every house party have at least one black guest.

But the white liberal is even more shattered by the redefinition of his role, or, more accurately, the rejection of his former role. Liberals have not hated us; they have loved us. It is the bigots who have hated us, and hate is its own bizarre kind of flattery; it pays its victims the high compliment of worthiness. But paternalistic love depreciates them. Hate says to a man that he is an equal; paternalism tells him he is a child. But what happens to paternalism when the child grows up?

The horror of racist programming in America, from womb to tomb, is that it has pictured the black man as an incompetent, a child—the "boy," "girl," and first-name syndrome—or at best it has viewed him as a little brother who must have his big brother as his keeper. Despite all protestations to the contrary, the historic Negro-liberal alliance, from the Abolitionists to today, has been on that basis. We blacks have been junior partners, not equals.

As a liberal friend wrote to me recently in response to my reply to his initial inquiry as to whether we had been wrong all these years he and I had fought together for integration, ". . . some of our long cherished cliches about the civil rights struggle do need updating. [But] . . . some things I continue to believe are absolute truths; among these is the fundamental truth that each man in fact be his brother's keeper, regardless of race . . ." Another cliche. And that is precisely the problem: liberals have been our custodians, guardians, handlers, *keepers,* but not our *brothers,* our eyeball-to-eyeball equals.

A middle-aged white lady, a mover in liberal causes for many years, asked me a few weeks ago why it is that now when the hand of friendship is offered to black people in the ghettos, often as not they bite it. I tried to explain that black people, especially of the lower economic strata, were hitherto silent, pliant, and largely invisible. But now they have found their voice. They are bursting with existence and are willing no longer to have their whole lives ordered by others. They insist upon making for themselves the decisions which determine their lives. They will make mistakes, but they must be their mistakes, their blunders. Free a man and he is not yet free. He must still free himself. This I viewed as a positive development toward participatory democracy. Help and cooperation, I argued, must be given on those terms, their terms, or not at all.

The worst result of the nation's racist programming is that even black people until now have absorbed the concept of themselves as inferior. It has stunted their growth. A child does not mature so long as he plays the role of a child. When he reaches adulthood, it is good that he leaves the household and rejects the parent if the parent does not begin to view him as an adult. Black people have now grown up in their self-image, and they have walked out of the house.

White liberalism has lost its relevance to the black struggle because it is emotionally and ideologically out of date. Some liberals have conquered their paternalism, and a few—a precious few— escaped the virus all along. But liberalism, on the whole, is weak in this respect.

To regain their relevance to the Negro struggle, white liberals must reorient their feelings and their thinking. They must get over seeing themselves as great white fathers and mothers, brokers of power and patronage for black people. They must learn that if they stoop down to offer, in the missionary way, the hand of friendship, the offer will be rejected, the hand bitten. If they offer it laterally, it will be circled warily, eyed suspiciously, then perhaps taken gingerly and tentatively.

The coming of age of the Negro has been psychological. But it is also political. The recent elections in Cleveland, Gary, Virginia, and several counties in Mississippi demonstrated that the black vote has matured in the grandest American tradition. The Negro electorate no longer is content to deprecate itself by having whites as its exclusive political custodians. It no longer is willing to be partner to the myth that political decision-making is white men's work. This shakes to its roots the urban coalition which has kept the Democratic kite aloft. The "tail" of the alliance has moved up front to join labor, liberals, ethnic blocs, and professional political machines as part of the kite itself. The Democratic Party must now accommodate to this new development or face disaster in 1968.

Black Self-determination?

The new black maturation, apparent for some time in the psychological sense and now visible in the political arena, has encompassed the economic and educational areas only in demand, not yet in performance. Economically the ghettos are still colonies; the income-producing properties are owned by absentees, and the inhabitants are consumers paying inflated prices. A balance of payments position like theirs would cause England's Prime Minister Harold Wilson to do more than devalue the pound.

Ghetto folk are now demanding that the outward flow of dollars be reversed and that economic control of their communities be turned over to those who share their woes and dreams. None but the lunatic fringe among them clings to the bootstrap illusion that Negroes can do it all alone. Most are keenly aware that they lack the boots—the capital, the technical know-how, the managerial skills. But help from whites must be consultative and advisory; the decisions must be made by the Negroes in the ghettos. They want industries to invest in their communities, and a few are beginning to do so—to build plants, to grant franchises, to train managers. It is mandatory, though, that such properties, when built, be turned over to the local community people—when trained—to run.

In Watts, Aerojet Corporation has built a subsidiary, the Watts Manufacturing Company, which makes tents and allied products. Watts people have been trained to run the plant from top to bottom. Plans are being made to allow the five hundred employees to purchase stock in the company. The Watts Manufacturing Company, alone, will not save Watts, but it is a start toward providing ghetto dwellers with some measure of control over their economic destiny.

The demand for control over their own future is nowhere so compelling as in the educational realm. After more than a decade of using every device available in a vain attempt to get their children into white schools, in the hope that white power would insure quality education because white children were their classmates, black parents have reversed their field. The demand, as yet unachieved, is now for local community control of ghetto schools. School boards have failed to integrate and failed to educate black children, so now black parents around the country are mounting insistent campaigns for decentralization of authority, giving them control over administrators and curricula in ghetto schools. They could hardly do worse than the school boards—witness the widening gap in learning, from grades one through twelve, between ghetto youngsters and others. They might do much better, for they have one thing which the school boards have lacked: a passionate concern for their children's education and future.

The debate will rage on between cohesiveness and dispersion. Ascendancy of one camp or the other will be determined ultimately not by rhetoric, and not even by leadership, as much as by events. Events today seem to be racing to the side of the spirited new force—cohesion—and I think that is right and good for the black man at this historical juncture.

JAMES FARMER, Professor of Social Welfare, Lincoln University (Pa.)

One Minute to Midnight

I think we've got to be perfectly honest about this situation. It is in fact one minute to Midnight. Time is, in fact, running out not just on people who are economically and educationally deprived, but time is running out in terms of people throughout the world taking America to be real and to be honest. But if we can say to the community, this is going to take 10 years but next year, this is what you can look for—everybody will have a job—everybody that is employable. And that's not hard to do, it just takes doing the same thing we did in 1932, when white folks were out of work. And overnight, overnight, we passed WPA, NYACC, FERA. No-

From an interview recorded March 3, 1968, by Public Broadcast Laboratories. Reprinted by permission of Whitney M. Young, Jr.

body said, Well we gotta wait, they don't have skills and they don't have motivation. They don't have the incentive. We just put these angry folks to work—shoveling air, sweeping air, just anything to put them to work.

And remember, I am asking you not just to hire the Phi Beta Kappas and the Lena Hornes. I am asking you also to hire dumb Negroes, like you do dumb white people. And mediocre Negroes, like you do mediocre white people.

WHITNEY M. YOUNG, JR., National Urban League

"If we can get the black community through this summer alive, we will have done a heroic thing. Our most urgent problem is survival until next fall."

ALBERT B. CLEAGE, JR.
(*Michigan Chronicle,* March 9, 1968)

"So you will find bitterness in the ghetto where you walk. Despair and cynicism—built on the hopes you raised and dashed—the promises you made and broke.

"What else will you find in the ghetto?

"You'll find a recognition—a broad awareness that the Civil Rights movement—the first phase of it—is over—is dead. We won the battle of the abstracts, the battle of moral principles, the battle of words. We won it in the battle fields of the south—on the picket lines, by sit-ins and marches and protests. We won it because litigation and the courts and the white man's legal system produced nothing but delay. No results. Only more hypocrisy."

FLOYD B. McKISSICK, Congress of Racial Equality

The Negro's Burden and America's Shame

And so being a Negro in America is not a comfortable existence. It means being a part of the company of the bruised, the battered, the scarred and the defeated. Being a Negro in America means trying to smile when you want to cry. It means trying to hold on to physical life amid psychological death. It means the pain of watching your children grow up with clouds of inferiority in their mental skies. It means having your legs cut off, and then being condemned for being a cripple. It means seeing your mother and father spiritually murdered by the slings and arrows of daily exploitation, and then being hated for being an orphan. Being a Negro in America means listening to suburban politicians talk eloquently against open housing while arguing in the same breath that they are not racists. It means being harried by day and haunted by night by a nagging sense of nobodyness and constantly fighting to be saved from the poison of bitterness. It means the ache and anguish of living in so many situations where hopes unborn have died.

After 348 years racial injustice is still the Negro's burden and America's shame. Yet for his own inner health and outer functioning, the Negro is called upon to be as resourceful, as productive and as responsible as those who have not known such oppression and exploitation. *This is the Negro's dilemma.* He who starts behind in a race must forever remain behind or run faster than the man in front. What a dilemma! It is a call to do the impossible. It is enough to cause the Negro to give up in despair.

And yet there are times when life demands the perpetual doing of the impossible. The life of our slave forebears is eternal testimony to the ability of men to achieve the impossible. So, too, we must embark upon this difficult, trying and sometimes bewildering course. With a dynamic will, we must transform our minus into a plus, and move on aggressively through the storms of injustice and the jostling winds of daily handicaps, toward the beaconing lights of fulfillment. Our dilemma is serious and our handicaps are real. But equally real is the power of a creative will and its ability to give us the courage to go on "in spite of."

Once when Ole Bull, the Norwegian violinist, was giving a concert in Paris, his A string snapped. Instead of stopping, Ole Bull transposed the composition and finished the concert on three strings. This is what the Negro confronts. Through years of unjust oppression and unmerited suffering our A strings of opportunity have snapped. But the performance of our lives must go on, and without self-pity or surrender we must go forward on three strings. Our lives will be comparable to the Battle of Marengo—in the morning an obvious defeat, in the afternoon a resounding victory. . . .

There is always the understandable temptation to seek negative and self-destructive solutions. Some seek a passive way out by yielding to the feeling of inferiority; or by allowing the floodgates of defeat to open with an avalanche of despair; or by dropping out of school; or by turning to the escape valves of narcotics and alcohol. Others seek a defiant way out. Through antisocial behavior, overt delinquency and gang warfare, they release their pent-up vindictiveness on the whole society. Meanness becomes their dominating characteristic. They trust no one and do not expect others to trust them. Still others seek to deal with the dilemma through the path of isolation. They have the fantasy of a separate black state or a separate black nation within the nation. This approach is the most cynical and nihilistic of all, because it is based on a loss of faith in the possibilities of American democracy.

The shattered dreams and blasted hopes of the Negro's daily life provide the psychological and sociological explanation for the choice by some of negative paths of escape. A society that has treated a whole race of people as flotsam and jetsam in the river of life cannot expect all of them to grow up healthy and well balanced. But in spite of these explanations the Negro cannot constructively deal with his dilemma through negative strategies. In spite of uncertainties and vicissitudes we must develop the courage to confront the negatives of circumstance with the positives of inner determination.

Somebodyness

One positive response to our dilemma is to develop a rugged sense of somebodyness. The tragedy of slavery and segregation is that they instilled in the Negro a disastrous sense of his own worthlessness. To overcome this terrible feeling of being less than human, the Negro must assert for all to hear and see a majestic sense of his worth. There is such a thing as a desegregated mind. We must no longer allow the outer chains of an oppressive society to shackle our minds. With courage and fearlessness we must set out daringly to stabilize our egos. This alone will give us a confirmation of our roots and a validation of our worth.

This sense of somebodyness means the refusal to be ashamed of being black. Our children must be taught to stand tall with their heads proudly lifted. We need not be duped into purchasing bleaching creams that promise to make us lighter. We need not process our hair to make it appear straight. Whether some men, black and white, realize it or not, black people are very beautiful. Life's piano can only produce the melodies of brotherhood when it is recognized that the black keys are as basic, necessary and beautiful as the white keys. The Negro, through self-acceptance and self-appreciation, will one day cause white America to see that integration is not an obstacle, but an opportunity to participate in the beauty of diversity.

Courage, the determination not to be overwhelmed by any object, that power of the mind capable of sloughing off the thingification of the past, will be the Negro's most potent weapon in achieving self-respect. Something of the inner spirit of our slave forebears must be pursued today. From the inner depths of our being we must sing with them: "Before I'll be a slave, I'll be buried in my grave and go home to my Lord and be free." This spirit, this drive, this rugged sense of somebodyness is the first and most vital step that the Negro must take in dealing with his dilemma.

Respect for Self and Kind

A second important step that the Negro must take is to work passionately for group identity. This does not mean group isolation or group exclusivity. It means the kind of group consciousness that

Negroes need in order to participate more meaningfully at all levels of the life of our nation.

Group unity necessarily involves group trust and reconciliation. One of the most serious effects of the Negro's damaged ego has been his frequent loss of respect for himself and for other Negroes. He ends up with an ambivalence toward his own kind. To overcome this tragic conflict, it will be necessary for the Negro to find a new self-image. Only by being reconciled to ourselves will we be able to build upon the resources we already have at our disposal. Too many Negroes are jealous of other Negroes' successes and progress. Too many Negro organizations are warring against each other with a claim to absolute truth. The Pharaohs had a favorite and effective strategy to keep their slaves in bondage: keep them fighting among themselves. The divide-and-conquer technique has been a potent weapon in the arsenal of oppression. But when slaves unite, the Red Seas of history open and the Egypts of slavery crumble.

This plea for unity is not a call for uniformity. There must always be healthy debate. There will be inevitable differences of opinion. The dilemma that the Negro confronts is so complex and monumental that its solution will of necessity involve a diversified approach. But Negroes can differ and still unite around common goals.

There are already structured forces in the Negro community that can serve as the basis for building a powerful united front—the Negro church, the Negro press, the Negro fraternities and sororities, and Negro professional associations. We must admit that these forces have never given their full resources to the cause of Negro liberation. There are still too many Negro churches that are so absorbed in a future good "over yonder" that they condition their members to adjust to the present evils "over here." Too many Negro newspapers have veered away from their traditional role as protest organs agitating for social change, and have turned to the sensational and the conservative in place of the substantive and the militant. Too many Negro social and professional groups have have degenerated into snobbishness and a preoccupation with frivolities and trivial activity. But the failures of the past must not be an excuse for the inaction of the present and the future. These groups must be mobilized and motivated. This form of group unity can do infinitely more to liberate the Negro than any action of *individuals*. We have been oppressed as a group and we must overcome that oppression as a group.

Through this form of group unity we can begin a constructive program which will vigorously seek to improve our personal standards. It is not a sign of weakness, but a sign of high maturity, to rise to the level of self-criticism. Through group unity we must convey to one another that our women must be respected, and that life is too precious to be destroyed in a Saturday night brawl, or a gang execution. Through community agencies and religious institutions we must develop a positive program through which Negro youth can become adjusted to urban living and improve their general level of behavior. While I strongly disagree with their separatist black supremacy philosophy, I have nothing but admiration for what our Muslim brothers have done to rehabilitate ex-convicts, dope addicts and men and women who, through despair and self-hatred, have sunk to moral degeneracy. This must be attempted on a much larger scale, and without the negative overtones that accompany Black Muslimism.

Since crime often grows out of a sense of futility and hopelessness, Negro parents, in spite of almost insuperable economic obstacles, must be urged to give their children the love, attention and sense of belonging that an oppressive society deprives them of. While not ignoring the fact that the ultimate way to diminish our problems of crime, family disorganization, illegitimacy and so forth will have to be found through a government program to help the frustrated Negro male find his true masculinity by placing him on his own two economic feet, we must do all within our power to approach these goals ourselves.

MARTIN LUTHER KING, JR.

The Concept of Black Power

"To carve out a place for itself in the politico-social order," V. O. Key, Jr. wrote in *Politics, Parties and Pressure Groups,* "a new group may have to fight for reorientation of many of the values of the old order" (p. 57). This is especially true when that group is composed of black people in the American society—a society that has for centuries deliberately and systematically excluded them from political participation. Black people in the United States must raise hard questions, questions which challenge the very nature of the society itself: its long-standing values, beliefs and institutions.

To do this, we must first redefine ourselves. Our basic need is to reclaim our history and our identity from what must be called cultural terrorism, from the depredation of self-justifying white guilt. We shall have to struggle for the right to create our own terms through which to define ourselves and our relationship to the society, and to have these terms recognized. This is the first necessity of a free people, and the first right that any oppressor must suspend.

The Importance of Self-Definition

In *Politics Among Nations,* Hans Morgenthau defined political power as "the psychological control over the minds of men" (p. 29). This control includes the attempt by the oppressor to have *his* definitions, *his* historical descriptions, *accepted* by the oppressed. This was true in Africa no less than in the United States. To black Africans, the word "Uhuru" means "freedom," but they had to fight the white colonizers for the right to use the term. The recorded history of this country's dealings with red and black men offers other examples. In the wars between the white settlers and the "Indians," a battle won by the Cavalry was described as a "victory." The "Indians'" triumphs, however, were "massacres." (The American colonists were not unaware of the need to define their acts in their own terms. They labeled their fight against Eng-

Stokely Carmichael and Charles V. Hamilton, *Black Power* (New York: Random House, 1968), pp. 34-56. Reprinted by permission.

land a "revolution"; the English attempted to demean it by calling it "insubordination" or "riotous.")

The historical period following Reconstruction in the South after the Civil War has been called by many historians the period of Redemption, implying that the bigoted southern slave societies were "redeemed" from the hands of "reckless and irresponsible" black rulers. Professor John Hope Franklin's *Reconstruction* or Dr. W. E. B. Du Bois' *Black Reconstruction* should be sufficient to dispel inaccurate historical notions, but the larger society persists in its own self-serving accounts. Thus black people came to be depicted as "lazy," "apathetic," "dumb," "shiftless," "good-timers." Just as red men had to be recorded as "savages" to justify the white man's theft of their land, so black men had to be vilified in order to justify their continued oppression. Those who have the right to define are the masters of the situation. Lewis Carroll understood this:

"When I use a word," Humpty Dumpty said in a rather scornful tone, "it means just what I choose it to mean—neither more nor less."

"The question is," said Alice, "whether you *can* make words mean so many different things."

"The question is," said Humpty Dumpty, "which is to be master—that's all." (Lewis Carroll, *Through the Looking Glass*. New York: Doubleday Books, Inc., p. 196.)

Today, the American educational system continues to reinforce the entrenched values of the society through the use of words. Few people in this country question that this is "the land of the free and the home of the brave." They have had these words drummed into them from childhood. Few people question that this is the "Great Society" or that this country is fighting "Communist aggression" around the world. We mouth these things over and over, and they become truisms not to be questioned. In a similar way, black people have been saddled with epithets.

"Integration" is another current example of a word which has been defined according to the way white Americans see it. To many of them, it means black men wanting to marry white daughters; it means "race mixing"—implying bed or dance partners. To black people, it has meant a way to improve their lives—economically and politically. But the predominant white definition has stuck in the minds of too many people.

Black people must redefine themselves, and only *they* can do that. Throughout this country, vast segments of the black communities are beginning to recognize the need to assert their own definitions, to reclaim their history, their culture; to create their own sense of community and togetherness. There is a growing resentment of the word "Negro," for example, because this term is the invention of our oppressor; it is *his* image of us that he describes. Many blacks are now calling themselves African-Americans, Afro-Americans or black people because that is *our* image of ourselves. When we begin to define our own image, the stereotypes—that is, lies—that our oppressor has developed will begin in the white community and end there. The black community will have a positive image of itself that *it* has created. This means we will no longer call ourselves lazy, apathetic, dumb, good-timers, shiftless, etc. Those are words used by white America to define us. If we accept these adjectives, as some of us have in the past, then we see ourselves only in a negative way, precisely the way white America wants us to see ourselves. Our incentive is broken and our will to fight is surrendered. From now on we shall view ourselves as African-Americans and as black people who are in fact energetic, determined, intelligent, beautiful and peace-loving.

There is a terminology and ethos peculiar to the black community of which black people are beginning to be no longer ashamed. Black communities are the only large segments of this society where people refer to each other as brother—soul-brother, soul-sister. Some people may look upon this as *ersatz*, as make-believe, but it is not that. It is real. It is a growing sense of community. It is a growing realization that black Americans have a common bond not only among themselves, but with their African brothers. . . .

More and more black Americans are developing this feeling. They are becoming aware that they have a history which pre-dates their forced introduction to this country. African-American history means a long history beginning on the continent of Africa, a history not taught in the standard textbooks of this country. It is absolutely essential that black people know this history, that they know their roots, that they develop an awareness of their cultural heritage. Too long have they been kept in submission by being told that they had no culture, no manifest heritage, before they landed on the slave auction blocks in this country. If black people are to know themselves as a vibrant, valiant people, they must know their roots. And they will soon learn that the Hollywood image of man-eating cannibals waiting for, and waiting on, the Great White Hunter is a lie. . . .

Only when black people fully develop this sense of community, of themselves, can they begin to deal effectively with the problems of racism in *this* country. This is what we mean by a new consciousness; this is the vital first step.

Politics of Modernization

The next step is what we shall call the process of political modernization—a process which must take place if the society is to be rid of racism. "Political modernization" includes many things, but we mean by it three major concepts: (1) questioning old values and institutions of the society; (2) searching for new and different forms of political structure to solve political and economic problems; and (3) broadening the base of political participation to include more people in the decision-making process. These notions (we shall take up each in turn) are central to our thinking throughout this book and to contemporary American history as a whole. As David Apter wrote in *The Politics of Modernization*, ". . . the struggle to modernize is what has given meaning to our generation. It tests our cherished institutions and our beliefs. . . . So compelling a force has it become that we are forced to ask new questions of our own institutions. Each country, whether modernized or modernizing, stands in both judgment and fear of the results. Our own society is no exception" (p. 2).

The values of this society support a racist system; we find it incongruous to ask black people to adopt and support most of those values. We also reject the assumption that the basic institutions of this society must be preserved. The goal of black people must *not* be to assimilate into middle-class America, for that class—as a whole—is without a viable conscience as regards humanity. The values of the middle class permit the perpetuation of the ravages of the black community. The values of that class are based on material aggrandizement, not the expansion of humanity. The values of that class ultimately support cloistered little closed societies tucked away neatly in tree-lined suburbia. The values of that class do *not* lead to the creation of an open society. That class *mouths* its preference for a free, competitive society, while at the same time forcefully and even viciously denying to black people as a group the opportunity to compete. . . .

But this same middle class manifests a sense of superior group position in regard to race. This class wants "good government" *for themselves;* it wants good schools *for its children.* At the same time, many of its members sneak into the black community by day, exploit it, and take the money home to their middle-class communities at night to support their operas and art galleries and comfortable homes. When not actually robbing, they will fight off the handful of more affluent black people who seek to move in; when they approve or even seek token integration, it applies only to black people like themselves—as "white" as possible. *This class is the backbone of institutional racism in this country.*

Thus we reject the goal of assimilation into middle-class America because the values of that class are in themselves anti-humanist and because that class as a social force perpetuates racism. We must face the fact that, in the past, what we have called the movement has not really questioned the middle-class values and institutions of this country. If anything, it has accepted those values and institutions without fully realizing their racist nature. Reorientation means an emphasis on the dignity of man, not on the sanctity of property. It means the creation of a society where human misery and poverty are repugnant to that society, not an indication of laziness or lack of initiative. The creation of new values means the establishment of a society based, as Killens expresses it in *Black Man's Burden,* on "free people," not "free enterprise" (p. 167). To do this means to modernize—*indeed,* to *civilize*—this country. . . .

Existing structures and established ways of doing things have a way of perpetuating themselves and for this reason, the modernizing process will be difficult. Therefore, timidity in calling into question the boards of education or the police departments will not do. They must be challenged forcefully and clearly. If this means the creation of parallel community institutions, then that must be the solution. If this means that black parents must gain control over the operation of the schools in the black community, then that must be the solution. The search for new forms means the search for institutions that will, for once, make decisions in the interest of black people. It means, for example, a building inspection department that neither winks at violations of building codes by absentee slumlords nor imposes meaningless fines which permit them to continue their exploitation of the black community.

Essential to the modernization of structures is a broadened base of political participation. More and more people must become politically sensitive and active (we have already seen this happening in some areas of the South). People must no longer be tied, by small incentives or handouts, to a corrupting and corruptible white machine. Black people will choose their own leaders and hold those leaders responsible to *them*. . . .

As the base broadens, as more and more black people become activated, they will perceive more clearly the special disadvantages heaped upon them as a group. They will perceive that the larger society is growing more affluent while the black society is retrogressing, as daily life and mounting statistics clearly show. . . . Black people will become increasingly active as they notice that their retrogressive status exists in large measure because of values and institutions arraigned against them. They will begin to stress and strain and call the entire system into question. Political modernization will be in motion. We believe that it is now in motion. One form of that motion is Black Power.

Close Ranks

The adoption of the concept of Black Power is one of the most legitimate and healthy developments in American politics and race relations in our time. The concept of Black Power speaks to all the needs mentioned in this chapter. It is a call for black people in this country to unite, to recognize their heritage, to build a sense of community. It is a call for black people to begin to define their own goals, to lead their own organizations and to support those organizations. It is a call to reject the racist institutions and values of this society.

The concept of Black Power rests on a fundamental premise: *Before a group can enter the open society, it must first close ranks.* By this we mean that group solidarity is necessary before a group can operate effectively from a bargaining position of strength in a pluralistic society. Traditionally, each new ethnic group in this society has found the route to social and political viability through the organization of its own institutions with which to represent its needs within the larger society. Studies in voting behavior specifically, and political behavior generally, have made it clear that politically the American pot has not melted. Italians vote for Rubino over O'Brien; Irish for Murphy over Goldberg, etc. This phenomenon may seem distasteful to some, but it has been and remains today a central fact of the American political system. . . .

The point is obvious: black people must lead and run their own organizations. Only black people can convey the revolutionary idea —and it is a revolutionary idea—that black people are able to do things themselves. Only they can help create in the community an aroused and continuing black consciousness that will provide the basis for political strength. In the past, white allies have often furthered white supremacy without the whites involved realizing it, or even wanting to do so. Black people must come together and do things for themselves. They must achieve self-identity and self-determination in order to have their daily needs met.

Black Power means, for example, that in Lowndes County, Alabama, a black sheriff can end police brutality. A black tax assessor and tax collector and county board of revenue can lay, collect, and channel tax monies for the building of better roads and schools serving black people. In such areas as Lowndes, where black people have a majority, they will attempt to use power to exercise control. This is what they seek: control. When black people lack a majority, Black Power means proper representation and sharing of control. It means the creation of power bases, of strength, from which black people can press to change local or nation-wide patterns of oppression—instead of from weakness.

It does not mean *merely* putting black faces into office. Black visibility is not Black Power. Most of the black politicians around the country today are not examples of Black Power. The power must be that of a community, and emanate from there. The black politicians must start from there. The black politicians must stop being representatives of "downtown" machines, whatever the cost might be in terms of lost patronage and holiday handouts.

Black Power recognizes—it must recognize—the ethnic basis of American politics as well as the power-oriented nature of American politics. Black Power therefore calls for black people to consolidate behind their own, so that they can bargain from a position of strength. But while we endorse the *procedure* of group solidarity and identity for the purpose of attaining certain goals in the body politic, this does not mean that black people should strive for the same kind of rewards (i.e., end results) obtained by the white society. The ultimate values and goals are not domination or exploitation of other groups, but rather an effective share in the total power of the society.

Nevertheless, some observers have labeled those who advocate Black Power as racists; they have said that the call for self-identification and self-determination is "racism in reverse" or "black supremacy." This is a deliberate and absurd lie. There is no analogy —by any stretch of definition or imagination—between the advocates of Black Power and white racists. Racism is not merely exclusion on the basis of race but exclusion for the purpose of subjugating or maintaining subjugation. The goal of the racists is to keep black people on the bottom, arbitrarily and dictatorially, as they have done in this country for over three hundred years. The goal of black self-determination and black self-identity—Black Power—is full participation in the decision-making processes affecting the lives of black people, and recognition of the virtues in themselves as black people. The black people of this country have not lynched whites, bombed their churches, murdered their children and manipulated laws and institutions to maintain oppression. White racists have. Congressional laws, one after the other, have not been necessary to stop black people from oppressing others and denying others the full enjoyment of their rights. White racists have made such laws necessary. The goal of Black Power is positive and functional to a free and viable society. No white racist can make this claim. . . .

It is a commentary on the fundamentally racist nature of this society that the concept of group strength for black people must be articulated—not to mention defended. No other group would submit to being led by others. Italians do not run the Anti-Defamation League of B'nai B'rith. Irish do not chair Christopher Columbus Societies. Yet when black people call for black-run and all-black organizations, they are immediately classed in a category with the Ku Klux Klan. This is interesting and ironic, but by no means surprising: the society does not expect black people to be able to take care of their business, and there are many who prefer it precisely that way.

In the end, we cannot and shall not offer any guarantees that Black Power, if achieved, would be non-racist. No one can predict human behavior. Social change always has unanticipated consequences. If black racism is what the larger society fears, we cannot help them. We can only state what we hope will be the result, given the fact that the present situation is unacceptable and that we have no real alternative but to work for Black Power. The final truth is that the white society is not entitled to reassurances, even if it were possible to offer them. . . .

Only a "Civil Rights" Movement

One of the tragedies of the struggle against racism is that up to this point there has been no national organization which could speak to the growing militancy of young black people in the urban ghettos and the black-belt South. There has been only a "civil rights" movement, whose tone of voice was adapted to an audience of middle-class whites. It served as a sort of buffer zone between that audience and angry young blacks. It claimed to speak for the needs of a community, but it did not speak in the tone of that community. None of its so-called leaders could go into a rioting community and be listened to. In a sense, the blame must be shared —along with the mass media—by those leaders for what happened in Watts, Harlem, Chicago, Cleveland and other places. Each time the black people in those cities saw Dr. Martin Luther King get slapped they became angry. When they saw little black girls bombed to death *in a church* and civil rights workers ambushed and murdered, they were angrier; and when nothing happened, they were steaming mad. We had nothing to offer that they could see, except to go out and be beaten again. We helped to build their frustration.

We had only the old language of love and suffering. And in most places—that is, from the liberals and middle class—we got back the old language of patience and progress. The civil rights leaders were saying to the country: "Look, you guys are supposed to be nice guys, and we are only going to do what we are supposed to do. Why do you beat us up? Why don't you give us what we ask? Why don't you straighten yourselves out?" For the masses of black people, this language resulted in virtually nothing. In fact, their objective day-to-day condition worsened. The unemployment rate among black people increased while that among whites declined.

Housing conditions in the black communities deteriorated. Schools in the black ghettos continued to plod along on outmoded techniques, inadequate curricula, and with all too many tired and indifferent teachers. Meanwhile, the President picked up the refrain of "We Shall Overcome" while the Congress passed civil rights law after civil rights law, only to have them effectively nullified by deliberately weak enforcement. "Progress is being made," we were told.

Such language, along with admonitions to remain non-violent and fear the white backlash, convinced some that that course was the *only* course to follow. It misled some into believing that a black minority could bow its head and get whipped into a meaningful position of power. The very notion is absurd. The white society devised the language, adopted the rules and had the black community narcotized into believing that that language and those rules were, in fact, relevant. The black community was told time and again how *other* immigrants finally won *acceptance:* that is, by following the Protestant Ethic of Work and Achievement. They worked hard; therefore, they achieved. We were not told that it was by building Irish Power, Italian Power, Polish Power or Jewish Power that these groups got themselves together and operated from positions of strength. We were not told that "the American dream" wasn't designed for black people. That while today, to whites, the dream may *seem* to include black people, it cannot do so by the very nature of this nation's political and economic system, which imposes institutional racism on the black masses if not upon every individual black. . . .

A key phrase in our buffer-zone days was non-violence. For years it has been thought that black people would not literally fight for their lives. Why this has been so is not entirely clear; neither the larger society nor black people are noted for passivity. The notion apparently stems from the years of marches and demonstrations and sit-ins where black people did not strike back and the violence always came from white mobs. There are many who still sincerely believe in that approach. From our viewpoint, rampaging white mobs and white night-riders must be made to understand that their days of free head-whipping are over. Black people should and must fight back. Nothing more quickly repels someone bent on destroying you than the unequivocal message: "O.K., fool, make your move, and run the same risk I run—of dying."

When the concept of Black Power is set forth, many people immediately conjure up notions of violence. The country's reaction to the Deacons for Defense and Justice, which originated in Louisiana, is instructive. Here is a group which realized that the "law" and law enforcement agencies would not protect people, so they had to do it themselves. If a nation fails to protect its citizens, then that nation cannot condemn those who take up the task themselves. The Deacons and all other blacks who resort to self-defense represent a simple answer to a simple question: what man would not defend his family and home from attack?

But this frightened some white people, because they knew that black people would now fight back. They knew that this was precisely what *they* would have long since done if *they* were subjected to the injustices and oppression heaped on blacks. Those of us who advocate Black Power are quite clear in our own minds that a "non-violent" approach to civil rights is an approach black people cannot afford and a luxury white people do not deserve. It is crystal clear to us—and it must become so with the white society —*that there can be no social order without social justice*. White people must be made to understand that they must stop messing with black people, or the blacks *will* fight back!

Next, we must deal with the term "integration." According to its advocates, social justice will be accomplished by "integrating the Negro into the mainstream institutions of the society from which he has been traditionally excluded." This concept is based on the assumption that there is nothing of value in the black community and that little of value could be created among black people. The thing to do is siphon off the "acceptable" black people into the surrounding middle-class white community.

The goals of integrationists are middle-class goals, articulated primarily by a small group of Negroes with middle-class aspirations or status. Their kind of integration has meant that a few blacks "make it," leaving the black community, sapping it of leadership potential and know-how. As we noted in Chapter I, those token Negroes—absorbed into a white mass—are of no value to the remaining black masses. They become meaningless show-pieces for a conscience-soothed white society. Such people will state that they would prefer to be treated "only as individuals, not as Negroes"; that they "are not and should not be preoccupied with race." This is a totally unrealistic position. In the first place, black people have not suffered as individuals but as members of a group; therefore, their liberation lies in group action. This is why SNCC —and the concept of Black Power—affirms that helping *individual* black people to solve their problems on an *individual* basis does little to alleviate the mass of black people. Secondly, while color blindness *may* be a sound goal ultimately, we must realize that race is an overwhelming fact of life in this historical period. There is no black man in this country who can live "simply as a man." His blackness is an ever-present fact of this racist society, whether he recognizes it or not. It is unlikely that this or the next generation will witness the time when race will no longer be relevant in the conduct of public affairs and in public policy decision-making. To realize this and to attempt to deal with it does not make one a racist or overly preoccupied with race; it puts one in the forefront of a significant *struggle*. If there is no intense struggle today, there will be no meaningful results tomorrow.

"Integration" as a goal today speaks to the problem of blackness not only in an unrealistic way but also in a despicable way. It is based on complete acceptance of the fact that in order to have a decent house or education, black people must move into a white neighborhood or send their children to a white school. This reinforces, among both black and white, the idea that "white" is automatically superior and "black" is by definition inferior. For this reason, "integration" is a subterfuge for the maintenance of white supremacy. It allows the nation to focus on a handful of Southern black children who get into white schools at a great price, and to ignore the ninety-four percent who are left in unimproved all-black schools. Such situations will not change until black people become equal in a way that means something, and integration ceases to be a one-way street. Then integration does not mean draining skills and energies from the black ghetto into white neighborhoods. To sprinkle black children among white pupils in outlying schools is at best a stop-gap measure. The goal is not to take black children out of the black community and expose them to white middle-class values; the goal is to build and strengthen the black community.

"Integration" also means that black people must give up their identity, deny their heritage. We recall the conclusion of Killian and Grigg: "At the present time, integration as a solution to the race problem demands that the Negro foreswear his identity as a

Negro." The fact is that integration, as traditionally articulated, would abolish the black community. The fact is that what must be abolished is not the black community, but the dependent colonial status that has been inflicted upon it.

The racial and cultural personality of the black community must be preserved and that community must win its freedom while preserving its cultural integrity. Integrity includes a pride—in the sense of self-acceptance, not chauvinism—in being black, in the historical attainments and contributions of black people. No person can be healthy, complete and mature if he must deny a part of himself; this is what "integration" has required thus far. This is the essential difference between integration as it is currently practiced and the concept of Black Power.

The idea of cultural integrity is so obvious that it seems almost simple-minded to spell things out at this length. Yet millions of Americans resist such truths when they are applied to black people. Again, that resistance is a comment on the fundamental racism in the society. Irish Catholics took care of their own first without a lot of apology for doing so, without any dubious language from timid leadership about guarding against "backlash." Everyone understood it to be a perfectly legitimate procedure. Of course, there would be "backlash." Organization begets counterorganization, but this was no reason to defer.

The so-called white backlash against black people is something else: the embedded traditions of institutional racism being brought into the open and calling forth overt manifestations of individual racism. In the summer of 1966, when the protest marches into Cicero, Illinois, began, the black people knew they were not allowed to live in Cicero and the white people knew it. When blacks began to demand the right to live in homes in that town, the whites simply reminded them of the status quo. Some people called this "backlash." It was, in fact, racism defending itself. In the black community, this is called "White folks showing their color." It is ludicrous to blame black people for what is simply an overt manifestation of white racism. Dr. Martin Luther King stated clearly that the protest marches were not the cause of the racism but merely exposed a long-term cancerous condition in the society.

STOKELY CARMICHAEL and CHARLES V. HAMILTON

So Little, So Late

For reasons that are both political and economic, other social institutions are becoming inclusive so rapidly as to make the church's voluntary labors seem so little and so late!

Only belatedly has the matter of local church inclusion been placed on the agenda because of deterring factors of isolation in white churches and cohesion in Negro churches.

All attempts at institutional inclusiveness in American social life tend to be anomalies because the basic fabric of living itself is one of fragmentation, occasional contacts and only very limited knowledge of those whom we would include. . . .

What do we really mean by inclusiveness? Is it really logical to assume that people who do not or cannot share any deep experiences with each other for six days a week will really have any illusions about the privilege of worship for one hour on Sunday?

JAMES S. THOMAS, Bishop of the Iowa Area
of the Methodist Church

From "Local Church: Exclusive or Inclusive," in *The Methodist Story,* January, 1967, p. 3. Reprinted by permission.

Racism: What It Is

Racism is mighty hard to define. It's like the story of that elephant being described by five blind men, each feeling a different part.

There are some who would point to the first grade readers and say: "Tom and Jane are always white. That's racism." Their slogan is "Color me Black." But if you did color Tom and Jane black in every primer in the United States, you would not have eliminated racism. The beast is bigger than that.

Others have other definitions.

The failure to teach Black history and culture in the schools. That's racism.

Segregation. That's racism. Except today, we have other names for it.

They call it the neighborhood school concept. And they draw the boundary lines very carefully. That's racism.

The track system. That's racism. They use culture biased, race biased, class biased tests to label Black children DUMB—except they don't call them DUMB. They call them culturally deprived and they put them in a grouping called "special academic."

Less money, less experienced teachers, less supplies, less facilities, less educational materials for Black schools. That's racism.

Assigning whites only to white schools, keeping Black children out of white schools, refusing to let Black educators hold top supervisory and administrative posts. All of that is racism.

FLOYD B. MCKISSICK, CORE

I Have a Dream

I say to you today, my friends, that in spite of the difficulties and frustrations of the moment, I still have a dream. It is a dream deeply rooted in the American dream.

I have a dream that one day this nation will rise up and live out the true meaning of its creed: "We hold these truths to be self-evident: that all men are created equal."

I have a dream that one day on the red hills of Georgia the sons of former slaves and the sons of former slaveowners will be able to sit down together at the table of brotherhood.

I have a dream that one day even the state of Mississippi, a desert state sweltering with the heat of injustice and oppression, will be transformed into an oasis of freedom and justice.

I have a dream that my four little children will one day live in a nation where they will not be judged by the color of their skin but the content of their character.

I have a dream today.

I have a dream that one day the state of Alabama, whose governor's lips are presently dripping with the words of interposition and nullification, will be transformed into a situation where little black boys and girls will be able to join hands with little white boys and white girls and walk together as sisters and brothers.

I have a dream today.

I have a dream that one day every valley shall be exalted, every hill and mountain shall be made low, the rough places will be made plains, and the crooked places will be made straight, and the glory of the Lord shall be revealed, and all flesh shall see it together.

This is our hope. This is the faith with which I return to the South. With this faith we will be able to hew out of the mountains of despair a stone of hope. With this faith we will be able to transform the jangling discords of our nation into a beautiful symphony of brotherhood. With this faith we will be able to work together, to pray together, to struggle together, to go to jail together, to stand up for freedom together, knowing that we will be free one day.

This will be the day when all of God's children will be able to sing with new meaning "My country 'tis of thee, sweet land of liberty, of thee I sing. Land where my fathers died, land of the Pilgrim's pride, from every mountainside, let freedom ring."

And if America is to be a great nation this must become true. So let freedom ring from the prodigious hilltops of New Hampshire. Let freedom ring from the mighty mountains of New York. Let freedom ring from the heightening Alleghenies of Pennsylvania.

Let freedom ring from the snow-capped Rockies of Colorado.

Let freedom ring from the curvacious peaks of California!

But not only that; let freedom ring from Stone Mountain of Georgia!

Let freedom ring from every hill and mole hill of Mississippi. From every mountainside, let freedom ring.

When we let freedom ring, when we let it ring from every village and every hamlet, from every state and every city, we will be able to speed up that day when all of God's children, black men and white men, Jews and Gentiles, Protestants and Catholics, will be able to join hands and sing in the words of that old Negro spiritual, "Free at last! Free at last! Thank God almighty, we are free at last!"

MARTIN LUTHER KING, JR.,
Southern Christian Leadership Conference

A Letter from Parish Prison
(New Orleans, Louisiana, Feb. 21, 1968)

Being a man is the continuing battle of one's life. One loses a bit of manhood with every stale compromise to the authority of any power in which one does not believe.

No slave should die a natural death. There is a point where caution ends and cowardice begins.

For every day I am in prison I will refuse both food and water. My hunger is for the liberation of my people. My thirst is for the ending of oppression.

I am a political prisoner, jailed for my beliefs—that black people must be free. The government has taken a position true to its fascist nature.

Those who they cannot convert they silence.

This government has become the enemy of mankind.

This can no longer alter our path to freedom. For our people, death has been the only known exit from slavery and oppression.

We must open others.

Our will to live must no longer supersede our will to fight, for our fighting will determine if our race shall live. To desire freedom is not enough.

We must move from resistance to aggression, from revolt to revolution.

For every Orangeburg, there must be ten Detroits. For every Max Stanford and every Huey Newton there must be ten dead racist cops. And for every black death, there must be a Dien Bien Phu.

Brothers and Sisters, and all oppressed people, we must prepare ourselves both mentally and physically, for the major confrontation yet to come.

We must fight.

It is the people who in the final analysis make and determine history, not leaders or systems. The laws to govern us must be made by us.

May the death of '68 signal the beginning of the end of this country.

I do what I must out of the love for my people. My will is to fight; resistance is not enough. Aggression is the order of the day.

Note to America

America, if it takes my death to organize my people to revolt against you and to organize your jails to revolt against you and to organize your troops to revolt against you and to organize your children, your god, your poor, your country, and to organize mankind to rejoice in your destruction and ruin, then here is my life. But my soul belongs to my people.

Lasima tushinde mbilashaka. We shall conquer without a doubt!

H. Rap Brown, Student Non-Violent Coordinating Committee

Are Negroes Ready for Black Power?

The theme of Black Power, in spite of much recent publicity, is not new on the American scene. Nor is it likely to die out in the foreseeable future, regardless of the outcome of the current debate concerning the propriety of the term "Black Power."

"Black Power" has been a continuing refrain in the history of the American Negro. The slave uprisings, which were more frequent than historians often relate, continually reiterated the Black Power theme. It was the clarion call of the rebel John Brown and of the abolitionist Frederick Douglass. The sophisticated and angered W. E. B. DuBois and the militant visionary Marcus Garvey addressed themselves to the issue of the black man's cooperative strength and dignity; and A. Philip Randolph's Brotherhood of Sleeping Car Porters came together, held together and became a major lever in American political and economic life through a commitment to what militants today speak of as Black Power.

What precisely does "Black Power" mean? In the Negro

Nathan Wright, Jr., *Black Power and Urban Unrest* (New York: Hawthorn Books, Inc., 1967), pp. 13-17. Copyright © 1967 by the author. Reprinted by permission.

churches, it has most often meant a kind of black solidarity in a holy war where in an imminent latter day the saints of light, who have witnessed the evil onslaughts of the powers of darkness, will receive their due reward. Howard Thurman in his recent and perhaps his greatest book, *The Luminous Darkness,* speaks of the perception of his early youth that white humanity was beyond the pale of his morality. Such widespread feelings of the mystical uniqueness of the Negro have been the backdrop for the political thrusts which we identify most often as Black Power. In its first several decades of militancy, the National Association for the Advancement of Colored People could have been fairly identified with the alleged dissidents of today who speak of the critical force of the Negro's united strength.

Such an idea today is frequently criticized for being open to misunderstanding, and subject to individual interpretation, and therefore possibly misleading. Since Black Power speaks—as it has done over several centuries—to the Negro's recognition and aggressive assertion of his own fundamental sense of dignity, integrity and worth, it must have flexible implications; for no two individuals can perceive and assert their own validity and place in precisely identical ways. The belligerent by nature will tend to express his own sense of being and relationship in bellicose ways; the more temperate will tend to use more temperate means. Nonetheless, there may be real danger in a mass rallying to the theme of Black Power. The Negro people over the years have been encouraged by many means to suppress and sublimate their natural feelings of conflict and frustration. With a long-postponed and new-found freedom, the potential catharsis inherent in the current call to the banners of Black Power may be fraught with painful excess. Black Power is a logical and much-needed expression of the Negro's awakening to self-awareness, a sometimes awkward stretching of his arms and flexing of his muscles as he looks half-bewildered at his newly felt but as yet untested and unmeasured political and moral strength.

On Being a Negro

Interestingly, those who oppose the use of the term "Black Power" have often raised the objection that Negroes court annihilation once Black Power comes face to face with white power. Such a vision of the armed conflict of two opposing and ludicrously unequal camps represents both a misreading of the intent of those who espouse Black Power and a failure to understand the necessary dynamics of social and moral progress.

Ethnocentrism, or the consciousness of in-group solidarity, with a consequent sense of pride and power, is one of the strongest of human sentiments. The nature of an in-group or an ethnic community is defined by the culture of which the group is a part. The American culture has defined a number of ethnic groups, including notably the Jews, the Irish and the Scotch-Irish, who represent religious, national or a combination of religious and national groupings. All of these groups have intense pride in their own membership; and they express this in a variety of ways. There are several singular and significant differences in the circumstances of the role of Negroes as an ethnic group in American life. The Negro's ability to express his sense of pride has been circumscribed.

Perhaps nowhere has this been more flagrant than in the wellnigh completely successful attempts of the white community, with the encouragement and complicity of the nation's social scientists, to have the Negro forget that he is by and large a European–American Indian–black African hybrid. The Negro has been encouraged to forget that the ancestors whose name he bears were of British stock, and that the varying shades of color and different textures of hair among his people are a reflection of a variegated ethnic ancestry. In culture almost completely, and in race to a fairly considerable degree, the overwhelming majority of American Negroes are of a European background. Yet the Negro's sense of racial and cultural pride has been restricted to his supposed African origins in a veiled and uncertain past. Rare is the writer of an American textbook in sociology or history who attributes to the Negro anything other than pure African descent, except in the semiderogatory sense of illegitimacy (although illegitimacy is common to all family strains).

"Black Power," then, may be seen to be a form of ethnocentrism, albeit falling into a trap set by the historically racist-bound American culture with the complicity of social scientists who inevitably tend to operate, hopefully with some objectivity, within the accepted framework of the society of which they are a part.

The Negro's sense of pride is further blunted by the un-American assumption that the Negro's position of social and economic inferiority is immutable. The "last-hired-first-fired" concept here may be seen to be not the result of individual prejudice but the logical expression of a way of life which rejects the Negro's worth. The Negro himself has purchased stock in this endeavor. Partly by recoil in self-defense and partly by imposed design, the American Negro has eschewed social equality. No major civil rights leader, even today, espouses as a major plank in his platform social equality, at the very heart of which is the matter of intermarriage. Yet economic survival and advancement, as well as a sense of pride, depend in no small degree upon relationships of a blood and legal variety.

Negroes today are isolated not only from the jobs at the bottom of the ladder, but also from those at the top, so desperately needed to begin a closing of the economic gap. Admittedly this isolation stems from an absence of contacts. Whom one knows is for white Americans as important as what one knows. For Negro Americans, the failure to know economically successful people in those intimate and familial relationships which spell care and concern and mutual economic responsibility means no less than a growing isolation from the economic and social fruits of American life, which are theoretically their due inheritance.

The renewed impetus toward the concept of Black Power reflects the apparent readiness of many Negro Americans to implement their now hoarse and hackneyed and desperate cry of: "All! Here! Now!"

The Greatest Show on Earth

A story is told of an advertisement for what was billed as the most unusual show on earth. The day finally came for the great performance, and an audience in curious expectancy was treated to a one-minute show of symbolic behavior. Twelve Negroes were simply tugging hard at a rope. When those who had come for the show demanded an explanation, the producer simply asked, "Where on earth have you ever seen twelve Negroes pulling together?"

What is true of the American Negro is true of all ethnic groups. Everyone is unique, and only at critical and measured points do corporate interests emerge. For the Negro this has been both bane and blessing. With the current controversy over the massive economic and social indications of the monumental use of the term Black Power, a consensus is sought where no agreement need legitimately exist. The fact is that, in spite of the failure of the American people to close the gap between Negroes and their white counterparts, many Negroes are content with the current drift and trend of things.

The willingness to speak to the affirmative implications of Black Power may be in a closely proportional relationship to one's conception of Negro progress. On this issue, Negroes are not, and doubtless will not be, agreed.

Negroes, like all Americans, are generally better off today than they were at the end of World War II. The awareness of this fact leads not only many Negroes typical of the "man in the street" but also a substantial portion of recognized Negro leadership to speak with apparent integrity of the "progress" and "gains" which Negroes are making. Yet the American economy generally has been growing by greater degrees than has the Negro's alleged "progress." This leads other Negroes of equal integrity to reject the term "progress" with as much disdain as that with which some have rejected the term Black Power.

NATHAN WRIGHT, JR.

The Negro Needs a Stake in the System

Let me make it real clear—I'm not a pacifist. I am not a nonviolent person. I am a very violent person, particularly as it relates to self-defense for myself and my family. And I'm not at all sure that I would not be an advocate of violence if I thought I could win. If the situation were reversed and we were in Nigeria or in Ethiopia or somewhere, I might well be an advocate of violence. But looking at the hard realities, unless somebody shows me something that I haven't seen yet, by way of superior weapons, then I at this point do not see this as a very sound tactic. And so

From an interview recorded March 3, 1968, by Public Broadcast Laboratories. Reprinted by permission of Whitney M. Young, Jr.

we are against violence. But I think the responsible Negro community has gone about as far as it can go in saying to its constituency be patient, be non-violent, be loyal. And not being able to produce tangible, concrete victories. The Negro must be given a stake in this system, in the same way that the business community at a time in history after great soul-searching and great anguish and grief managed to begin talking with labor leaders and finally gave them a stake in the system, to the degree that when I was in Miami not too long ago, at an AFL-CIO executive council, I walked in the hotel and all of the executive buyers were walking around with pekinese dogs, mink coats and chauffeured cars waiting outside and elaborate, well stocked suites. They were in no mood to talk about revolution.

WHITNEY M. YOUNG, JR., National Urban League

Study in Black and White

It is conceded by all observers that Senator Eugene McCarthy's New Hampshire primary total was due in no small part to the work of student volunteers. They came from New Hampshire and from colleges in other states. Some left school for the duration of the campaign. The word was passed to the youth on the campuses that their man, McCarthy, needed help in his campaign based on his—and their—opposition to the Vietnam war. They answered, in person.

For their cause and for the men who voiced their views they wrote letters, ran mimeograph machines, arranged conferences, ran errands, manned telephones, distributed literature, rang doorbells and argued persuasively with New Hampshire voters.

Some of them did more. They had their long hair cut. They shaved off their beards. They put on clean shirts and some even donned ties! They did this because they wanted to appeal to voters, not to repel possible McCarthy supporters with the treasured peculiarities of individual students. In other words, they put the

From *New York Amsterdam News,* March 30, 1968. Reprinted by permission.

cause first (getting voters on their side) and their personal dressing habits second.

Hundreds of these veteran student workers have moved into Wisconsin and reports are that perhaps as many as 7,000 will work there for McCarthy.

Take Possession

What a contrast to the intemperate dogmatism and personal invective of the "militant black students"! While the white students were busy helping their man round up delegates in opposition to the policy of President Johnson, a black student group at Howard University was taking possession of the Administration building.

What high purpose moved these Howard students to throttle a university and to attempt to dictate administrative and educational policy?

Well, they were moved by a conviction that student demonstrators who injected themselves into the recent Charter Day observance of the University should not be charged. This says: "We can do what we please, whenever we please, but we must not be punished."

The white students, confronted with solving a problem for their standard-bearer, took the action that would win friends and influence voters in New Hampshire. The black students were so busy "taking over" a university and denouncing what they call "Uncle Toms" that they have lost sight of what should be their main objective: winning friends for the changes they wish to bring about at Howard.

Under Their Noses

There are mountains of tasks among their people that cry for the attention of these students. Right there in Washington under their noses, is the national legislature of the United States, the Congress. If the Howard students have done anything to press the needed Republican Congressmen to support the Senate-passed open housing bill, the secret has been well kept.

It is more important from the standpoint of 22 million Negro Americans for them to get votes for the bill than to shake their fists at the president of Howard University. Their dedication would be more admirable if it were for "the people" whom they profess to love instead of being for their egos.

The white students are going for the political jugular vein according to the campaign rules; the black students are just going—mostly in response to their own repetitive harangues.

ROY WILKINS, Executive Director, NAACP

On the Police State

Whenever you have to pass a law to make a man let me have a house, or you have to pass a law to make a man let me go to school, or you have to pass a law to make a man let me walk down the street, you have to enforce that law—then you'd be living in a police state. America right now is moving toward the police state.

MALCOLM X

From *Who Speaks for the Negro?*, ed. by Robert Penn Warren (New York: Random House, 1965) p. 261. Reprinted by permission of the publisher.

Some Personal Reflections and Observations on the Negro Middle Class

by Muriel Snowden

I finally decided that I would talk with you as frankly and as honestly as I can about a minority *within* a minority, about the group characterized as the Negro Middle Class. As a member of this group, which *also* lives, works, and functions inside the urban ghetto, I want to try to sort out fact from myth in a way which is admittedly highly personal and experiential. Who are we? Where do we stand? How do we relate to the "militants"? What are our problems?

In years past, before Michael Harrington's *Other America* emerged into the spotlight, attention was often directed toward those black Americans who managed to live comfortably. They were cited as shining examples of the opportunities this democracy offers *all* of its citizens. And for good measure, you could always throw in Ralph Bunche, Marian Anderson, Lena Horne, Jackie Robinson, George Washington Carver, *et al.*

There was a phoniness about this which nobody ever bothered to talk about. The yardstick used in measuring "success" dealt only in material terms and completely ignored the all-important psychological ones.

To pursue this point a little further: today, the pendulum has swung to the other extreme. The middle class—"successful" people, including just the average black Joe and his family—are either ignored or dismissed because they are removed from the poverty level, or else maligned by both whites *and* blacks for having managed to "escape." An attitude like this consigns us to the no-man's land of South Africa's Cape Coloureds. (This analogy may be totally inaccurate because I do not know any Cape Coloureds, nor do I have any way of determining where their open or secret identifications lie.) What I *do* know, though, is that a vital point is seemingly being missed today by many of those claiming racial expertise in their failure to recognize that a far greater number of middle-class Negroes, more than are given credit for it, *do* identify with the black revolt on the level of the quest for psychological security. In at least this one respect, we are all have-nots whether we admit it or not—and more and more of us are starting to admit it, if only to each other.

My husband and I lived through the nightmare of the ghetto explosion in Boston last June. We were on the scene during the build-up. We got caught in the by-play between the police and the protesting on-lookers. We joined the militants in meetings around unity and strategy and opened up for them some of the direct lines to the city authorities. Our meeting facilities at Freedom House were made available, and we even operated an emergency medical station there at their request.

We also met with other Negroes in our community, people not identified with the militants, and we struggled for hours about what public position we could or should take regarding the "rebellion."

We finally ended up by saying nothing. We didn't want to join the chant of "deploring the violence," and we wanted to do more than merely affirm the validity of the complaints of the Mothers for Adequate Welfare or point a finger at the police who here, as in Watts and elsewhere, indisputably triggered the whole thing by their panicky action. I suspect, too, that behind it all, there lurked in our minds the secret, reluctant thought that maybe a June 2nd [riot] was what it took. After all, all the years of our attempts at calm, reasoned appeals had accomplished nothing.

And so the white power structure in our town bemoaned the "strange silence" of what they like to refer to as "the stable Negro leadership," and they berated us for our "abdication of responsibility." One Massachusetts State Senator, with a reputation as an outspoken, fair-minded white liberal who has initiated and/or supported legislation such as the Massachusetts Racial Imbalance Act and reorganization of the welfare system, spoke last October at a conference at Radcliffe College. He went so far as to state that not only had the Boston Negro community failed to produce effective leadership but that those who could do the job had been "compromised" by taking federal and state positions.

Let me make one more point. Apparently there always has been and always will be a generational gap in human society. You are removed from your parents in many ways, and *my* parents did not understand my brother and me either. They were disappointed when I elected to take my nice Radcliffe education into a job as an old age assistance worker in Newark's then toughest district— its Third Ward. When I quit after five years because I could no longer stomach running around making believe that old people could really live on $30 per month, they felt that I was making another mistake. Their hardest blow came from my brother, their only son, who steadfastly refused to follow our father into dentistry and instead became deeply involved with Norman Thomas Socialists, the Fellowship of Reconciliation, and the War Resisters League. Later, he was to spend almost four years in a federal penitentiary as a conscientious objector in World War II.

With a little more insight, my parents would not have been surprised to realize that they, themselves, had made it possible for us to reject the superficialities of their world of creature comforts in the search for more meaningful values of our own.

And this backbone-stiffening process goes on. Think about it. How did these fire-eating black young people get that way? In many instances, they are the children of the moderate Negroes of my generation. These kids didn't pull their anger, their concepts of self and dignity and manhood out of thin air. We produced them. We taught them.

I am reminded of the scene in *Guess Who's Coming to Dinner* where Sidney Poitier confronts his father with the statement that the latter thinks of himself as a black man while he, the son, thinks of himself as a man. The movies haven't quite caught up with the movement though, because a more accurate statement would have been, I think, "Father, you think of yourself as black; I think of myself as a black *man!*"

This is what my husband remembered when he joined the group from Boston that went to march in Selma. There was a woman walking close beside him, and he asked her about being afraid since she lived and worked in Selma. Her answer, as she pointed to her two kids who were marching in front of her, was this: "Sure, I am, but I'm marching for *them.*"

The point that I think I am trying to make is that the many experiences which both my husband and I recall vividly are those in which we saw our parents stand up and fiercely protect us from racial hurt and slurs. This had a great deal to do with how we were taught to think about ourselves and with what we were able to pass along to our own daughter—and certainly ours are not isolated situations.

Further, even though everybody tries to make a big thing out of the fact that only a small percentage of urban Negroes engage in riots, the silence of the "others" undoubtedly stems from their vicarious venting of their own inner rage and hostility toward the police, toward exploitation, toward denial.

There is a great deal of ambivalence in all of this, and I would be willing to wager that there are as many shouting matches going on elsewhere as there are in Boston among black people of every level and class about what "black power" really means and the best ways in which black Americans can and must make themselves felt and respected.

Despite the widely different approaches espoused by these different elements in the black community, a few common denominators are beginning to show up. One that seems for sure is the universal resentment we *all* feel toward that white person who tries to out-black power the extremists in an effort to establish himself as a sympathizer—or worse yet, as someone who knows and understands better than any of us the plight of the poor black community. It is my opinion that this type will soon be neutralized or totally eliminated from our scene.

There is also pretty generalized negative reaction to those whites who attempt to solve their own ego needs and psychological hang-ups by running to us. We tend to agree with Ron Karenga or whoever it was on the West Coast who said: "Brother, we ain't runnin' no therapy sessions here."

Personally, I have to make distinctions between those whites for whom "we ain't runnin' no therapy sessions" and those who are or can be true allies. I am not yet prepared to suspect, distrust, disbelieve every individual whose skin is white. My own life experiences won't permit that even though I have to admit that in times of severe stress, I find myself guiltily harboring doubts about the depth of sincerity of white friends.

Middle-class Negroes must contend with a cruel paradox: Having played the game by all the rules—you know, "work hard," "be thrifty," "get an education," "mind your manners," "watch your language," "wear the 'right' clothes," etc., etc.—we are *still* outside the pale. We have to learn what the alienated black reformers are trying to teach us—that we are still, first of all, black, in a racist society. In other words, we have to face the fact that *we* are the living proof that white America's pious pronouncements are still just a sham.

This means that more and more of us need to admit loudly and publicly our own hostility and alienation and refuse to be the pawns in an evil game. This, from conversations with my now-22-year-old daughter, is what I gather the young black students in Ivy League schools, for example, are talking about and why they have formed the black student groups.

It means, too, that more and more middle-class Negroes must find the ways to reopen the channels of communication so that they may be more intimately and productively involved in this common struggle in which our fates are so inextricably interwoven. I think the turmoil, the tension, and the realities are moving the black community toward a kind of cohesion which I am sure will never be total, but one which will, I hope, be able to take advantage of all our strengths *wherever* they exist.

Muriel Snowden is Associate Director of Freedom House, Boston, Massachusetts.

"The man tell you who your enemy is in Vietnam. I'll tell you who your enemy is. It's Lurleen Wallace. You're a fool not to shoot George, Lurleen, or little junior. The honkie is your enemy."

H. RAP BROWN, SNCC
(quoted in *The Harvard Crimson,* October 20, 1967, p. 53)

"I'm a *bad nigger*. The only language these white folks understand is an eye for an eye, a tooth for a tooth. Every time a black man gets killed, you ought to try to get two honkies. You spendin' all this money on expensive clothes and hairdos. You better buy yourself some guns and ammunition. You gonna need them."

WILL ROGERS, SNCC
(quoted in *The Harvard Crimson,* October 20, 1967, p. 53)

Al Cleage, Jr., on Black Power

What is the nature of Central Church?
We have all kinds of people here—and they come on the basis of a commitment or a conviction about the kind of Christianity we preach. A lawyer doesn't expect to be treated differently because he is a lawyer. An ADC mother who comes into the church doesn't expect to be treated differently because she receives ADC. . . .

From "Interview: Al Cleage on Black Power," in *United Church Herald,* Vol. II, No. 2, February, 1968, pp. 27–30. Reprinted by permission.

Has your preaching about the nation increased in intensity recently?

I wouldn't say "increased in intensity." It has developed. You don't all of a sudden realize that most of the things you learned in the seminary about Christianity are false. It take a little time. Your preaching develops. Gradually you find a form in which the concepts are clarified. . . . You can be a pretty good preacher but not know what to preach. As situations give you a message, you can make Christianity relevant. If you're able to grasp what the message is for your day, then your preaching takes on an entirely new significance.

You seem to welcome black militants into your church. Is this part of the style of your ministry?

Yes, we welcome black militants. By militants I presume you mean black people who are tired of oppression and who have given up on the assumption that you can talk white people into changing. Those black militants who are committed to change and who want to do something about it—activists—we welcome them. And Central is about the only church in Detroit where respectable black militants can come without shame.

Are these persons ready for violence if that is necessary?

I think any black person—militant or non-militant—except the extreme Uncle Tom (and there aren't many of them left)—is ready for violence if it is necessary. Just like any white person is ready for violence if it is necessary.

Under what conditions would violence be necessary?

You take the situation here at the present time. We know very well that in the peripheral sections of the city which are predominantly white, and in the suburbs, mass meetings are being held—weekly—to arouse white people to the danger of the black inner core of the city.

Every kind of provocation and lies are given. Extremist groups speak of Communism fomenting riots in the inner city. All this is going on and gun clubs are organized. Thousands and thousands of guns are going into the suburbs, and these are not just rifles and shot guns. These are carbines—rapid fire carbines—machine guns, and hand grenades. All being accumulated in the outer city, largely through the deliberate manipulation of white extremists. They are utilizing the fear of white people about black power, which they don't understand. These extremists know there is no threat from the black inner city—except in terms of black people wanting to control their own destiny.

How close would black militants be to violence? If the outer suburbs for any reason would try to invade the inner city, there would be widespread violence. In '43 white people invaded the black community. They tried to march into it by hundreds. If they did it today everyone would be slaughtered. In that situation there would be violence.

Have guns been coming into the black community too?

Not in the way they've gone into the white community, because black people don't have access to arms the way white persons do. A white person can get a permit for a hand gun in 24 hours. A black person would be lucky to get it in 12 months. You try to get a National Rifle Association gun club charter in the black community! It would take you 100 years.

Do you suspect that some of our suburban laymen are active in these gun clubs?

I would suspect so. I don't see any reason why our churches would be different from others. . . .

Is [white fear and panic] unique to Detroit or do you think it is widespread?

It is widespread in most metropolitan areas. Part of the reason for the rapid population shift—white people from urban areas to suburbs—is because they're afraid to stay in. It is a peculiar, almost absurd thing (like most human conduct). Suburban folk feel threatened today just when there is less reason for fear than at any time in the history of the black struggle for freedom. Today we don't want anything they have. We don't want to move out there. We don't want to go to their schools. We don't want bussing. We don't care anything about open occupancy.

We want our *own* community. We want everything in it equal. Only through outright lies can black power be interpreted as a direct threat to white people in the suburbs. . . .

Are you then preaching a separatist doctrine? And is it a permanent thing or a way station along the road—is it a strategy or is it the goal itself?

That's another bad question. I don't have to work for separation. The white man has done too good a job. I was separated from the day I was born. Every area of my life has been separate. Church? I always went to a black church. They were acting white but it was a black church. Schools? Predominantly black. Essentially all the people I know are black.

You can't ask me if I'm advocating separation. I don't know anything else. I know all about separation. But I didn't do it. I just inherited it.

Some of us, however, are working for the time when these conditions do not prevail. Otherwise the United Church Ministers for Racial and Social Justice wouldn't have come to General Synod with requests for open membership in the churches, for free movement of pastors, and for social change. You seem to be describing a kind of separatism which they are not talking about.

They are talking about separatism that exists. They recognize that black people are separate in America and in the church. They say, "Let's end that separation. Let's make some definite concrete steps toward ending it."

I say this separation exists and you won't end it with conversation. You may make some token steps. But we're not going to end the separation—which white men have made—by conversation. We're only going to end it when black people escape from powerlessness.

If there is some transferral of power to black people, then black people will be able to negotiate and deal with white people upon some basis of equality. That's the only basis upon which separation can be ended. . . .

What does the phrase "black identity" mean? And how does your church seek to help reclaim the worth of blackness?

Black consciousness. Black pride. The search for black identity. This is a people seeking mental health. We've been sick a long time. We lost our identity when we were brought to this country as slaves. We were told we were inferior. They cut us off from each other and from our African traditions.

The white man has always asserted that black is ugly. It's written into the language. Anything distasteful is black. It was a black day. You're blackballed in a fraternity. Everything black is vicious. So there must be a candid acceptance, if you're going to have black and white coexisting, that black is just as beautiful as white. And as good.

But it is even more important for black people to go through this process. The black man can't wait for the white man to decide that black is beautiful. He's got to decide for himself that black is beautiful. . . .

Do you welcome the fact that there is an increasing number of Negro pastors holding positions of responsibility in the church?

Oh yes! Certainly. It's high time. But we're just beginning. Too much still is tokenism. There must be black ministers in really responsible positions throughout the church. We need black people in every department.

You've talked about the nation-within-the-nation. Would you say a word about the church-within-the-church? . . .

I believe black people need to have a black caucus in every institution in which they function. In labor unions rank and file black people must decide what labor should do for the black man. The same thing holds for the church.

For too long our church has been sitting off with some white man in an office in New York deciding what ought to be done in black communities in Detroit, Chicago, Washington, Los Angeles. And they couldn't have found their way into a black community in any one of those cities that they were issuing statements about. . . .

This a moment of decision for the self-conscious part of the black church. There are some black churches which are irrelevant. They still jump up and down and cross the Red Sea every Sunday. But there aren't many of those left. They are relics. Dinosaurs. The new church that is coming into being is made up of pastors and congregations who realize they've got to minister to the real needs of the ghetto—the need for black identity and consciousness.

There is a feeling that if the denominations cannot accept the realities of what's happening today, then we must create a new superstructure so the churches can function to give increased power and strength.

The black churches are caucused within every denomination, struggling to be significant. But if the denominations merely give them lip service, then one day there will be a national conference of Negro churches and you'll see a new black church. It's almost inevitable unless denominations take seriously what is happening across the country. The white denominations must realize what is happening and that they have to make a decision. They've only got a year or two. . . .

What do you think is the future of the civil rights movement?

It's pretty well washed up. Not that they won't do some good things. But King is a symbol of the fact that it's washed up. Black people today say that if we're citizens we don't need any more legislation. Just enforce the Constitution. For all people.

Actually it's been a farce that all constitutional guarantees must be especially extended to black people. Supose you had to pass special laws for Jews or the Irish or Catholics. America would be a shambles, with no possibility for life. The Constitution would cease to have any significance. Either black people are citizens or they are not. If they are, we don't need any more legislation. Just enforce the law. . . .

What's going to determine our struggle is the transference of of power, self-determination, and the nation-within-the-nation. That's what must be dealt with. If the civil rights movement will accept that, then the movement has a future.

Some people allege that Communism has made inroads in the civil rights movement and the black ghetto. Have you seen any evidence of this?

These are allegations of Birchites and the American Nazi Party and a few local psychopaths.

There have been no inroads made into any black community in the past 10 years.

Communism is defunct in the black community. They couldn't even hold a meeting.

A black Comunist today would be considered an Uncle Tom because he is still talking about black and white unite and fight. Communists are completely lost in the ghetto. No influence, nothing to do with anything in the freedom movement from coast to coast.

America Will Do What Is Right

Germany set out not to destroy a few blocks in our cities, they set out to destroy all of America. They didn't succeed, but they did destroy hundreds of thousands of American lives. But nobody raised a whimper when we, you know, allocated billions of dollars to rebuild West Germany. There are no slums in West Germany today. No unemployment in West Germany.

But if we can do this for Germany, we ought to be able to do it for our own citizens.

I believe that we've seen the handwriting on the wall. And that we will not wait to be embarrassed, to be pushed, to be bludgeoned into being decent. We will do this because it's right, not because 3% of the Negro citizens of this country rioted. But because 97% kept the faith, and said that they believe in America.

WHITNEY M. YOUNG, JR., National Urban League

From an interview recorded March 3, 1968, by Public Broadcast Laboratories. Reprinted by permission of Whitney M. Young, Jr.

A Drum Major for Justice

Every now and then I guess we all think realistically about that day when we will be victimized with what is life's final common denominator—that something we call death.

We all think about it and every now and then I think about my own death and I think about my own funeral. And I don't think about it in a morbid sense. And every now and then I ask myself what it is that I would want said and I leave the word to you this morning.

If any of you are around when I have to meet my day, I don't want a long funeral.

And if you get somebody to deliver the eulogy tell him not to talk too long.

And every now and then I wonder what I want him to say. Tell him not to mention that I have a Nobel Peace Prize— that isn't important.

Tell him not to mention that I have 300 or 400 other awards— that's not important. Tell him not to mention where I went to school.

I'd like somebody to mention that day that Martin Luther King, Jr. tried to give his life serving others.

I'd like for somebody to say that day that Martin Luther King Jr. tried to love somebody.

I want you to say that day that I tried to be right and to walk with them. I want you to be able to say that day that I did try to feed the hungry. I want you to be able to say that day that I did try in my life to clothe the naked. I want you to say on that day that I did try in my life to visit those who were in prison. And I want you to say that I tried to love and serve humanity.

Yes, if you want to, say that I was a drum major. Say that I was a drum major for justice. Say that I was a drum major for peace. I was a drum major for righteousness.

And all of the other shallow things will not matter.

I won't have any money to leave behind. I won't have the fine and luxurious things of life to leave behind. But I just want to leave a committed life behind.

And that is all I want to say. If I can help somebody as I pass along, if I can cheer somebody with a well song, if I can show somebody he's traveling wrong, then my living will not be in vain.

If I can do my duty as a Christian ought. If I can bring salvation to a world once wrought.

If I can spread the message as the master taught.

Then my living will not be in vain.

> Martin Luther King, Jr.,
> from a sermon preached at Ebenezer Baptist Church

Martin Luther King and Malcolm X

I was not a follower of Dr. King, I did not agree with things he SAID, but I respected him because of his sincerity and because, no matter what he SAID about non-violence and redeeming white people through black suffering, the things he actually DID always set up black-white confrontations in which black people could begin to see what white people are really like.

Every time he set up a black-white confrontation, black people came out of that confrontation more united and with fewer illusions about white people. When we look back at the Montgomery Bus Boycott 13 years ago, we can remember how fearful and disunited we were before a black woman, Mrs. Rosa Parks, refused to move to the back of the bus and the Montgomery black community was willing to stand with her as black people had never stood together before. . . .

You can say, if you like, that black people were engaged in redemptive suffering as they walked for more than a year. Or you can say that the economic boycott in Montgomery was the first effective use of Black Power. But we look back now and see that what black people were really doing was learning to work together and to be unafraid.

They were learning to do the things necessary to mobilize Black Power to win the basic rights that they were demanding. Dr. King was teaching black people the simple elementary meaning of Black Power. . . .

Black people marched and protested, determined to continue until white people understood that they would not turn back. . . .

White people beat us, they turned police dogs and fire hoses on us, and they jailed us. White people used every kind of barbaric violence against us. But day after day black folks continued to march and to confront white people as black people had never confronted white people before.

Dr. King was preaching non-violence, passive resistance and redemptive suffering, but what he was saying really had no relationship to what was happening in the minds and hearts of black people. As we marched, we were becoming a united people. Our identification with white America was being broken.

Even as Dr. King described his dream, for most black people the dream of integration was dying. As black people were brutalized by white violence, the black man's faith in non-violence was dying.

Dr. King was saying one thing, and black people were learning another. They were learning that white people are not superior beings, and that no matter how many police dogs, cattle prods and fire hoses they could mobilize, they are not invincible. . . .

Dr. King created the situations in which we were able to learn. He created the situations which Malcolm X interpreted. We needed both of them, and the things they taught were only contradictory if we listened to their words rather than analyzing their effects upon black people. . . .

Nobody would have listened to Brother Malcolm if Dr. King had not created the situations in which we began to learn that we could FIGHT and that we could WIN. Our victories did not consist of the pitiful little civil rights which we won but the changes which took place in us as we struggled.

This was Dr. King's basic contribution. Even as he was saying "We Shall Overcome" and "I Have a Dream," he was systematically destroying all our myths and dreams about the goodness and invincibility of the white man. . . .

Every cattle prod, every fire hose, every jail, every violent cruelty inflicted upon us by white people revealed to us the real nature of the enemy we face. Now the final violence of Dr. King's murder has severed the last link in the chain of illusions which bound us in second-class citizenship.

Dr. King laid the foundation for the emerging Black Nation. White people will never admit it but they created the Moses who led us out of bondage and pointed us in the direction of the Promised Land.

Rev. Albert B. Cleage, Jr.
(*Michigan Chronicle,* April 13, 1968)

Martin Luther King, Jr.

On death: *"The quality, not the longevity, of one's life is what is important. If you are cut down in a moment that is designed to save the soul of a nation, then no other death could be more redemptive."*

"It may get me crucified, I may even die. But I want it said even if I die in the struggle that 'He died to make men free.' "

Last public utterance: *"I'm happy tonight. Mine eyes have seen the glory of the coming of the Lord."*

On nonviolence: *"Let's not burn America down. Let's take her like she is and rebuild her. We must maintain and advocate and promote the philosophy of nonviolence."*

On the relationship of white men and black men: *"The black man needs the white man to free him from his fear, and the white man needs the black man to free him from his guilt."*

On hate: *"If you think I came to tell you to hate white people you have the wrong man. Our goal is not to defeat or humiliate the white man, but to win his friendship and love."*

On the 1954 U. S. Supreme Court decision: *"In every generation a Negro leader has risen up and cried out like Moses of old, 'Let my people go,' but their cries have been met by hardened hearts until May 17, 1954, when the Supreme Court opened the waters of the Red Sea toward the promised land of desegregation."*

On the future of mankind: *"We must live together as brothers or perish together as fools."*

On love: *"I've decided to stick with love . . . Hate is too great a burden to bear."*

These quotations are from *Jet*, April 4, 1968.

Subsidies for the Poor? Why Not?

Many of the plans for ending poverty and putting people to work rebuilding our decaying cities call for government subsidies. These would be either outright grants, or tax breaks to motivate companies and individuals to take on socially useful projects.

From the howls that have gone up from critics you would think nothing has ever been subsidized before. Some even say that the tax structure has to be "protected" from rebates given for anti-poverty programs. Don't they know it is too late to "protect" it? It is already riddled with special interest loopholes.

The fact of the matter is that subsidies are as American as the flag. I don't know of anyone who is well-to-do who doesn't benefit in some way from federal subsidies. Only the poor get a very small slice of the subsidy pie; everyone else gets a good helping.

Just look at the Mississippi Delta, where Negro sharecroppers and tenant farmers are literally starving. In one county only 27 farmers were paid more money in federal crop subsidies than the whole poverty program in that county got for the year. Because of this subsidy, farmers cut back on acreage and laid off workers. These farm workers then had to plead for anti-poverty assistance and surplus food or leave for big city ghettos.

In the last two years alone, cotton farmers got $1.8 billion in price supports. But this money went to farm owners who, in effect, got a guaranteed annual income for not growing cotton. I'm not against this welfare program for well-off landowners. I just want to see it extended to cover the poor as well.

The basic purpose of subsidies is to encourage the development of economically useful projects. For example, it is considered a good thing for the U.S. to have a large fleet of ships at its disposal. So the government subsidizes more than half the ships built to carry foreign trade. Some people think a supersonic plane would be a good thing. So the government subsidizes the private companies building it to the tune of two or three billion dollars. . . .

The average middle-class American is heavily subsidized. In-

From *New York Amsterdam News*, March 30, 1968. Reprinted by permission.

terest on his mortgage and his local property taxes are deductible on his federal tax. But when these sums are included in the rent poor people pay in the slums, they can't deduct it. Mortgages themselves, are often backed by federal guarantees. Commuter railroads are often heavily subsidized, as are the highways suburbanites need.

Many Americans climbed into the middle class by virtue of subsidies like the GI Bill, which enabled them to go to college. And white middle-class citizens are often favored in property tax charges. A recent study in Boston showed that homes in affluent areas are assessed at only a third of their real value, while homes in the Roxbury ghetto are assessed at 75 per cent of their true value.

Business is subsidized to purchase new machines. Such investments are eligible for a seven per cent tax credit.

I'm all for this. But if we subsidize middle-class homeowners, expanding businesses, and farm corporations who are paid not to grow crops why can't we also subsidize the poor, who need it most?

We ought to subsidize industry for building homes and plants in the ghetto, and we ought to subsidize training costs for companies who hire the unemployed as well as living costs for trainees and students.

Subsidies work because they encourage money and effort to go into the subsidized areas. They are a form of investment. Let's invest as much in people as we invest in machines. Let's subsidize industry to tackle poverty and bad housing, the way we subsidize them to build ships and planes. The nation can only benefit from it.

WHITNEY M. YOUNG, JR., National Urban League

PART TWO

The People Speak for Themselves

Martin Luther King at Oslo

White America insists on viewing the civil rights movement (as it views The Race itself) as an unarticulated homogeneous monolith. The Reverend Dr. Martin Luther King has been appointed concrete chieftain of its ghostly image of the black opposition. Dr. King, as *the* Negro leader of the decade, has walked the tightrope for eight long years. Steadily rising winds, in this country and elsewhere, have made the tightrope increasingly unsteady, and Dr. King has fallen repeatedly in recent years. He fell again, perhaps fatally this time, at Oslo on December 11, 1964.

Dr. King seemed to be presented with a clear mandate; Oslo was a platform from which he might have attempted to express the climate of impending crisis that hangs over the communities of black America. His acceptance speech might have served to heighten the world's awareness of the real and growing tensions between the races in America and points East. He chose instead to speak to the complacency of white America—and indeed of the entire white world. He chose to smooth ruffled feelings and to calm quite realistic fears. He chose to ignore completely the mood of the masses he purports to represent. In so choosing, he irrevocably defined himself as a leader whose basic responsibility is focused upon the United States Information Agency and the "Great Society" rather than upon the Negro people who despair of sharing in its Greatness.

It should come as no surprise to the reader that nonviolence is not the coming thing in Afro-America. It comes as a bit of a shock to Negroes in 1965 to learn that they will continue to "take suffering upon themselves instead of inflicting it on others . . . [and that they] . . . will do this peacefully, openly and cheerfully, because . . . [their] aim is to persuade." It is simply not true—and Dr. King knows that it is not true that we in the United States "have witnessed the gradual demise of the system of segregation." He knows furthermore that very few Negroes are basking in the

Claude Weaver, in *The Harvard Journal of Negro Affairs*, Vol. 1, No. 1, 1965, pp. 31–32. Reprinted by permission.

light of "that glowing day a few months ago when a strong civil rights bill became the law of our land."

Reverend King, with a doctorate, must be able to see what any jobless Negro on the corner can see: that after eight years of challenge and struggle the old racial patterns of the United States remain basically intact; that the desegregation of the schools has degenerated into a farce of tokenism; that the civil rights bill—in the unlikely event of its firm enforcement—will strike nowhere near the core of the basic problems involved; that the Administration, the Congress, and the whole of white America are interested obviously and solely in pacifying their troublesome children with as much as is necessary to "get them off the streets."

Reverend King must be able—even from Bimini or Norway—to sense the mounting sense of futility; the old hopelessness closing in again. He too must feel the cold dread we all feel at the prospect of a series of covert African-American colonial wars. We are, all of us, while Dr. King preaches in his insipid and sunny sermons, sailing into a storm. . . .

It is not, in the final analysis, what Dr. King *said* that is outrageous—it is rather what he did not say. His description of the cloud-cuckoo land may have pleased his listeners, but it did not prepare them in the least for the rude shocks soon to come from an unhappy and deeply divided world. In shirking reality at Oslo, the Reverend Dr. King has done us all a great disservice.

CLAUDE WEAVER

No Love for Nonviolence

"We hold no love for nonviolence—it is a philosophy that was bankrupt a long time ago. We simply don't believe in having black people slaughtered—going up against armed policemen with their bare hands just because they're angry. Before we go to war we should know we are fighting from a position of strength, not weakness."

VIC SOLOMON, CORE
(quoted in *The New York Times,* April 6, 1968)

Riots Are Here

"Riots are here. Riots are part of the ugly atmosphere of our society. I cannot guarantee that riots will not take place this summer. I can only guarantee that our demonstrations will not be violent . . . if riots take place, it will not be the responsibility of Martin Luther King or the Southern Christian Leadership Conference . . . There's no point in turning to us."

> MARTIN LUTHER KING, JR., (quoted by Walter Rugaber, in *The New York Times,* March 31, 1968)

"I don't give a damn about Martin Luther King or the Black Nationalists. I want to stay alive and hold a job, and they don't do either of those things for me."

> A MIDDLE-AGED MAN, New York

"Every governmental program on which some jobs could be gotten for black youth is being cut back so that the pressure on black youths to go into the Army becomes greater."

> CONRAD J. LYNN, New York Attorney

You Win or You Die

"Individuals should make phone calls to the police department during an uprising (telling of emergencies such as being robbed, shot at or someone's being killed, a store or bank being broken into etc.). The address that you give to the police department should be outside the area of revolt but in the same borough. Also report snipers that do not exist in areas outside the revolt. Women are good for this type of job."

> FROM A PAMPHLET CIRCULATED IN NEW YORK (quoted by Jimmy Breslin, *New York Magazine,* April 8, 1968)

"Violence—it's very beautiful. It wakes the white man up. It says to him, you like violence and here it is. But it's bad when the brothers and sisters burn down their own stores. They are cutting off their own food supply. They ought to go somewhere else, where they don't hurt themselves."

> DANNY WILLIAMSON, house cleaner, Pasadena, California
> (quoted in *Fortune* magazine, January, 1968)

"We must fight for the right of self-determination, race pride and pursuit of blackness. We must believe in our cause and be willing to die for it and we should stop reading other people's literature and write our own, and stop pretending revolution and make it."

> RON KARENGA, US, Los Angeles
> (quoted in *The Washington Post,* September 28, 1967)

"I did not join the movement because of love, but because of hate. I hate racism and am out to smash it."

> STOKELY CARMICHAEL

Don't Blame the White Man

As a former resident of Detroit, I was appalled, as were most other Americans, by the recent riot. This insurrection, instigated by hoodlums, infected otherwise sane, intelligent citizens to forget their responsibilities to family, country and race. . . . The time is long past when we can place all the blame on the white man. I personally feel that you should take a definite stand. We cannot condone anarchy. Demonstrations such as Father Groppi's in Milwaukee are to be encouraged, but senseless lawlessness advocated by Stokely Carmichael and fellow travellers should be openly condemned.

> JACK WASHINGTON, Plattsburgh, AFB, N.Y.
> (*Ebony* Magazine, November, 1967)

Whose Society Is This?

If I were trying to run things my way, I would do everything that I could to teach everybody that they were not able to run things like me. I would teach that to build something else meant that whoever wanted to do it would have to become like me. I would finally teach that I was the only person who knew enough to make other people like me. If I could manage all that, I wouldn't have to let people know that they were slaves. It would be very important that the slavery I imposed be couched in my definition of freedom, and remain unseen in order that rebellion remained stifled, and my control intact.

CHARLIE COBB, SNCC

From "Whose Society Is This," *The New Republic*, December 18, 1965. Reprinted by permission of *The New Republic*, © 1965, Harrison-Blaine of New Jersey, Inc.

Work for Welfare!

I am an average married Negro woman who would like to use my American rights to express my views about rioting.

Welfare is a wonderful organization and I know many families could not exist without it. But I believe the things we appreciate most are things for which we work. These people should work for the welfare they receive in jobs created by the government paying lower wages than regular jobs. I think this would encourage some to feel they don't really need welfare and go look for better jobs. I feel this would not only give them pride and dignity, but less idle time, as well. . . .

MRS. JAMES WOODSON, Roslyn Estates, L.I., N.Y.
(*Ebony* magazine, November, 1967)

Go Home and Do Your Homework

A Negro youngster out on the street participating in a demonstration who is not doing anything in his school work, who is gaining nothing in the way of a cultural background and who knows it, is going to go home that night and know that he is still just as much an outcast from American society as he was before he went out on that street and expressed his anger. Heaven knows, when people are talking militancy, and some are even talking violence, you aren't necessarily the most popular man in the world when you say, "All right, go and participate in that sit-in, but when you get through go home and do your homework, because you may ram open the door to the table where the white man is feasting, but if you go in and sit down at that table and are uncertain as to which fork to pick up, you're still going to feel like a man on the outside."

CARL ROWAN, Washington, D. C.

Quoted in Thomas F. Pettigrew, *A Profile of the Negro American* (Princeton: D. Van Nostrand Company, 1964), p. 307. Reprinted by permission.

A Blueprint for Change in the Detroit School System

Black Children Prepared for ADC and Vietnam

According to their own statistics, the Detroit Board of Education and school administration have failed to educate our inner city children. Comparisons of achievement levels in Detroit schools consistently place inner city schools at the bottom—whether testing for aptitude, basic skills, or the number of above average senior high students. . . . Obviously inner city schools do not prepare our children and young people either for the world of work or for college entrance. They prepare our children only for ADC and the war in Vietnam.

Albert B. Cleage, Jr., in *CCAC* [Citywide Citizens Action Committee] *News,* February, 1968. Reprinted by permission.

In our opinion the Detroit Board of Education and the office of Superintendent have not given Detroit inner city schools strong, sincere, administrative direction. These schools have been left directionless and for the most part entirely in the hands of principals who have felt no sense of urgency or accountability either to the Superintendent or to the Board of Education. Many of these principals have approached their task with the conviction that inner city children are incapable of learning and have transmitted this race prejudice to their teaching staffs by indicating that not much in the way of achievement can be expected from children who are either innately or culturally inferior.

We charge that this continuing failure to educate inner city children reflects a deliberate policy of racial discrimination which makes it impossible for the Detroit school system to educate them until basic changes are made in its structure and orientation. We absolutely reject the rationalization, based upon Nazi-like theories of racial inferiority, which shifts the blame to Afro-American parents and children by labeling them "culturally deprived," "socially disadvantaged" or "lacking in motivation." We also reject the philosophy of white supremacy which seeks solutions in federally or foundation-financed programs designed to indoctrinate inner city children with the standards and values of a middle-class white culture.

White Teachers Destroy Black Pride

We charge that the basic reason for the failure to educate inner city children stems from the schools' deliberate and systematic destruction of the Afro-American child's self-image and racial pride. Numerous aspects of Board policy contribute to this systematic destruction of our children's belief in themselves. The policy of providing superior 'open schools' in the white outlying areas to which small numbers of privileged inner city children may be permitted to go and the policy of bussing Black children to 'white schools,' for example, express the underlying philosophy that quality education cannot be provided in inner city schools because if you mix Black with Black you can get only stupidity, whereas if you mix Black with white you must get something superior to anything all-Black and somewhat inferior to anything all-white.

The basic threat to the Afro-American child's racial pride and self-image is the preponderance of white administrators and teachers in inner city schools. These individuals serve not only as teachers and administrators but also as white power symbols. The fundamental sickness afflicting inner city residents, both children and adults, is the sense of inferiority which stems from their powerlessness and the knowledge that they have no control over their own destiny. They do not own the stores where they buy. They do not control the banks which cash their checks. They do not own the apartment houses in which they live. They do not control the political structure which dominates their communities. A Black child growing up in this situation needs a school which counteracts the influences of a white community which constantly threaten to engulf and destroy him. He must find in the school symbols which give him self-pride, self-confidence and a hope for the future. If he is forced to attend a school in which there is a preponderance of white teachers, white principals, white department heads, white counselors and white administrators, he finds himself in a situation which can only underscore his sense of powerlessness and inferiority. These white administrators, aided and abetted by biased textbooks which present a distorted picture of the Afro-American child's history and culture, serve to rob him of any motivation to learn and to develop because he sees nothing around him to make learning and self-development seem to offer either an avenue of escape from the conditions in which he lives or an instrument with which he can change these conditions.

White Administrators Over-represented Because of Race

Two-thirds of the twenty-one high school areas in Detroit are predominantly Afro-American, and Afro-American children constitute nearly 57% of the Detroit school population. Yet white administrators constitute 76.0% to 96.2% of supervisory staff.

These white administrators do not hold their positions because of the superior quality of their work, but just the opposite. In the face of their continuing failure as educators, they continue to hold their positions and to have the power to determine who else may teach or administer in inner city schools *only because of their race*. White administrators who enjoy the power and patronage inherent in the right to hire and fire for federally financed programs like Head Start and Teachers Aides cannot be expected to eliminate themselves from their high-paying, prestigious and powerful positions merely because they are unable to do the job for which they are being paid. Stated quite simply, these white administrators have quite naturally used their power to create and maintain a discriminatory system of selection and promotion whereby they are able to perpetuate themselves, their friends, and their relatives in their positions, while systematically excluding qualified Afro-American applicants.

In the application for the position of Assistant Principal, for example, the written test counts for only 30% while the oral interview, in which a principal's word or evaluation can be decisive, counts for 70%. In the application for Principal the written test counts for even less. Quite obviously, a system which is weighted so heavily in favor of a non-objective or oral test and against a written or objective test offers a ready-made vehicle for racial discrimination and personal abuse.

Inasmuch as the Detroit school population is now approximately 57% Afro-American, as two-thirds of the high school areas are now predominantly Afro-American, and as the self-image of the Afro-American child requires that he *not* be taught by white teachers or attend schools administered largely by white administrators, we propose that the Detroit Board of Education take the following steps to institute a completely new program for the selection and promotion of administrators:

a. Fill all administrative vacancies with Afro-Americans until such positions have been filled with Afro-Americans in proportion to the number of Afro-American children and young people in the Detroit school population.

b. Appoint Afro-Americans to fill all of the nine positions of Region Assistants which have just been created.

c. Fill all administrative vacancies in inner city schools with Afro-Americans. We have been informed that new evaluations for assistant principals and secondary principals are scheduled for early fall. We urge that new evaluations should be undertaken more quickly to make possible the appointment of Afro-Americans to fill existing vacancies so that inner city parents can be assured during the summer interim that there will be more Afro-American principals, assistant principals, counselors and department heads in inner city schools by the opening of school this fall.

d. Take immediate steps to remedy the present glaring inequality in the racial distribution of administrators in the field of physical education, where young Afro-Americans provide so much of the skill that results in financial income from competitive sports. There are no Afro-Americans in the top positions of the Physical Education Division and only one department head for senior boys and one for senior girls. This racial discrimination is also apparent in the selection of coaches and referees for sporting events.

New Testing Machinery for Administrative Promotion

To equalize the percentage of Afro-American administrators the Detroit Board of Education must employ a method of selection and promotion which removes from the hands of the present administrators the power to protect their own vested interests and to provide preferential treatment for their friends. For this reason we propose that the State Board of Education be asked to set up new machinery for the testing of all administrative personnel, in cooperation with Michigan state universities, and that the Detroit Board of Education agree to appoint and promote in terms of this objective evaluation.

State-wide Minimum Achievement Standards

We are convinced that curriculum deficiencies and widespread distribution of inadequate teachers and indifferent administrators throughout inner city schools necessitate immediate action by the State Board of Education to provide minimum achievement standards for each grade level and achievement tests covering minimum standards for each grade level from 3 to 12. These tests should be given at the end of each school year under the supervision of the State Board in cooperation with Michigan state universities. The results of these annual tests should be made public in order that school administrators may be held accountable for their educational accomplishments. Administrators who are unable to keep inner city schools up to grade level can then be replaced without undue delay.

Equal Distribution of Uncertificated Personnel

The Detroit Board of Education presently employs 1,070 ESRPs (Emergency Substitutes Regularly Placed), a large proportion of whom are uncertificated and poorly prepared, and a disproportionately large number of whom are placed in inner city schools. We recommend that the number of uncertificated and poorly prepared personnel be reduced as quickly as possible. We feel that the strategy of hiring unqualified teachers at a lower pay schedule in order to increase the total number of teachers available is too costly in terms of the educational deprivations imposed upon our children. We demand that, so long as non-certificated and unqualified personnel are permitted to remain in the school system, they be equally distributed between inner city and outlying schools and that the percentage and distribution of such personnel be made public each semester.

New Texts and Problem-centered Classes

We believe that if Afro-American children are to be given motivation and are to be helped to develop a desirable self-image, the inner city schools must realistically seek to compensate for all the disadvantages which are foisted upon inner city residents by a white society and which tend to make inner city children feel that they are inferior. To this end, we propose that inner city schools be given a different educational orientation from outlying schools. Inner city schools must become creative centers capable of giving Afro-American children and young people a knowledge of their history, their culture and their destiny. To do this, the schools and their teachers must have flexibility in the selection of textbooks and in the utilization of creative teaching techniques. Standard textbooks which ignore or demean the contributions of Africa and Afro-Americans certainly must be supplanted by books which teach our children their worth and value. More classes must be problem-centered in terms of the discussion and understanding of the everyday urban problems which must eventually be solved under the leadership of Afro-Americans. The creative abilities of Afro-American children in the arts, dance, and creative writing must be developed but not at the expense of academic studies. In all these respects an effective school curriculum for inner city schools would differ markedly from the curriculum of the outlying schools. This must not be interpreted to mean that inner city schools will not be required to meet the same grade level achievement as outlying schools. Rather, it means that this is the only method by which inner city children will be able to meet the objective achievement standards which we have proposed be set by the State Board of Education.

This new orientation for inner city schools not only requires Afro-American administrators and teachers in inner city schools but also the transfer out of these schools of white personnel who are unable or unready to teach within this educational framework. There are too many white teachers now teaching in inner city schools who cannot possibly give Afro-American children a sense of pride and belief in their own destiny because, consciously or unconsciously, they believe in the inferiority of all non-whites.

Separation for Black Advancement

After 400 years of the white man's enforced separation, Black people are rejecting the dream of integration as the goal for their struggle and are instead finding pride in their own history, culture and power, seeking to develop their own independent leadership, organizations and programs, and determined that the separation which the white man has forced upon them shall now be used for their advancement rather than for their exploitation. After 400 years of self-defeating 'individualism' born of oppression and the psychological need of the oppressed to identify with the oppressor through the search for status, special privileges and crumbs from the master's table, Black people are coming to realize that the Black man's freedom from oppression and exploitation is not an individual thing to be fought for and won person by person— but a group accomplishment to be secured only through the power of a united Black people.

We feel strongly that no city can long endure if it refuses to face realistically the problem created by its continuing failure to educate more than 50% of its population. We are confident that our proposals are realistic and constructive and can halt the steady disintegration of this urban community.

ALBERT B. CLEAGE, JR.

The White Man Knows

"The original premise held by Negroes was that we had a chance to change white people if they realized what they were doing to us. Now the black man knows that the white man is aware of what has been done to black people. The black man no longer has faith in the white man to give aid and comfort. The black man knows that if things are to change black people need strength and power."

OSWALD SYKES, Harlem Rehabilitation Center

Afro-Americanism at Harvard

"I don't believe in romanticizing the ghetto, but part of the cost of living in the kind of environment I came from is not to have had the broadening experience of knowing other Negroes and not to be sensitive to them. Soon after I got here, I grew up. I had to revise some of my basic assumptions."

TOM WILLIAMSON, JR., Harvard College
(Look magazine, October 31, 1968)

"There are at least two kinds of nationalists on the street today. One is 'do-rag brother' and the other is the oratorical nationalist.

"The only thing keeping the whole business from blowing wide open, right now, is the oratorical nationalists. They are out there trying to keep it cool. They blow against 'Whitey' and how bad he is, but this is how they gain the respect of 'do-rag' brother. Those nationalists that everybody is condemning are saying to 'do-rag' all of the time, 'Keep cool, brother, keep it cool.' They are the best friends America has."

A BLACK NATIONALIST, Watts, California

What I want, what I am, what you force me to be, is what you are

For I am you, staring back from a mirror of poverty and despair, of revolt and freedom. Look at me and know that to destroy me is to destroy yourself. You are weary of the long hot summers. I am tired of the long hungered winters. We are not so far apart as it might seem. There is something about both of us that goes deeper than blood or black and white. It is our common search for a better life, a better world. I march now over the same ground you once marched. I fight for the same things you still fight for. My children's needs are the same as your children's. I too am America. America is me. It gave me the only life I know—so I must share in its survival. Look at me. Listen to me. Try to understand my struggle against your racism. There is yet a chance for us to live in peace beneath these restless skies.

GORDON PARKS
(*Life* magazine, March 8, 1968)

Healed by Stripes

Mainstream religion's theme is *katallagete!*—"be reconciled!"

But instead of obedience to this kingdom demand established by God for every human group and person, mainstream religion has been superseded by established white folk religion, whose kingdom is a direct contradiction of the Kingdom of God.

This kingdom of and for whites is the ultimate concern of the dominant group in America. It is all the more demonic because its irrational pretension to mainstream Christianity perverts as it represses the demand of reconciliation. This racist heart is proliferated and compounded in what the critics of popular religion ("peace of mind cult") and church attendance call "culture re-

Joseph R. Washington, Jr., *The Politics of God* (Boston: Beacon Press, 1967), pp. 153–155. Copyright © 1967 by the author. Reprinted by permission of Beacon Press.

ligion." These critics see "racism and nativism" as characteristics of culture religion, failing thereby to distinguish between white folk religion and culture religion. Culture religion we will have with us always, at least until white folk religion is expunged from the preconscious and conscious minds of whites. It is this dastardly endeavor to storm the Kingdom of God and make it subsidiary to the kingdom of whites we have declared anathema, not only because it is the presupposition of the dominant white folk churches but because this (irrational) spiritual preconsciousness has spirited the entire social-cultural matrix of American life. In this respect, there has never been separation of church and state in America.

The only radical human challenge to white folk religion and its social-cultural establishment is the Negro. The element of reconciliation has been primary in the genuine religion of the Negro folk. They have joined it with the democratic creed. Both have been at the heart of the Negro folk; they have accepted the authentic declarations of these religious and secular creeds. Freedom and equality with and for all are for the Negro folk both an affirmation of mainstream religion and the creed of democracy as well as a protest against their repudiation in white folk religion. The heart of Negro folk religion is the heart of mainstream religion which, however, has been perverted by white preconsciousness. This perversion has repressed the heart of the religion and democracy, initiated by the "chosen people" and set forth in the Old Testament, which Jesus declared as established in the Kingdom of God—the preconsciousness of the Kingdom is *katallagete!* The Anglo-Puritans preconsciously declared biblical religion and democracy applicable to whites only and a minority of whites at that, forcing its willful and minority spirit upon the majority.

Freedom and equality with and for all—Negro folk religion—is the genius of the Negro folk. Developed not out of an elite breakthrough of its minority but the suffering of its majority, it parallels the genius of religion and democracy rooted in biblical faith. As a result of this suffering by a whole people for four centuries and placed in the perspective of the Bible, we contend here that the Negro cannot be understood or understand himself except as another "chosen people." By their stripes may all be healed. . . .

JOSEPH R. WASHINGTON, JR.

A Sea of White Protestants

Once I was a Catholic. I was baptized, made my first Communion, my Confirmation, and I wore a Cross with Jesus on it around my neck. I prayed at night, said my Rosary, went to Confession, and said all the Hail Marys and Our Fathers to which I was sentenced by the priest. Hopelessly enamored of sin myself, yet appalled by the sins of others, I longed for Judgment Day and a trial before a jury of my peers—this was my only chance to escape the flames which I could feel already licking at my feet. I was in a California Youth Authority institution at the time, having transgressed the laws of man—God did not indict me that time; if He did, it was a secret indictment, for I was never informed of any charges brought against me. The reason I became a Catholic was that the rule of the institution held that every Sunday each inmate had to attend the church of his choice. I chose the Catholic Church because all the Negroes and Mexicans went there. The whites went to the Protestant chapel. Had I been a fool enough to go to the Protestant chapel, one black face in a sea of white, and with guerrilla warfare going on between us, I might have ended up a Christian martyr—St. Eldridge the Stupe.

ELDRIDGE CLEAVER

Eldridge Cleaver, *Soul on Ice* (New York: McGraw-Hill, 1968), p. 30. Copyright 1968 by the author. Reprinted by permission of the publisher.

Black Jesus, Black Church

"It was impossible in the past for black people to think of Jesus as black, because they hated themselves and their color. But now it is becoming impossible for black people to worship a white Jesus, and historically they are right. Jesus definitely was non-white, and the whole teaching of the New Testament deals with a non-white nation's struggle for power against a white colonial oppressor, the

Romans. Now it is for us to evolve a theology and a black church. that speaks to black people in this twentieth century, and that is what we are evolving here."

> THE REVEREND ALBERT B. CLEAGE, JR.,
> Central United Church of Christ, Detroit
> (*Fortune* magazine, January, 1968, p. 151)

"Even if somebody did rise up on Easter, it would just be another white man to kick us."

> LAROI DREW ALI

Black Freedom Won't Wreck the Culture

I wish that we could break this thing down so that it could be seen that desegregation isn't going to stop people from being Southern, that freedom for Negroes isn't going to destroy the main current of that way of life, which becomes, like most ways of life when we *talk* about them, more real on the level of myth, memory and dream than on the level of actuality anyway. The climate will remain the same, and that has a lot to do with it, the heroes of Southern history will remain, and so on. The economy will probably expand, and a hell of a lot of energy which has gone into keeping the Negro "in his place" will be released for more creative pursuits. And the dictionary will become more accurate, the language a bit purified, and the singing in the schools will sound better. I suspect that what is valuable and worth preserving in the white Southern way of life is no more exclusively dependent upon the existence of segregation than what is valuable in Southern Negro life depends upon its being recognized by white people—or for that matter, by Northern Negroes.

> RALPH ELLISON, New York

Quoted in *Who Speaks for the Negro?*, ed. by Robert Penn Warren (New York: Random House, 1965), pp. 334–335. Reprinted by permission.

A Remedy for Crime

The phrase "crime in the streets" is used by the press and public to mean "Negro crime." The police and National Guard of several localities have purchased special equipment and have been given special training to suppress expected rioters. Preachers of hate are doing their best to polarize the races.

No one stops to differentiate between the hoodlums and thugs (of which every race has a number) and the dope addicts (who must steal to satisfy their cravings), on one hand, and the great majority of law-abiding black people on the other. Statistics show that 80 to 85 per cent of crime committed by blacks is committed against blacks. These are rarely publicized.

It is a way of life for crime by blacks against blacks to be ignored. Indeed, it is almost a way of life to be mugged or robbed in Harlem. Worse still, statistically speaking, are the house robbers. I know one doctor whose office in the past month was thoroughly cleaned of everything from his microscope to the FM radio in his waiting room. Within the next three weeks his office was cleaned twice more.

Daylight sidewalk muggings are now a common thing among my patients. One leading church has canceled its Wednesday Lenten services this year. Prayer offers no protection from the muggers. God is on a holiday.

Things are so bad that the decent people of Harlem have been intimidated. They see nothing, hear nothing and say nothing. They are afraid of retaliation.

When this summer comes and the expected explosion occurs, the procedure will be as always—to club every black face that is seen on the streets into submission or to experiment with Mace, tranquilizer darts or some of the other new devices about which instructions are now being given.

It matters not whether the face belongs to a thug or a Ph.D. History reveals that no other method of restoring "peace" has been devised in America.

May I make one plea before things get beyond possible correction? Attack the causes. Stop thinking of "cooling-off" measures.

Open the unions and give black people jobs. The New York Times recently told of 1,000 stevedore jobs going begging on the Jersey side of our harbor due to International Longshoremen's Association restrictions. No college degree is needed here. (The I.L.A. does hire blacks, but their racial policy, quantitatively and qualitatively, leaves much to be desired This particular case is not race prejudice per se, but it is a union blocking 1,000 unskilled workers while massive unemployment exists.)

Adopt the recommendations of the New York Academy of Medicine, given long ago, to stop drug addiction.

Protect the law-abiding Harlem inhabitants from that 85 per cent of the crime they are having inflicted upon them by their fellow residents.

I raise my voice to seek protection for the black masses who are unable or too terrorized to speak, and especially for those who are aged and weak, many of whom I X-ray every day, their bones often fractured from the violence that accompanies muggings. This is a different matter from civil rights—don't mix the two—although a fantastic unemployment rate is a factor common to both. It is a matter of protection for the citizens who suffer most. Free us from violence.

GEORGE D. CANNON, M.D., New York
(*The New York Times,* March 30, 1968)

The Proper Uses of the Black University

The black student is being educated in this country as if he were being programmed in white supremacy and self-hatred. Aside from the usual problems of inadequate everything, the black student is being educated in a racial information vacuum. The vast majority of Negro college students are not even aware of the true nature of the race problem and know nothing of our rich cultural heritage. It is no secret that black men and women are

Ernest Stephens, in *Freedomways,* Second Quarter, 1967, pp. 131–138. Reprinted by permission.

oppressed in this country. Why then should we not deal openly with our oppression as a unified group within our own educational structures? How long will it be before black leaders and educators take hold of Negro colleges and transform them from "training schools for Negroes" into universities designed to fit the real needs of black people in this nation?

The educational system of this country is designed to fit the needs of the society, a society which has never been willing to meet the needs of black people. The orientation of the educational system is directed toward assimilation of the college graduate into the society, the assumption being that an educated man with the proper background and credentials can take his place in the system and contribute to its betterment as well as to his own. This assumption is for the most part correct, unless the man is black. If the man is black the problems he confronts are categorically different. The educated black man must satisfy all academic requirements, and yet contend with the problem of his color. This is evidenced by the fact that the average lifetime earning potential of a Negro male who finishes four years of college is less than that of a white with only an eighth grade education. Therefore, if the black student is educated to make the same assumptions about the society as the white student, he is being duped.

Too often the role of the black student is tacitly defined as assimilation into the society through attaining only the skills essential to his profession. The college degree is looked upon as being the great equalizer. The basic assumption here is that the possession of a degree will render a racist society blind to the color of an man's skin. This assumption is false.

Color Is Constant

The educational structure of the entire country is divided into black and white sections, which is no more than a mirror image of the society. Given this black and white division, the educational policies should be directed toward serving the needs of each group; yet, the educational design of both categories operates as a constant and color as a variable. On an individual basis, however, color is in fact the constant. Therefore, if one is educated without regard for his color, and the society constantly handles the individual on the basis of his color, the individual is being handicapped and educated in a vacuum.

Considering the existing division of the educational structure, we must question the nature of education in the primary and secondary school as well as in the university. Aside from the fact that black elementary and high schools function as indoctrination centers on black inferiority, the direction of education is oriented toward memorization and recall rather than observation and analysis. No basis, therefore, is provided for independent thinking. The black student is taught to parrot rather than to think. If he ever reaches the university, he enters *programmed* and not educated.

Socially, politically, and culturally, black people in this nation have never been regarded as equal to white people, and the white society's programmed education for black people psychologically reinforces our inequality. Negroes are on every level of society excluded at some point from the mainstream. In an attempt to overcome the problem of color, black people must constantly strive to enhance their qualifications. In spite of the fact that the black educational level is accelerating at a more rapid rate than that of the whites, the average income level of the Negro as a percentage of that of whites is decreasing—from 62 per cent in 1950 to 57 per cent in 1960 to 54 per cent today. Thus, black people in this country are on a socio-economic treadmill.

It is apparent from the downward socio-economic trend of the Negro that if education is a way to liberation, the existing system does not adequately speak to our needs. In spite of this fact, little or no emphasis is placed upon realistic analysis of the Negro's plight at the black university. His development toward a new ideology is stifled, and his ideological development is encouraged only within the existing social and cultural structure.

In terms of the free expression of new ideas and concepts, there is not one black university in this country which functions as an institution of higher learning. The present situation within black universities is one reflective of an archaic and repressive ideology. Independent thinking is discouraged; diversity is stifled. Instead, the black student is trained to be a reactionary android who will quietly take his place in society never to know the reality of the destructive forces which isolate and suppress him.

White History for Black Students

Instead of encouraging racial pride through analysis and discussion of black people's rich cultural heritage, the black student is told that he is "culturally deprived," while Western culture is shoved down his throat. In history the horrors of slavery are watered down and sketchily covered so as not to enrage the complacent black student, while the period following Reconstruction is covered as if the Negro had strangely disappeared from the face of the earth. Abraham Lincoln is portrayed as the essence of integrity rather than as a clever politician, while George Washington, who once traded a slave for a keg of molasses, is portrayed as the pillar of democracy. Frederick Douglass is for all practical purposes ignored, while the only thing pointed out about W. E. B. Du Bois is that he became a communist. Economics is taught as if government and big business were two separate institutions. Political science is taught as if democracy were a reality, while the fundamental principles of democracy are smashed against the heads of black human beings daily. Revolutionary ideologies are discouraged even from discussion. Thus, the black student is programmed in the maintenance of the status quo.

The black student attending a Negro university in the South is usually the product of a family just above the poverty level. A college education is normally an opportunity not afforded his parents. He is therefore anxious to attain the precious academic degree at any cost, the degree being looked upon as the passport to equality. If the black student challenges the system, he is subtly reminded by the administration that he is "jeopardizing the great opportunity afforded him."

The administrative policy of the majority of black universities is based upon a system of rigid control of the student body. As a means of maintaining this control, the administration capitalizes on the impoverished background of the students and the overcrowded conditions of the school. Many schools send warnings of expulsion to the parents of students involved in protest activities. Others are even less subtle and simply expel or suspend large numbers of students for their participation in protest activities. By accepting more students than the school is equipped to handle, the administration can create a running appeal for more funds due to inadequate facilities, and since the enrollment is large enough to sustain a mass expulsion if student unrest becomes too acute, the administration can exercise rigorous control. The student body can therefore be whipped into line by expelling the activists, removing the leadership, and terrorizing the remaining student population into submission.

Indoctrination is employed at the black university as a more subtle vehicle for controlling the students. The black university is plagued with programs of compulsory ROTC, compulsory religious services, and ludicrous curfew regulations. On many black campuses students are not only confined to their dormitories after dark, but they are restricted to the confines of the campus during the day. This indicates acceptance of the white mythology that Negroes are more sexually promiscuous than white people and should therefore be kept under close supervision. Black students are regimented and encouraged through the ROTC program to further the cause of American imperialism throughout the non-white world. The university, black or white, is simply not the place for a military outpost. Furthermore, according to the concept of democracy, supposedly fundamental in this country, religion or the lack of it is a matter of choice. Compulsory religious and military activities are examples of indoctrination, not education.

The university is not supposed to be a church, an army base, or a prison.

The assumption made to justify the policy of rigid control is that the black student, having been "culturally deprived," is incapable of making sound decisions concerning the direction of his development. Consequently, much emphasis is placed upon the maintenance of a great deal of restraint and the projection of a particular well defined image designed to impress the white society, thereby making the process of assimilation much less chaotic. It is almost as if black people are being sold into slavery again on the basis of their ability to become unrecognizable from white people. The tragic paradox is that no black person escapes the stigma of his color within a racist society, for white people determine the criteria for acceptance.

Revolutionary Philosophy Would Stimulate Thinking

The society itself has defined the role and stature of all persons not forming a part of the elite white group. If, therefore, a man is considered to be a Negro, he and all his progeny, present and future, are placed in the same category. Should we black people then continue to strive for white acceptance, or should we begin to make ourselves acceptable to ourselves? If we are to assume the latter philosophy, we must view white acceptability as being irrelevant to our purposes. Our acceptability by whites must be based upon what we are and not what we can never be.

In an attempt to provide a more realistic direction and tone for the education of black students, we must consider fundamentally altering its present orientation. The orientation should be toward directing black college graduates back into the black community. Today's direction of Negro graduates into the mainstream of society causes a resource drain within the black community. The black professors who are "good enough to teach in white schools" should be given cause to reconsider the premise implied by their actions. The orientation should be toward betterment of the race through cooperative service within the black community as opposed to integration into the white community. Underlying this type of orientation would be a far more meaningful form of brotherhood than exists today.

The present concept of brotherhood for black men and women has meaning only within the context of white sanction. Black fraternities, sororities, and other socially inclined groups are not only condoned but encouraged, yet black political parties, black controlled economic bases, and black controlled educational structures are considered out of the question. If we entertain ideas of uniting black people in an effort to attain power (the lack of which is subjecting black people to genocide in this country), we are called racists. Essentially, it is the white folks who determine the line between brotherhood and racism for black people, and their right to do so is legitimatized at the black university. The concept of brotherhood and cooperation must therefore be expanded within the black university to fit the needs of the black population.

American universities are designed to directly reinforce the system of this country, a system founded upon oppression and exploitation. White people control the system; therefore, if the tone of education at Negro universities strays too far from white sanction, the universities will suffer financial loss. This loss will be due to the fact that Negro universities are largely financed and supported by white people, who do not sanction ideas of black people coming together to help other black people. Since the structure of the black university is based upon the structure of the white, it too reinforces the system and thereby reinforces oppression and exploitation.

The administration of the black university responds to the needs of the white power structure which acts through the white dominated Board of Trustees, and forces the black student to mimic the reactionary stance it takes. In this manner, a tight system of control is maintained with the student being the initial victim and the black community the ultimate victim of exploitation. In this context the black university functions as a subtle instrument of suppression against the total black society of this country. The black university should speak to the needs of the nation by speaking *first* to the needs of its oppressed black population. As it stands, the black university supposedly speaks to the needs of black people via speaking to the needs of the nation. This is, at best, a farce.

The curriculum throughout the black educational structure must be subjected to thorough and highly critical analysis. It is from the area of liberal arts and more specifically the social sciences that new concepts and ideologies will emerge. Every black student should have the opportunity of exploring thoroughly and realistically the history of exploitation to which black people in this country have been subjected for over 350 years. There can be no realistic solutions to black oppression until the problems are clearly understood. This understanding could be brought to bear within the framework of the basic social sciences which are required subject matter at most secondary schools and colleges.

Revolutionary philosophy should be taught, not to provoke anarchy, but to stimulate the independent thinking essential to initiating meaningful changes. It is within this framework that the urgent social problems relating to the riots or violent rebellions can be held up to critical analysis. It must be understood that these are simply forms of protest born of the frustrations of suppressed black people. The black man in the ghettos of this nation has recognized the enemy and the enemy has acknowledged the black man. It is time for us as a unified black people to recognize that the white value system is absurd and awaken ourselves to the task of self liberation. Attention must be directed toward solution of the basic problems underlying the riots rather than toward the riots themselves. The militancy of protest must correspond to the intensity of the oppression.

The Task of Freedom

If these changes are to become a reality in the black university, students themselves must initiate them. Initiation of these changes will erupt from recognition of the inadequacies of the system, which are becoming more apparent daily. The above point raises a question concerning the extent to which the student has the right to determine the nature and content of the educational process through which he must go. The university is a system based on mutual dependence between students, faculty, and administrators; it does not function solely to pay the salaries of its personnel. Hence, the black student must come to grips with asserting his power at the university.

The black student must begin to discuss the nature of the racist philosophy of this country. Here the student could delve into the question of why the society expects the Negro to be more moral than the white person. The idea here is that the black man must avoid being racist at all costs, while the white man flaunts his racism and institutionalizes it within the structure of his society. Black people are taught that we must achieve equality through dignity and restraint rather than indignity and action. The chains of total physical enslavement have been removed, but the black man is now subjected to a mental bondage that is even more savage. The mental bondage inhibits and restrains the abilities of black people to produce a functional philosophy of liberation independent of the existing racist philosophy. When the principles of logic and reason learned in the white society are turned against the oppressors the result is a horrified white response. *The black student is taught to react to the response of white people and not to the problems of black people.*

The frightening product of this entire process is the confused black college graduate, thrust out into a hostile racist society and handicapped by tunnel vision and a self-negating perspective. He faces the society a living example of his white indoctrinated sense of inferiority. He knows little of his rich cultural heritage, has little racial pride, and often looks with contempt at his own less fortunate, uneducated brothers and sisters.

We must understand that black people's struggle in America is a struggle for economic survival and the right to live as men. We must determine what it means when the substance of our struggle for liberation is suppressed within the very framework of our own black educational institutes. We must understand what it means when affluent whites can muster support within the framework of their own educational structures, not for a movement for human survival, but for the right to curse and smoke "pot."

Black students, in order to formulate a program of action on black campuses to implement the struggle for liberation of black Americans must confront not only the problem of how to accomplish this, but must also be prepared to grapple with the reactionary administration, the faculty, and yes, even sections of the student body, for the right to pursue this course. Let us awaken our minds to the task of freedom and move to speak to the white society from a position of power. Let us move to end the white world's paternalistic slavery of our minds. In the words of W. E. B. Du Bois, "We have no right to sit silently by while the inevitable seeds are sown for a harvest of disaster to our children."

ERNEST STEPHENS, Editor,
Black Thesis, Tuskegee Institute, Alabama

Where the Truth Is

You send the best of this country off to be shot and maimed. They rebel in the street. They will take pot and they will get high. They don't want to go to school because they're going to be snatched off from their mothers to be shot in Vietnam.

The main reason for juvenile delinquency today is because their parents are angry and their parents are angry because they are so highly taxed and because there is a war going on they do not understand.

We have to realize where the truth really is.

The children of America are not rebelling for no reason. They are not hippies for no reason at all. We don't have what we have on Sunset Boulevard for no reason. They are rebelling against something. We all seem to camouflage something. This is very basic. We pay taxes and we are very resentful of those high taxes.

There are so many things burning the people of this country, particularly mothers. They feel they are going to raise sons—and I know what it's like, and you have children of your own, Mrs. Johnson—we raise children and send them to war.

EARTHA KITT
(*The New York Times,* January 19, 1968)

"I don't believe in this rioting, personally. One of my best buddies in this outfit is a white from Mississippi. We eat out of the same mess tin. If I go to the PX, I share whatever I get with him, and he does the same for me."

PFC. WILBERT LATIN, Shreveport, Louisiana
(*Newsweek,* November 20, 1967)

"McNamara likes to say the reason for the bombing of North Vietnam is to force it to halt its aggression against the South. White America has been committing aggression against the Nation of the black man since 1619. If bombing cities halts aggression, I'm willing to try Chicago and New York."

A CHICAGO BLACK NATIONALIST

For a Cause

We're fighting for a cause over here, both to protect the U.S.—in the long run—and to protect the rights of the South Vietnamese people. Mr. Muhammad Ali along with Mr. Carmichael and Dr. King would not be able to tell the Negro youth to refuse to fight if our Communist enemies were running the U.S.

How about telling the ones at home that are protesters, and the ones in the riots to get with us and see to it that we get the supplies we need to win this thing over here and come home to our wives and loved ones.

T/SGT. ALBERT GLENN, JR., APO San Francisco
(*Ebony* magazine, November, 1967)

"I saw quite a few dead soldiers, white and Negro. It was awful. I figure if some of these race haters, the black ones and the white ones, encountered that, maybe they'd change their minds. If I were a white man, I think I could predict my future. But as a Negro I just have to wait it out."

EMMETT BEARD, Chicago
(*Newsweek,* November 20, 1967)

Black Survival Curriculum

Should target practice and lessons in weaponry be given to black children in the public schools? Should the math lessons relate directly to such matters as muzzle velocity and windage? And should the home economics course stress how to survive when supplies to the black community are cut off?

Yes, writes Herman B. Ferguson, an assistant principal in the city public schools who was suspended last year after being accused of plotting to murder moderate Negro leaders.

Writing in The Guardian, which calls itself an independent radical weekly, Mr. Ferguson has outlined a "black survival curriculum" for schools in which Negro children will learn "self-determination, self-control and self-defense."

The day will start, he said, with a pledge of allegiance to a red, black and green flag, the banner of black nationalists.

The student's pledge would be something like LeRoi Jones's "We Are Beautiful People," Mr. Ferguson explained.

Physical Training

"After the morning classes are over," he went on, "he [the student] goes to physical training where the first part of the period is devoted to target practice on the school shooting range.

"Following this he reports to a nearby classroom for instruction in weaponry, gun handling and gun safety.

"His next class takes place in a gymnasium where he is given a lesson in one of the Eastern martial arts of self-defense.

"To make his study of original languages more functional and to motivate him to master his native tongue, all instruction in the self-defense and the weaponry are conducted in Swahili and Yoruba."

Self-defense and weaponry will be the "prestige courses," Mr. Ferguson said.

Pride in His Blackness

"Inasmuch as a good course in weaponry must include basic information from such disciplines as math, physics, chemistry and biology, and since his physical training will deal with developing his neuro-muscular system to a high degree of efficiency, a total curriculum could be planned using these two areas as the core or base," he wrote.

"As our black student moves about the building, loudspeakers placed in the ceilings continuously bathe him with the quiet sound of Malcolm X speaking, LeRoi Jones reading one of his poems, Aretha Franklin singing a soul song and other black heroes speaking to him and filling him with a constant pride in his blackness.

"His afternoon is spent studying the traditional subjects of reading, writing and arithmetic."

The reading material would focus on the life stories of black heroes like Malcolm X, Garvey, H. Rap Brown, Stokely Carmichael, LeRoi Jones, Nat Turner and others, Mr. Ferguson said. Math problems would focus on "mathematical considerations involved in firing, repairing and making weapons."

Period of Silent Meditation

"The school day ends with a 15-second period of silent meditation in memory of the millions of black heroes who have given their lives that we may survive for another day," the article said.

Mr. Ferguson said the school he described would be controlled by an elected parent group fully responsible for setting standards, hiring and dismissing all personnel, evaluation of the program and budget control.

The graduate of such a school, he said, "will not be found dying in far-off places in an army that represents the same forces that oppress and exploit him daily. He will know exactly where his battlefield is."

HOMER BIGART
(*The New York Times,* March 14, 1968)

"I'm not here to prepare for a 32nd vice niggership at General Motors."

A GRADUATE STUDENT, Columbia University

"The only time things gonna change is when Negroes and po' whites get together. They got po' whites worse off than you. They tell 'em they better than niggers to keep 'em fighting us."

LI'L MALCOLM, Atlanta
(*The Harvard Crimson,* October 20, 1967)

"Negroes don't fear bad talk, but the white man does. He wants to fear us. He has called us animals and cannibals. This helps him to rationalize his retaliatory moves."

JUANITA MYERS
White Plains, N. Y.

The Word Was Not for a Nigger

My Nigger Son:

I take this time to write this missive, that you might better understand, therefore better endure, the long suffering of becoming a man without ever learning what or who you are in the present scheme of things.

Much of this you might lay to the fault and sins of the Alabaster Man. But you must not blame him altogether for your plight. "The fault . . . is not in our stars, but in ourselves, that we are underlings." The most grievous fault lay in language. Words. His order of words which was never meant to include your kind or the likes of you. His language and philosophy began with a word—and there is where it ends. How can you, my Nigger Son, find your identity, articulate your experiences, in an order of words? Language. Which was created and conceived by a people who did not even know of your black existence or Earthly presence?

Note how the Myth of this Genesis reads, my Son:

"In the Beginning was the Word. And the Word was God. And the Word was with God."

So say the Ancient Scriptures, Judeo-Christian. Holy, Sacred, Hebrew, Latin, Caucasian approved. Nigger adopted! Bullshit!

We all know that the Word was never the beginning of anything. Neither God nor Man could have begun with a word, for in the beginning of everything was first the Experience. The Word came later. For what else are words but man's feeble attempt to articulate or record his original experiences with God?

But thereafter, my Nigger Son, came forth more words. Grunting sounds. Groans from the pit of his bowels, expelled from his throat, trippingly on his tongue. . . . Words. Noises and symbols for noises, repeated the Alabaster Brother in his pathetic attempts to articulate his questionable experiences. . . . In the Beginning the Beast became more preoccupied with his invention of more words. Understand, my Nigger Son, all that he recalls of the Beginning was the Word. Of course, this was long before he came

Robert H. deCoy, *The Nigger Bible* (Los Angeles: Holloway House, 1968), pp. 21–26, 39–45. Reprinted by permission.

to discover the Blacks and to enslave your kind. For in his Beginning with words, our Alabaster Peer could conceive nothing of a Race or Beings who could exist independent of his own paltry few, way back. There and then. When?

It was a long time after his Beginning, "With his Word that was God and with God," before our Alabaster became conscious of your existence. Surely his words could never be used to articulate the experiences of our particular Black beginnings. Which certainly did not coincide with his words.

It was shortly after he had been "given the Word," my Nigger Son, that the Alabaster Brother became conscious of your existence and sailed forth to contaminate your native Continent, confuse your Minds and Spirits with his Tongues of limited words. He conquered the wealth of your lands, captured the health of your Black bodies and curtailed your experiences with a God. He castrated your men, as a tribute to his White Whores' vanity, while [taking] the Black Bodies of your women, beneath the altars of Christian concubinage. All these things he was forced to do, my Nigger Son, in order to give meaning to his words. Did not his beginnings commence with the Word God? Do not his other words say that he was the image of God in Christ?

How then, my Nigger Son, can you ever hope to express what you are, who you are, or your experiences with God, in a language so limited, conceived by a people who are quite helpless in explaining themselves?

When we were brought forth, my Nigger Son, depicted as "Beasts of Burden" in his World, upon this Continent, there were still no words invented to describe you. God had given the Alabaster Peer the words, 1. White. 2. God-like. 3. Captor. 4. Master. 5. Christian. 6. Benefactor. 7. Rulers. 8. Caucasians. 9. Patriot.

None of the above words were conceived for you, my Nigger Son, but in equal contrast none of the following words can be applied as a description of him: As you can read and see, each, by corresponding number, is in direct antithesis to what has been reserved for the Alabaster kind: 1. *Black*. 2. *Godless*. 3. *Captive*. 4. *Slave*. 5. *Heathen*. 6. *Beggar*. 7. *Servant*. 8. *Colored*. 9. *Negro*. *Nigger*.

My Son, you have a choice of being of the latter two, Negro or Nigger, though there are those Bastards amongst us who would say, "It is simply a matter of your conduct and behavior in the presence of white folks." This does quite often distinguish which title the Alabaster Ones will bestow upon you. Note however, there are no contrasting, or counterparts, of such words to describe them. Negro or Nigger? The first is the closest that their language can afford to come, in acknowledging your resemblance to Being— that is, Human. The latter word, "Nigger," is bestowed only upon you to better delineate your differences, as distinctively apart, from the Alabaster Peers. Whatever these two sounds, words, imply, my Son, remember, you have a choice of being either. For "Negro" will never become a reality.

Your Being as a Nigger is closer to your inherent Black nature.

There are no redeeming factors in being accepted as "Negro," for this word was manufactured to describe those Niggers who would waste their existence in the hopeless void of eventually dying as Christian Caucasians.

The Alabaster man invented the word, "Negro," to imply that he could make a Nigger "Grow," that is, become a race which even his own God saw no reason to Create. Should the Negro ever become a reality, then, my Nigger Son, the Alabasters will have proved themselves Creators of Human Beings, equal to the very God Whom they are sworn to perpetuate. . . .

To those Niggers who would be integrated:

I write that we may come together to bury a Monster that we have come to know as "Integration" and discard the Yoke of Humiliation that has kept it alive. Consider, my Niggers. It is the Separatist aspects of this society which has brought us thus far. Mark my words, it will be the Separatist aspects of our nation which will save us Niggers as a race of people.

This thought occurred to me one evening as I sat watching an all too familiar scene on the television News. Throngs of our almost lost and misguided Nigger children and youths, marshalled into line behind Black Preachers, "Their Leaders" exhorting them in hymn and prayer on behalf of an Illusion called Integration, which they will never come to know.

It was not this part of the scene that bothered me, my Brothers. I have witnessed it before many a time and heard the threats of their lamentable hymns from the day I came forth from the pit, my Black Mother's womb. Rather the thing that caught my attention was the incredulous faces of the Alabaster Peers, both young and old, who had lined the streets and walks to watch them. More so was the retaliating jibes of the indignant white youths in response to the hymns and prayers which our Niggers were chanting.

> "Two, Four, Six, Eight!
> We don't want to Integrate."

Our Black Preachers turned back to their throngs and stepped up the repetition of the ancient hymn line, from the throats and faces of their followers:

> "We Shall Overcome . . .
> We Shall Overcome . . .
> We Shall Overcome . . . Some Day . . ."

I felt the tears well and course down my cheeks. The anger lumped up into my throat. Not at the Caucasian tormentors, my Nigger friends! No! I was more angry at our poor singing and praying Niggers. I wanted to jump through the television set. Admonishing, that our youths would climb from their knees and answer back at the taunting jingle:

> "Two, Four, Six, Eight!
> We don't want to Integrate.
> For we all know our destined Fate
> Is to make amends and Separate."

But they rather went on singing a lamentable statement, which none of them could possibly believe:

> ". . . Deep in my Heart, I Do Believe.
> We Shall Overcome . . . Some day . . ."

We should call for a Separation by Treaty, my Brothers. . . .

I would have it that on the local level that we have our own civic agencies, police forces, fire department, etc. with complete autonomy, but working in close conjunction with other such agencies of our cities, states and nation. Our own courts and jails, our own schools. Not to forget, our own tax collections and franchise supervision as to businesses and real estate ownerships.

Elijah Muhammed exclaims: "There is no people without land . . ." The Old Prophet is wrong. I rather say, "There is no people without their minds and spirit." For thousands of years the Jews survived, some even flourished, without a native land. But, they had their own minds and spirit. They also kept Jehovah, a God of their own. . . .

The Jews first freed their minds and spirits. After that, the Exodus under Moses was inevitable. The Promised Land was awarded them by their God only after they elected to be free in mind and spirit.

Their Scribes and Prophets were wise enough not to give them THE TEN COMMANDMENTS until after "The Israelite Children" were a safe distance from the hordes of the Pharaoh. It is easy to see why. One of the Commandments stated "Thou Shalt Not Steal." When the Hebrew Children fled captivity, Moses had encouraged them to take all of the Gold, Treasures, that they could lay their hands on. Their God and Prophet did not consider this stealing. It was, rather, a payment in reparations for their long period experienced under bondage.

SO, they took gold, my Brothers. Lots of gold. Enough to melt down to make themselves "Images." Calves of Gold!

I have often wondered, my Brothers, were the Pharaoh and his armies in such hot pursuit to recapture the slaves, or rather more anxious to recoup the Treasures in gold which the Hebrew children had "borrowed" and fled with?

Oh, but to create a Nigger God like that of the Jews, and a Leader with the guile, mind and spirit of their Moses!

You, my Nigger Converts, are born inheritors of this very same God and His Commandments. "Thou (Niggers) Shalt Not Steal." If so, this God shall not be your deliverance! You will incur his wrath and damnation if you but break his Commandments. How will you ever be free when this has been implanted in your minds and spirits? Yet, these commandments did not apply to those who created this God of Antiquity.

Now, you will ask me, my Niggers: "How does a people go about freeing their minds and spirits?"

And I will answer you with FIVE WORDS: *Look. Listen. Analyze. Dissect. Reject. Look*, to see the defects in the Gods and systems that you have been taught to worship and serve. *Listen,* to the Preachers, Teachers, followers who acclaim the powers and goodness of this God. *Analyze,* compare what defects you have seen with their explanations and accounts as to how it all came about. *Dissect,* what promises this God has made to you, through your Nigger Preachers and Teachers, to that which he has already awarded to the Chosen People who conceived him. *Reject,* the doctrines of any God who would have his Nigger Ministers preach to you that "Your time is forthcoming" and others have you join in singing, "We Shall Overcome."

When, you have rejected the unnatural aspects of such a God for your Black desires and aspirations, then *what* happens? Immediately, you will be free of him, in mind and spirit. Amen.

After all, does not freedom mean a state of separation, exemption from slavery, servitude, confinement, constraint in mind and spirit?

Remember, my Nigger Brothers and Sisters: "A man exists a slave, only through his spiritual acknowledgment of a Master." A Captor cannot be Master where his Captive rejects him Mentally and Spiritually. The Physical rejection is a matter of course. Not time.

Digest these words well, my Niggers, and you will readily see that a Treaty of Separation, implemented with equal guarantees and racial autonomy, would solve our American Nigger Dilemma much sooner and easier than the present course we pursue. But we have got to free our minds and spirits before we will bring about or even see what the Christian calls, "The Millennium."

Robert H. deCoy

"This walk right, talk right, smile right, smell right program . . . [is] crap. . . . Why can't a dirty black man walk in for a job like a dirty white man and have the same chance?"

Alvin Echols, Philadelphia
(*Newsweek,* November 20, 1967)

A Negro Is Still a Nigger

Clearly, it is as a measure of self-defense that the black community has begun to draw together and even to discuss separatism. Let every liberal white American ponder this. . . .

Whereas the black masses, both those in the rural South and those who have flooded into Northern cities in the past quarter century, aspire primarily for a higher standard of living and for freedom from the indignities and oppressions which their blackness has attracted to them, the middle-class Negroes have developed more subtle tastes. To varying degrees, these Negroes have become "assimilated" into white society and lead lives which are spiritually dependent upon the white community in a way that the mass of Negroes could never comprehend. For them, an integrated America is fast becoming a reality and the thrust of their effort is to extend the integration concept to every corner of the country. Their schizophrenia arises from the inescapable reminders of their vulnerability. Even with a Ph.D., a Nobel prize, a Congressional Medal of Honor or a vast fortune, a Negro is still a "nigger" to many (most?) white Americans and the society does not let him forget it for very long. Nor does the sensitive Negro really want to forget it; he wants to change it.

R. S. BROWNE (*Ramparts*
magazine, December, 1967)

"Black" Is Arrogant

Anything except that odious word, "Negro" which has such a ridiculous heritage of mockery. We were not dropped into America; we were forcibly dragged from Africa. So what else are we? Words are the greatest avenue of communication and much more reliable than signs. They are forceful symbols! Words, that is.

Besides all of this I have a sinking feeling that the dear old Boers, or whatever they are in South Africa, would just love to RIGHTLY own the name Africans; they tried to get as close as they could. Let us all rally around Afro-American. I think Black has connotations of arrogance.

VIRGINIA J. HARDEN, Detroit, Michigan
(*Ebony* magazine, January 1968)

"Negro," Anyone?

One by-product of the black power movement is an assault on the word "Negro."

"Negro is a slave word," said H. Rap Brown of the Student Nonviolent Coordinating Committee. He, Stokely Carmichael and other black power spokesmen insist on the word "black" and often refuse to talk to reporters who speak of "Negroes."

Prominent leaders such as Dr. Martin Luther King of the Southern Christian Leadership Conference and Roy Wilkins of the National Association for the Advancement of Colored People have been heckled and denounced for using the word "Negro."

Keith Baird, the coordinator of the Afro-American History and Cultural Center of the New York City Board of Education, said: "This is not a minor semantic dispute. It engages the emotions and intellect of a vast number of people, from Southern campuses to the corner of 125th Street and Seventh Avenue in Harlem."

Hoyt W. Fuller of *Negro Digest* says "Afro-American" is being promoted by internationally minded men as a semantic reminder that the fate of the black struggles today in America and in Africa are closely linked.

In recent years, the greatest pressure for the word "black" has come from the Nation of Islam (Black Muslims) and the late Malcolm X, who referred contemptuously to "so-called Negroes" who refuse to struggle for their rights.

This usage has caught on widely. Ossie Davis, the playwright-actor, wrote recently: "A black man means not to accept the system as Negroes do, but to fight hell out of the system as Malcolm did."

Mr. Fuller said: "There is definitely a generation gap in usage. Those who have adjusted to things as they are use 'Negro'; those that haven't, use 'black and Afro-American.'"

He said *Negro Digest* was under "great pressure" to change its name.

Mixed usage has become common. Dr. Ralph J. Bunche, Under Secretary for Special Political Affairs in the United Nations Secretariat, says he now used "black" as often as "Negro," though he attributes little significance to the dispute. C. Eric Lincoln, the sociologist, now at Union Theological Seminary said:

"I use 'black' when talking to young people, and 'Negro' when addressing those past 40 who are comfortable with that term. In writing, I find myself shifting from 'Negro' to 'Black American.'"

Mayor Lindsay rarely uses the word "Negro" any more, using "black" instead.

Because "black" has become associated with militancy, few prominent Negroes seem willing to attack the new usage publicly. However, John Morsell of the N.A.A.C.P. said:

"I don't think it's worth such a storm to replace a well-established word. 'Negro' is a precise and useful word. And, after all, 'black' is just as much a reminder of the slave period as 'Negro.'"

Dr. William E. B. Dubois, one of the founders of the N.A.A.C.P., used the terms "black," "Negro" and "Afro-American" interchangeably.

Current clamor for a more "meaningful" label began with the parade to independence, in the late nineteen-fifties, of black African nations. With the end of the myth of dark, uncivilized Africa, Negroes became more willing to identify with that continent.

JOHN LEO (*The New York Times,*
February 26, 1968)

Indian, Caucasian . . . and Negro

I have no qualms about being identified as a Negro. I regard that designation as nothing more than an impersonal, factual description of one of the major branches of humankind. The unfavorable connotations that have grown up around the word are unfortunate, I feel, but hardly worse than those associated with many ethnic names that do not even identify a race—merely a nationality.

I am aware that my own ancestry includes individuals of American Indian and Caucasian blood, but since my Negro ethnic characteristics predominate, I will not deny that I am, primarily, a Negro. The use of such terms as "Afro-American" or "African-American" would seem, to me, to remind one that his ancestors were dragged from their homeland. I would much prefer "Negro American" which only signifies my race and the fact that I am an American citizen.

JUDY E. CUMMINGS, Staten Island,
New York (*Ebony* magazine, January, 1968)

Power for Black Americans

In the wake of the April riots it must be realized that the explosive situation in our cities is primarily racial. This is not to deny that there are masses of poor, powerless whites; there are. But the economically deprived whites do not perceive their condition as the result of deliberate policy calculated to suppress them as a group—ethnic or racial. Many blacks *do* have such a view.

Therefore, black people react differently, and that reaction is one of the reasons our cities are powder kegs of dynamite today. Blacks are becoming increasingly alienated; they no longer trust "the System," generally, or individual white decision-makers. Black people are beginning more and more to see their failure not as the function of some individual defect of their own labors but as the result of racist white America's deliberate and successful attempt to deny them upward mobility.

This means several things. Poor blacks are much more susceptible to mass acts of rage and expressive violence. They are much more willing than poor whites to organize and to challenge the structures of power. Poor whites still believe in the Ethic: if you work hard, you will achieve; and if you do not achieve, it is because of some individual failure on your part. Poor blacks no longer have such illusions about the myth of individualism in a mass, complex industrialized society.

The problem is not simply one of an equitable distribution of goods and services (more jobs, better houses, more schools), because blacks will still be *recipients,* dependent totally on whites. Blacks will accept these things and still remain distrustful (perhaps less explosively, but still there will be the lack of confidence), because they know that those who giveth can also taketh away.

How to overcome this and to create a real sense of belonging and participation? By embarking, in addition, on an equitable distribution of decision-making power. This will mean power to black groups qua black groups; and this is true at this time precisely because that is where much of the *legitimate* leadership is.

These black-power-oriented leaders are close to the frustrations and aspirations of their people. They talk in terms of emphasizing this history and culture of black people—and this is relevant. They talk in terms of developing group pride and power—and this is necessary.

At the same time, the power possessed by the black power leaders must not be sham. It must not be merely white power once removed. Black power leaders must clearly possess the power to determine decisions affecting the black community: schools, urban renewal, law enforcement, jobs, etc. If this power is only apparent, not real, it will simply be aggravating an already explosive situation. And black power leaders who accept dictates from outside the black community will quickly be isolated and dumped.

This may seem to be an emphasis on decentralization, a further fractionalizing of the society. In fact, it is a developmental process. It is a way to restore faith and confidence. It is a way to bring alienated black people into a viable political community, because it is clear that these pockets of black power cannot survive without overwhelming economic suport from the outside: Federal Government, private industry and foundations.

The relationship must be seen as reciprocal: blacks receive economic support and political power; whites receive a chance to live in a healthy, developing, equitable society. The *quid pro quo* is there. The partnership to improve the black ghettos that should be talked about should not be simply between government and business, but it must include legitimate local black power leaders.

Unless the society is prepared to deal in this kind of transformation, it is probably merely playing at school.

If power is legitimately shared in this way, the society might find that black people will be more understanding of the protracted nature of some of the solutions. As legitimate participants, they will see and be involved in the working out of their problems. As it is now, procrastination is interpreted as insincerity and unwillingness to act. And their experiences lead them to believe that such conclusions are entirely valid. Black power, as described here, is an alternative; it provides the opportunity for a new validity.

CHARLES V. HAMILTON, Chairman of
the Department of Political Science,
Roosevelt University, Chicago.
(*The New York Times,* April 13, 1968)

Take Some of Them With You

"We must get ready for the black and white confrontation which seems certain to come.

"We must get ready too. Whitey is also getting ready to rain down on us. He can't drop the H-Bomb on us because we're here and he's here with us. But, go out and get something to protect yourself with."

HERMAN FERGUSON, Harlem, New York

Be Ready to Die

"The federal government now has become a police department. It has stockpiled armies and new deadly equipment to be dispatched at anytime and anywhere to use on us. Let's be ready to die. If they kill us blacks, who are outnumbered, take some of them with you. The kinds of death they have planned for us will be quick. The pain won't last long."

HERMAN FERGUSON, Harlem, New York

Heed Wilkins, or Face Rap Brown

"I'm not throwing any bricks. I'm not looting any liquor stores. But I understand why my 'brother' does. I don't go along with the radicals. But they are necessary to let people know how we feel. If white people don't want to heed Roy Wilkins and Martin Luther King, if we can't get whites to help, we've got to follow Rap Brown.

"At one time I believed this militant talk was detrimental. Now I believe it's the only thing that will get a reaction. I don't worry about the so-called backlash. When I see our real enemies in Congress scuttling civil rights bills, I feel like joining up in a black backlash."

A Bus Driver in New York

Sold Like A Mule

"It wasn't necessary to kill the American Indians. If we were going to steal this country, we could of at least shared it. It also wasn't necessary to enslave the Black Man who was stolen from a much more civilized country and brought here, bred, worked and sold like a mule. He was not a mule. He was a man.

"If this nation is to be saved, it will be saved by black people, even though we are treated the worst. We don't want a generation of blacks to die in the streets. Try to save as many as you can."

James Baldwin, New York

The Black Man Is Justified

"You, the black youth of today here in America don't have to justify the position that you find yourself in. Long before the paleolithic period and white men came here thinking that the world was flat your forefathers made contributions to advance world culture.

"Your forefathers made this the richest country on earth. To say this is not teaching hate. It is only letting you, our children, know that they contributed more or as much to making America and the world as great as anyone.

"You don't have to justify taking welfare or anti-poverty money. It is yours to have. It is your right to have it. It belongs to you because your forefathers paid for it with interest. If it were not for you, the white man would not be throwing his superiority around so lavishly and freely."

SISTER BETTY SHABAZZ,
widow of the late Malcolm X

"It became obvious to me for the first time in my life that the business of the police in a black community is genocide. They seem to feel a need to kill black people. Their hatred was unbelievable."

A BLACK WOMAN, Detroit

"If they don't get those bastards out of the Negro neighborhoods, there's going to be a war. I look at them and feel like I want to kill. Tell you, if my kid comes home from school and tells me the teacher told him the policeman is his friend, that teacher is going to be in a whole lot of trouble with me."

A BLACK FATHER, Chicago

A god was begged,
Yet allowed the taking
Away at the end of
A shotgun muzzle,
Harnessed in a yellow-helmeted
Coward's grasp of
Authority.

DONALD FERGUSON, Chicago

"I ain't got no whole lot to say, but I will say this. It gets harder all the time to be black and a cop. Very hard, baby."

A BLACK POLICEMAN, New York

"Ain't no use. Man gonna get me, kill me off, no matter what I do. Here in the street one night, maybe. Maybe on the Freeway, he stop me: BAM. Or maybe over there, ya know, Vietnam. That's the cool way. Me and the Vietcong out there. Bang. Bang. Me dead. Or the Vietcong dead. Either way, the white man won."

A 17-YEAR-OLD, Los Angeles

Negritude in America

On certain occasions the Negro lower class, unlike the middle class, has embraced movements, cults, and symbols which were consciously embedded in its experience of being black in American society. This grasping at their blackness was, and still is, necessarily chauvinistic. White society offered the Negro masses no other mode of wresting their essence from the utter cruelty of their slave and caste status in that society.

When viewed from this vantage point, there is a curious commentary upon man's inhumanity to man whenever white Americans deliver that callous insult to the Negro's long-standing injury by questioning the validity of his chauvinistic or racist mode of retrieving his blackness. No doubt the black chauvinist mode of self-renewal is as mundane and vile as any other chauvinism at any period of human history. But it is no less an historically valid expression, for the history of white America's relationship to the Negro provided few meaningful alternatives. And for the poorer Negro the alternatives are meaningful only if they respect his blackness. . . .

Martin W. Kilson, in *The Harvard Journal of Negro Affairs*, Vol. 1, No. 1, 1965. Reprinted by permission.

The Middle-Class Response

In general, middle-class Negroes have been ambivalent toward the Negro American sub-culture and the African heritage. In the process of becoming integrated, after a fashion, into the American mainstream, they incline toward a lack of identification with their blackness, if not an outright denial of it. Everything that distinguishes the Negro American sub-culture is outwardly avoided for the presumably better traits of white society. Thus, the typical middle-class Negro shuns the mode of speech, forms of humor, physical motor skills, and sundry other traits or patterns distinguishable in the Negro sub-culture.

Insofar as a large portion of the Negro middle class has been of mixed racial ancestry, even the Negro's black skin is denigrated. The mulatto and brown-skinned Negro has been, in fact, the main carrier of middle-class values and traits in the Negro sub-culture. . . .

It must be noted, however, that despite the tendency of the Negro middle class to dissociate itself from the Negro sub-culture, there has always been a segment among this class which has endeavored to retrieve its blackness, often out of self-interest but equally out of humanistic or intellectual inspiration. Mulatto or not, the middle-class Negro is still viewed by white society as part of the Negro sub-culture from which he yearns to escape. There is thus an upper limit to the middle-class Negro's tenuous stake and general acceptability in American society, and it is this upper limit which causes some Negroes of this class to maintain close ties with the Negro sub-culture. . . .

Blackness and the Future

I am convinced that blackness—negritude—as a conscious category of Negro American (and Negro African) thought and behavior in modern society is here to stay. There is increasing evidence of this among the Negro masses, chauvinistic as it may be, and even middle-class Negroes are more attuned today than ever to retrieving the essential human values of the Negro sub-culture. This is especially true for the younger generation of educated Negroes who reject the crass ideals of so much of middle-class America and affirm Langston Hughes' injunction that our inspiration should come from "the low-down folks. . . ."

And the sweet, subtle spirit of Countee Cullen will never forgive us:

> But time to live, to love, bear pain and smile,
> Oh we are given such a little while

MARTIN W. KILSON

The Dreamer and the Dream

"I am a black woman and every black man, woman and child must stand up proud and say that I am proud of being black. I have a purpose and a direction because yesterday I discovered me.

"I'm black and I'm beautiful. I'm the singer and I'm the song. I'm the player and I'm the music. I'm the dreamer and I'm the dream and as a black woman, I hold my head proud and high."

VAL GRAY, Chicago

Stay Out of the Army

"White kids are taught white nationalism. Black kids must be taught black nationalism. . . . It hurts me everytime I see a black GI in Vietnam there killing the Vietnamese brother. They are our brothers. It is the white murderers who do not deserve to live. Whitey is the enemy of the future of all mankind.

"We must stay out of the Army. We must delay and block the man as much as possible. To send our black boys off to the Army is to help and perpetuate the same kind of slavery that got them into the Army in the first place. Let our boys stay home and find a meaningful life right here."

CONRAD LYNN, New York Attorney

Fox-hole Integration

It appalls me to read ever-so-often the printed words uttered by some black soldier in the jungle who says there is complete integration in the fox-holes when the fighting gets thick. Sounds like a survival statement. What Uncle Sam doesn't print are the many Negro complaints and incidents of hatred by white, young GIs who hate Malcolm X, despise Carmichael, don't understand Martin Luther King's anti-Viet Nam stand; and won't believe that Muhammad Ali has the Faith, Baby. The brothers who feel secure with a career in the Armed Forces and really believe Viet Nam is a melting pot of racial indifferences ought to realize that they are still being called nigger behind their backs as frequently as a Vietnamese is called a gook. And to show you how hatred spreads, an 8-year-old Vietnamese boy ran up to me and said he and his friends were told that a "soul brother killed Kennedy." The Warren Commission missed something, evidently.

> SP/4 NOBLE SISSLE, JR.
> APO San Francisco
> (*Ebony* magazine, November, 1967)

A Fighting American

This letter is directed toward the protesters and demonstrators against the Viet Nam policy. I am a Negro soldier, now serving in the Republic of Viet Nam. The demonstrations on the Viet Nam policy back there in our country are very disturbing to all of us here. I wish some of those demonstrators and protesters would think twice before carrying signs in the street.

I would like to give my opinion or view of why we are here in Viet Nam. The answer to the question is simple. I am here because Communism threatens not only my country, but the rest of the free world. There is an international drive to impose Communism on every country in the world, including ours. The Americans fighting over here, both black and white, understand, even if some of our clergy and intellectual demonstrators and protesters don't. I am a Negro and a fighting American who is proud of his country. Thank God for that. (*Ebony* magazine, November, 1967)

Killing Too Long for "The Man"

"If my grandson is going to die, I'd rather he died right here on this street and not off in somebody's 'Veetnam.' He ain't got no business in them Chinese folk's backyard noway.

"These folks in Detroit now. All that burning an' lootin an' everybody saying folks shouldn't be violent. How you goin' tell people, little people, not to be violent when the whole United States is kickin' them little Chinese so awful. Don't make no sense, none a t'all. . . .

"Them little boys. Devils. No place to go and play, nobody to teach 'em what it's all about. Mothers on the welfare, you know. Poppas gone. And the young men can't find no jobs so they join the Army and go to Veetnam. Shouldn't be no black folks shootin' no brown folks for no white man. We been killing too long for the white man, tha's all. I seen those boys goin' off in the '42 war to kill Germans an' them Japs. I watched them off this street when they went off to Korea. Now they're goin' to Veetnam. Black folks ain't got nothin' out of all these white people's wars. Nothin' but a whole lot of hell."

A CHICAGO GRANDMOTHER
(quoted by Robert C. Maynard in
The Washington Post, September 27, 1967)

"I went over there to fight 'Charlie Cong' and one day in a bar in Saigon, a cracker from Texas called me 'nigger' for coming in the place. Soon after that it dawned on me that I was fighting the wrong 'Charlie.' My enemy is not 'Charlie Cong.' It's 'Mister Charlie.' "

A VIETNAM VETERAN

Negroes Being Used

You see, it is a legitimate aspiration of Negroes, as with all Americans, to own and succeed in their own businesses. Stokely Carmichael talks about businesses owned by Negroes, but how can you improve your economic level by burning down what individual Negroes, working hard and acting sensibly, have gained? It turns out that the revolutionaries aren't interested in improving our lot at all, but we are being used to terrify and prepare the American people for guerrilla warfare in the streets. King has stated that only Marxism has the revolutionary spirit. Okay. He's made it quite clear where he stands.

REV. E. FREEMAN YEARLING,
New York, Founder, National
Negro Congress of Racial Pride

Quoted in *American Opinion,* March, 1968, p. 40. Reprinted by permission.

Patience and Magnanimity

Because both Negro men and women are judged in the mirror of white society, their identity model becomes an impossible one to attain. Ego strength is derived from a mutuality of confirmation between an individual and his social environment. This mutuality is denied to Negroes.

In a lifelong battle against identity diffusion, burdened with an accumulation of unresolved personality conflicts, finding nowhere the paths to psychological peace, the Negro turns to angry protest, and is met with counsels of moderation. After years of learning patience and humility, after years of living Christian virtues in a naive manner decidedly un-Christian, American Negroes are supposed to learn magnanimity too.

PAMELA BLAKE, Lexington, Massachusetts

From *The Harvard Journal of Negro Affairs,* Vol. 1, No. 1, 1965, p. 16. Reprinted by permission.

The Olympics and Black Americans

Nothing on the sports scene recently has caused more high-level arm-flapping than the announced decision of many black athletes not to participate in next October's Olympic Games in Mexico City. The athletes who have joined our organized boycott, Olympic Project for Human Rights, have been termed misguided, ungrateful, self-defeating and unpatriotic.

We don't mind. Our motive is a simple one. For 36 of the 72 years that the modern Olympics have been staged, American Negroes have contributed greatly to U.S. victories. And while they were winning medals, they were also being hailed before the world as symbols of American equality—an equality that has never existed. We are putting Washington and the world on notice that they can no longer count on the successors of Jesse Owens, Rafer Johnson and Bob Hayes to join in a fun-and-games fête propaganized as the epitome of equal rights, so long as we are refused these rights in white society.

One of the boycotters, Tommy Smith, put it this way: "I'm not only willing to give up participating in Mexico City, but I'd give up my life if necessary to open a door or channel to reduce bigotry." Smith, a 23-year-old California collegian, is known as the world's fastest human. His world mark of 0:19.5 for 220 yards and 200 meters and his 0:43.8 for one leg of the 440-yard relay are the fastest ever registered. In agreement with Smith are Lee Evans, the national A.A.U. quarter-mile champion; 27-foot broad-jumper Jerry Proctor, one of the finest young prospects we have; John Carlos, an 09.3 sprinter; Lew Alcindor of U.C.L.A., generally recognized as the best college basketball player in years; Otis Burrell, who can high-jump 7' 2", and who might well have won a gold medal at the Mexican Games; and Henry Jackson, one of the top three or four triple-jumpers in the world. Each of these men knows he may be hurting his own career but is prepared to sacrifice

Harry Edwards, in *The Saturday Evening Post*, January 13, 1968, p. 6. Reprinted by permission.

his personal opportunity at the Olympics in order to win some recognition for the plight of his race. . . .

We believe that many more will join the boycott in coming months. And frankly, any Negro athlete who doesn't, is, in my opinion, a cop-out and a traitor to his race.

> HARRY EDWARDS, Professor of Sociology,
> San Jose State College, California

Olympic Boycott Supported

"It is unmistakeable that black athletic participation in American international competition is image building only in hoping to conceal this programmed racist society. This cheap device is exposed to the eyes of the entire non-white world, by the black athletes in the boycott."

> A RESOLUTION OF THE
> BLACK STUDENTS' CONFERENCE (1968),
> Central State University, Ohio

"These so-called middle-class Negroes think they're going to escape. There ain't gonna be no escape when that man is ready with his ovens. You black, you burn. That's all."

> A BLACK NATIONALIST, Watts

On Muhammad Ali

"I view society as a group of institutions. And the Negro heavy-weight champion has long been an institution in the Negro community—tantamount to the president of the United States.

"But Negro champions before Muhammad Ali always rationalized their success in white terms. Now Ali has sharpened it and turned it into what it really is—a racial stronghold and very black.

"Ali symbolizes the new Negro—self-reliant, self-assertive, standing up to the white man and rationalizing his success in black terms. Ali identifies with the ghetto. When he is in Los Angeles he always comes to Watts and walks its streets. He is unlike many ghetto Negroes who are wards of the welfare system, offenders in jail, Negro males dependent on Negro females. Ali is everything the ghetto Negro isn't but yearns to be."

> STANLEY JOSEPH SANDERS, a Rhodes scholar from Watts
> (*The Christian Science Monitor,* November 6, 1967)

How It Looks from the Off-side

Because the greatest obstacle to racial peace is the communications barrier, it is vital to keep the lines open between the white majority and Negro minority. This advice came from one of the Nation's most outspoken Negro firebrands, Ernie Chambers, a bearded, bushy-haired Omaha barber specializing in Afro cuts and civil rights agitation, who sounded off at a closed session of the President's Commission on Civil Disorders.

This column has obtained a copy of his confidential advice, which is must reading for whites who are trying to understand how the black militants feel and what they think.

In a voice charged with emotion, Chambers told the Commission fiercely: "We have marched, we have cried, we have prayed, we have voted, we have petitioned, we have been good little boys and girls. We have done every possible thing to make this white man recognize us as human beings. And he refuses . . .

"You can understand why Jews who were burned by the Nazis hate Germans, but you can't understand why black people who have been systematically murdered by the government and its agents—by private citizens, by the police departments—you can't understand why they hate white people . . .

"A policeman is an object of contempt. A policeman is a paid and hired murderer. And you never find the policeman guilty of a crime, no matter what violence he commits against a black person. In Detroit, you were shooting 'snipers.' So you mounted a .50 caliber machine gun on a tank and shot into an apartment and killed a four-year-old 'sniper.' " . . .

Black vs. Peace Power

Chambers kept talking: "Black people doing ordinary, reasonable, peaceful things in this country are attacked by the police; and the police are praised for it. And you talk about giving the police more money and more power . . .

"You will appropriate all kinds of money to give the National Guard increased training in how to wipe us out. And it's a funny thing that in all these so-called riots, the police and National Guard kill far more people than the so-called rioters. And as for the sniping, don't you believe that. Why are no cops killed? I believe the National Guard should be fought like they are telling us we should fight in Vietnam . . .

"We are being forced by police misconduct to get together to fight the police. You know when I'll believe that singing 'We Shall Overcome' is an effective way to fight the police? When I see you send your Marines, your airmen and your infantrymen into Vietnam led by the Mormon Tabernacle Choir.

"We are going to fight your people like you fight us. And don't say I'm revealing too much, because if something happens to me, there are other people who come up. They killed Malcolm X and produced Stokely (Carmichael) and Rap (Brown). You kill Rap; he will multiply. You kill Stokely; he will multiply. Now you don't know me; so maybe you don't want to kill me. You might just want me in jail. But you get me off the scene, and I'll multiply . . .

"Here is what you are going to give my child. I am going to send him to school and teach him to respect authority. So here is a Cracker teacher standing in front of my child making him listen to 'Little Black Sambo.' See, that's the image the school gives him when he's young to teach him his 'place.' A caricature, wearing outlandish clothing that even the animals in the forest don't want to wear . . .

"So he goes through the caricature like I did when I was a small child in grade school. And I don't forget these things. I wasn't born with the attitudes I have now. They were put in me by Crackers. I sat through Little Black Sambo. And since I was the only black face in the room, I became Little Black Sambo . . ."

Sit and Take It

"He gets a little older, so he can't be Little Black Sambo because he's too old for that. So you turn to good old Mark Twain, one of your great writers. And the black child grows from Little Black Sambo into Nigger Jim. And the white kids read this stuff and they laugh at the black child; and he's got to sit there and take it . . .

"They use the term 'Nigger' on the floor of Congress. And look at Sen. Dodd—good old Christian Sen. Dodd; and then old black Adam Clayton Powell. Dodd had more charges against him than you can shake a stick at, and in black and white from his own documents what he had done. And you people sat around debating 'whether we are going to censure him or whether we are to reprimand him' . . . Then here is Adam Clayton Powell where the charges are very nebulous and uncertain. But the real problem is that he was a black man with too much power. And he was uppity. And he acted just like you have always acted. So you kick him out and say he is a bad man."

DREW PEARSON AND JACK ANDERSON
(*The Washington Post,* October 24, 1967)

"Look here, brother, you go back and tell that white man we got nothing to say to him. When we do have something to say—when we get it together, see—we'll let him know. We'll contact him on the Detroit-Newark Bell System . . . He always answers on that line."

A BLACK NATIONALIST, Chicago

Freedom Is Not Free

I am very alarmed about the lack of teaching of courtesy, discipline, punctuality and truthfulness in our schools. I'm not so interested in a boy having a Master's Degree as in a fellow being able to put in a good honest day's work for a good day's pay, and to have some pride and dignity in work which you can do. I am interested in children learning to develop their potential and learning to recognize their limitation. We are not all equal because we weren't all cut out of the same cookie cutter; but ability has nothing to do with race.

I am interested in the schools teaching that freedom is not free. You work at it from the time you are born till the time you die. Our schools have to teach that someone has to pay the bill for everything. This idea of expecting a "Great White Father" to hand you something for nothing is an economic impossibility and has created a class of irresponsible Welfare slaves. The idea that all you have to do is satisfy your gullet, get drunk and have children, throw them out onto the community and someone will care for them, must be dispelled.

MRS. MATTIE CONEY, Indianapolis

"We assert the right of Black students who are experiencing political and violent suppression to respond in kind. We see the Orangeburg Massacre as a lesson which teaches the necessity of self-defense. Our motto is: Avenge Orangeburg."

A RESOLUTION OF THE BLACK STUDENTS'
CONFERENCE (1968), Central State University, Ohio

Listen or Perish

I think it comes as news to a great many of my co-citizens that the reason that black people are in the street has to do with the lives they're forced to lead in this country, and they're forced to lead these lives by the indifference and the apathy and a certain kind of ignorance, a very willful ignorance, on the part of their co-citizens. Everybody knows, no matter what they do not know, that they would not like to be a black man in this country. They know that, and they shut their minds against the rest of it, all the implications of being a black father or a black woman, or a black son, and all of the implications involved in a human being's endeavour to take care of his wife, to take care of his children, to raise his children to be men and women in the case of a structure which is built to deny that I can be a human being, or that my child can be.

The great pressure in the country has been, all these years that I've been living here—and I was born here, 43 years ago—is 'what does the Negro want?' and this question masks a terrible knowledge. I want exactly what you want, and you know what you want. I want to be left alone; I don't want any of the things that people accuse Negroes of wanting, and I don't hate you. I simply want to be able to raise my children in peace and arrive at my own maturity in my own way, in peace; I don't want to be defined by you. I think that you and I might learn a great deal from each other if you can overcome the curtain of my colour, the curtain of my colour is what you use to avoid facing the facts of our common history, the facts of American life. It is easy to call me a Negro or nigger or a promising black man, but in fact, I'm a man like you; I want to live like you. This country's mine, too; I paid as much for it as you. White means that you are European still, and black means that I'm African, and we both know, we've both been here too long.

You can't go back to Ireland or Poland or England, and I can't go back to Africa, and we will live here together, or we'll die here together, and it is not I who am telling you. Time is telling you. You will listen, or you will perish.

JAMES BALDWIN, New York

James Baldwin, in an interview (March 3, 1968) recorded by Public Broadcast Laboratories. Reprinted by permission.

A Dissent from the Kerner Report

The white Establishment took a major step forward with the publication of the report of the President's Commission on Civil Disorders. Yet it seems to me that we will make a serious error if we merely applaud this effort and do not subject the report to serious scrutiny.

I am very distressed that the report—addressing the *obvious* and *urgent* but not the *important* and *fundamental*—calls for nothing more original and novel than the expansion of the current conventional approach to racial improvement in the black ghettos. Like previous reports of its kind, the Kerner Report suggests that the road to black-white conciliation is to be achieved by having the white community treat the *consequences* of *their own white racism* in the black community.

What is most disturbing about the report is that while it recognizes white racism to be the fundamental cause of black-white hostility in our cities, it makes no recommendations for dealing with it. This raises a most relevant question: How can we reasonably expect America to develop the will and commitment to implement the programs recommended by the report unless and until we have begun to deal realistically with racism in the *white,* not black, community.

We repeat a grave error if we continue only to propose programs designed to improve the physical lot of blacks. God knows, no one can deny that such programs are necessary. But to neglect the need of whites to overcome their hang-ups and to improve their mental health is a grave oversight.

In articles published four years ago I stated that whites are mentally ill with respect to race and that white racism is a collective mental illness that needs systematic treatment. This means, for one thing, that such programs as are recommended by the commission cannot be mounted—so long as the power to initiate and implement such programs rests with the white community and until

James A. Tillman, Jr., in *Christianity and Crisis,* April 1, 1968, pp. 62, 66. Reprinted by permission.

whites have begun to come to grips with their own insecurities, which cause them to need—and to live by—racism.

Therefore, the commission's failure to make proposals and recommendations to this end is a significant loss. Confession and contrition on the part of the white Establishment is simply not enough!

JAMES A. TILLMAN, JR.

Reports, Legislation; No Change

I don't know whether the [Kerner] report is going to accomplish anything or not. I think that there have been previous reports which have been as hard-hitting as this one. In the 1940's, the Myrdahl study was a magnificent report, and the Myrdahl study dissected the anatomy of American racism ruthlessly and skillfully, but I don't think there have been significant changes in the predicament of the Negro in America from 1940 to 1947, or from 1947 to 1968. We have had judicial decisions, we've had legislation, we've had occasional commitment to change, and more recently, we have had commitment even coming from the White House, and still, the man in the ghetto sees very little change in his day-to-day life.

DR. KENNETH CLARK

Kenneth Clark, in an interview recorded (March 3, 1968) by Public Broadcast Laboratories. Reprinted by permission.

No Change Without Investing Money

I think that the [Kerner] report has new elements. Number one, a cross-section of prominent Americans are now saying what enlightened Negro leadership has said for many years, that the basis

Bayard Rustin, in an interview (March 3, 1968) recorded by Public Broadcast Laboratories. Reprinted by permission.

of this problem is economic and social. Number two, the report deals with the backlash, which has been built on the basis that these riots were a conspiracy. It is made quite clear that they are not a conspiracy.

Number three, Americans have thought that by just being 'nice people' maybe they could do away with the problems of the ghetto. This report says, unless you are prepared to invest billions and billions of dollars, even to the point of increasing taxes, nothing will change.

I have no crystal ball, but I am saying all things are ultimately changed by people getting new insights. Now, I would hope that the American people will now see the choice: whether they are going to invest these billions and stop American fabric from being torn apart, or whether they want race war.

Now, I would assume the American people have sense enough not to want race war. That is the stark choice which this commission reports to us.

BAYARD RUSTIN,
A. Philip Randolph Institute

The War Will Be Here

You know, it's very hard to say what you want to say when after you've said it, somebody gets up and acts like you haven't been talking. But you know what? I got a son in the Hundred and First Airborne that you're going to kill, probably—because he's going to Vietnam. I've got a nephew just came back from Korea that was wounded three times. And the first thing that happened when he went home—a cop beat the hell out of him with a pistol butt.

Now, you get this straight. You can kill all the black folks you want to, baby, but you will not kill the freedom of black folks. It's coming, we're going to get it. You think you're so indestructible. You think you're so great because you got all these weapons. I remember Mao Tse-tung once said—he wondered where he'd get his

Russ Meek, in an interview (November 5, 1967) recorded by Public Broadcast Laboratories. Reprinted by permission.

weapons from, and then we armed Chiang Kai-shek—and he said, "Thank you, Jesus," you see.

So don't misunderstand us, baby. We're dead serious. This country was founded on revolution. Those little settlers out there in the northeast section of this country had some muskets and some sticks and some stones, and they whipped the mighty professional British army, baby. And five thousand of them were black, and one black woman disguised herself as a man and fought with you all. And we don't have our freedom yet. We fought in every one of your damned lousy wars, baby, and you give us nothing.

Now, the war is going to be here, because we're going to be free. Now, you kill all you want to—but we kill too. And we don't frighten. We don't frighten at all . . .

RUSS MEEK, Chicago

"I can't lose by rioting. Done lost. Been lost. Gonna be lost some more. I'm sayin' to the Man: 'You includin' me in this game or not?' And I know his answer, so I'm gettin' ready to get basic."

A GANG LEADER, Oakland, California
(*Newsweek* magazine, November 20, 1967)

"Why is it that people never pay any attention to what we ordinary Negroes think? Let Stokely Carmichael or somebody come into town to raise hell, and you can't see him for reporters. People get the impression that he's speaking for us. He's not, but we don't have any way to make our voices heard."

A HOUSEWIFE, Washington, D.C.
(*Newsweek* magazine, November 20, 1967)

"We've been working hard for years, and we have won a lot of respect in the city. Yet our statements are ignored, while the press gives full play to anything a radical Negro has to say."

NELSON C. ROOTS, Washington, D.C.
(*The Washington Post,* June 5, 1967)

Prepare for the Attack

CONCERNING STORAGE OF WATER—Water boiled for ten minutes and placed in sterile bottles with cap on tight can be stored for six months without refrigeration. Distilled water will keep up to a year. At the beginning of trouble, all available containers should be filled with water, bathtubs, sinks, buckets, bottles, etc. This is to be used for toilet flushing and washing purposes. Water in hot water tank can be used for drinking. If and as necessary, conserve on water as best you can.

GET TOGETHER WITH YOUR BLACK BROTHERS AND SISTERS IN YOUR COMMUNITIES AND GET YOUR *THANG* TOGETHER FOR SURVIVAL. Should a neighbor be uncooperative or discordant, let him be. Beware of those who oppose such preparation. Certainly do not allow yourself to become discouraged by it.

PLEASE forget the hate you might have for a *Brother* or *Sister* in the community and get together.

WE MUST UNITE NOW FOR THE ATTACKS UPON OUR COMMUNITIES FROM THE POLICE, ARMED FORCES AND THE WHITE COMMUNITIES.

SURVIVAL IS NO PLAYTHING.

From a mimeographed broadside
distributed in a black community

"I want to burn down every building in this town. Let me do that and I'll be grateful to the white man for the rest of my life. All you guys want to give is a dollar an hour. Man, I can *beg* more than that right on this corner. Y'know, if I was back in Vietnam, I'd shoot every white guy I could find. They didn't tell me that I was going to be just another nigger when I got back here."

J. T. Watkins, Chicago
(*Newsweek* magazine, November 20, 1967)

More Leaders, White and Negro

I think it rather unreasonable, if not unjust, suddenly to thrust the control and containment of deep-seated Negro feelings and attitudes on a few Negro leaders.

Admittedly, the recent emergence of so-called Negro leaders has served to provide a means of communication between the lowest class of Negroes and the white community, and has provided a better sense of direction (hopefully) to the severely impoverished Negro.

Yet I consider it premature to criticize these leaders for the recent outbursts of Negro resentments against society, particularly law-enforcement agencies, and to accuse these leaders of not being able to control their people.

No more should they be expected to control Negro attitudes built up over years of oppression than the white liberal law-enforcement officers can be expected to exercise complete control over the activities of the Ku Klux Klan and other die-hard segregationist groups, night riders or bigoted Southern politicians. And last but not least, the analogous but less dramatic Northern "equal-opportunity" employer.

Die-hard segregationists continue to plague Southern Negroes seeking equality and their sympathizers, the white youths and religious leaders attempting to assist them in this effort.

The deep-seated hate that gives impetus to the Klan activists may be compared to the seething, smoldering fury built up within the Negro over years of oppression and deprivation.

As a Negro I am deeply ashamed and embarrassed at the Los Angeles rioting and looting. Yet I can't help but feel that unless more effective means of constructively releasing these pent-up emotions are established, more of these outbursts may be imminent.

As the situation stands today there are far too few Negro leaders to reach the poor, uneducated, undirected mass of Negroes, frequently the ones involved in this kind of asocial behavior. A stepped-up program of leadership, including both whites and Negroes, must be instituted.

M. JACQUELINE GORDON, New York
(*The New York Times,* August 30, 1965)

"If I had integration and an Edsel and I wanted to sell one of them, it would be easier to sell the Edsel."

                                        A HARLEM BLACK NATIONALIST

God Helps Those . . .

"We made it because we had a goal, and we were willing to work for it. Don't talk to me of your 'guaranteed national income.' Any fool knows that this is insanity. Do we bring those who worked to get ahead down to the level of those who never gave a damn? The world owes nobody—black or white—a living. God helps the man who helps himself!"

                            ARCHIE MOORE,
                            former light-heavyweight champion

"The ghettos in America are like the native reserves in South Africa. They symbolize the Negro as unacceptable, inferior and therefore kept apart."

                            RALPH BUNCHE
                            (*Newsweek* magazine, November 20, 1967)

Thinking Black: What It Is

"Thinking black" is Huey Newton and his rage—a rage so blinding he can look on white America comfortably only through the cross hairs of a gun. "Guns are very, very political," says Newton, the 25-year-old "defense minister" of an Oakland, Calif., Negro splinter group called the Black Panther Party for Self Defense. "A gun makes me immediately equal to anyone in the world." Not quite. Before dawn one October morning, Newton staggered into an

Oakland hospital, clutching at a hole in his belly. Behind him lay two cops who had rousted him out of his car for a routine stop-and-frisk. One was dead, the other wounded. Newton—himself hit in the exchange—was charged with both shootings.

"Thinking black" is the kids with their "natural" coifs and their Afro clothes and their lessons in Swahili, taking a joy in blackness as exaggerated as the shame of blackness has always been in white America. It is the young elders of CORE—a mostly white and militantly integrationist group scarcely three years ago—studying a map of Indonesia and pondering quite seriously whether America's urban ghettos, too, can be forged into an independent "island republic." It is the reverie of tall, angular civil-rights lawyer Howard Moore, 35, stepping off a plane in Dar es Salaam, telling a traveling companion, "This is it, I'm home, baby"—and sustaining himself back in the U.S. on the dream that he will someday repatriate to the motherland.

And "thinking black" is a perfectly reasonable sort like Donald R. Hopkins going to bed one night a Negro and waking up the next morning a black man. Hopkins, at 30, is making it: he is assistant to the executive vice chancellor at Berkeley. But making it, for increasing numbers of the middle-class Negro young, no longer means taking flight from the problems of the black poor. Hopkins is not interested in guns or costumes or going back to Africa. But he has come to believe that Negroes must separate in spirit before they can integrate in fact—that they must break their old ties of dependency on whites, develop political and economic sinew of their own and then move for integration as a "coalescence of equals." This view seems to frighten whites only when it is advertised as "black power"—a label the new black thinkers nonetheless heartily accept. "I've seen my wife come home crying because of the police stopping her on the street and asking her if she's a prostitute," says an Indianapolis poverty worker. "As a human being, I believe in human power. But as a black man, I have to believe in black power because I've lived under white power too long."

NEWSWEEK MAGAZINE (November 20, 1967)

"We all grew up with the feeling that somehow Mr. Charley was going to save us—a 'rescue fantasy,' in psychoanalytic terms. To think white is to say that my salvation is going to be Mr. Charley. To think black is to say I'm the only one who is going to save myself."

> DR. PRICE M. COBBS, San Francisco
> (*Newsweek* magazine, November 20, 1967)

The Lion That Roared

"There once was a pet lion, and this pet lion lived behind a nice white picket fence. He didn't roar and he didn't bite. But one day a big lion happened to come by that fence, and when he saw the quiet pet inside, he let out a huge roar. The pet lion rushed towards the fence, and suddenly he realized that he was a lion too and he roared."

> KENNY GRUSON
> (*The Harvard Crimson,* October 20, 1967)

Black solidarity manifestly cannot be created by white leadership. Nor can power for black people be developed on white steam.

The white leaders of America who wish America to come into its own must therefore recognize the need for black pride, black solidarity, black self-development, and black respect for its own potential under the guidance of its own leadership.

> NATHAN WRIGHT, JR., Newark, N.J.
> (*Concern* magazine, October 1, 1967)

Where It's At

You know, in Augusta, Georgia, I used to shine shoes on the steps of a radio station, WRDW. I think we started at three cents, then we went to five, and six—never did get to a dime. But today I own that radio station. You know what that is? That's black power. Right here. It's not in violence. It's in knowing what you're talking about. Being ready.

Now, I say to you, because I'm your brother. I know where it's at. I been there. I'm not using it from imagination, I'm going —I'm talking from experience.

Let's live for our country. Let's live for ourselves. Please go off the streets.

JAMES BROWN, Soul Singer

Stop the White Lawlessness
That Ignores Basic Needs

The President of our country has strongly stated that lawlessness must be stopped, that law and order must be restored. We who live in the black ghettos of our nation's cities also want lawlessness to stop. We want to stop the lawlessness of racial discrimination in housing and that of white landlords who greatly overcharge for dilapidated, rat-infested slum apartments. We want to stop the lawlessness that ignores basic needs in the inter-city schools; that allows merchants in Negro communities to sell their goods at exploitation rates, and to receive interest rates and carrying charges three to four times higher than the value of the items sold. We want to stop the lawlessness that permits police officers to beat the heads of Negro boys merely to amuse themselves, and the lawlessness of law enforcement agencies who allow the numbers racket, houses of prostitution, and "blind pigs" to operate openly in our neighborhoods for the amusement and profit of white suburban dwellers.

ARCHIE L. RICH, Pastor, Berea Methodist Church,
Detroit (*Concern* magazine, October 1, 1967)

Not This Time, Baby

Hell
We are on
To you whitey
trying to off
yellow power
with black power
(killing two birds
with one stone) . . .

NORMAN JORDAN, Detroit

"I hope it [the Kerner Report] will change things, but I know it won't. People just don't want to face up to it. American whites must realize that American blacks are citizens, and any 'revolt' would be because they want to be full-fledged citizens like anyone else. . . . It's going to take a total effort by the government and the whole country, right down the line."

MELVIN JACKSON, Los Angeles

On the Gut-Level

Unfortunately, the white community does not understand that dehumanization only breeds dehumanization. Therefore, their participation in the "Black Revolution" has been, to date, peripheral. Their participation has been, in many cases, on the outside altogether. It has too often involved them as opponents of the inevitable. The "Black Revolution" has only been seen by them as a thing for black men. They question blacks: What is it that you

From *The Union Seminary Quarterly Review*, Spring, 1968. Reprinted by permission.

want? What can we do for you? What should be our role relative to black power? How can I understand how you feel? And so they ask *ad nauseam,* never realizing that the revolution is for all Americans. Each American who adjudges the system to be evil must find his role in revising the system.

Too much of the burden for strategy has been placed on the shoulders of black men. He has been made responsible for coming up with solutions for a problem created by white men. He is at once the *problem* and the problem-solver. The need is for the white man to see the crisis in human relations as his problem, for him to deal with it at the gut-level.

What about separatism? The white liberal in this day finds himself caught in "no man's land." He has, by virtue of the stance he has taken, separated himself from the white community. He is not wanted there. The black community is saying that there is no place here for him either. What, then, does he do in his dilemma? Until now, his role has been one of working with the black community and often leading the movement. The *mood ebony* says that way is no longer acceptable.

Separation is an interim strategy through which the black community experiences its own integrity. A "strategic retreat" is to reshape the image of the black man, not in the image of the white man, but to exhibit the fact that the worth of black men is in no way related to his whiteness. Also, it is an attempt to bring about some unity of purpose and some consensus about goals. The white man's role is not that of redefining the black community. He cannot participate in that process.

On the other hand, he can define and develop strategies for the white community, recognizing that separatism is not a personal rejection, but an ideological one. There is certainly a need for men, having made a serious commitment to the revision of the system, to give leadership in their communities for the ultimate goal of an integrated society. The revision of the order in the black community alone cannot achieve this goal.

The Role of Violence in the Black Revolution

The happenings of Watts, Detroit, Harlem, Newark, Bedford-Stuyvesant, etc., have spoken more eloquently and have been heard more clearly than the courts, the Urban League, the NAACP, or

SCLC. The Rat Bill was a congressional joke, until the disturbances of last summer. H. Rap Brown is correct when he suggests that violence is the American way—that it is as American as cherry pie. Unfortunately, the Congress, the state and municipal governments seem to respond to crises clarified by the so-called "riots" more readily and speedily than to those petitions and appeals to conscience. It is a true statement, but a sad commentary, that "the better (or worse) riot you have, the more anti-poverty funds will be made available to you"—that is, to a specific community. Whether or not we believe violence to be a legitimate expression of the powerlessness, hopelessness, and despair evident in the ghettos of the nation, it produces concrete results. These results are both negative and positive: negative in the despondent, desperate calls for "law and order"; positive in the concrete measures proposed for the alleviation of the problems.

The members of the United States Conference on Church and Society in Detroit last October made some attempts to deal with this question from the point of view of the Church:

The church is ill-prepared to examine violence as an approach to social change because the tragic urban situation which faces America today can, to some extent, be blamed on the church. Violence in our land is inherent in value structures and social processes which the church itself undergirds and participates in as a social institution.

We churchmen find ourselves in this dilemma. Further:

There are situations where Christians may become involved in violence. . . . It must be recognized that there is no guarantee that the actual results of the use of violence will be those intended by its initiators. The question . . . emerges today whether the violence which sheds blood in planned revolutions may not be a lesser evil than the violence which (though bloodless) condemns whole populations to perennial despair.

Dietrich Bonhoeffer, who had some experience in the question of the ethics of violence, reminds us that the free man

. . . has not to decide simply between right and wrong and between good and evil, but between right and right and wrong and wrong. As Aeschylus said, 'right strives with right!' Precisely in this respect responsible action is a free venture; it is not justified by any law; it is performed without any claim to a valid self-justification, and therefore also without any claim to ultimate knowledge of good and evil. Good, as what is responsible, is performed in the ignorance of good and in the surrender to God of the deed which has become necessary and which nevertheless, or for that very reason, free; for it is God who sees the heart, who weighs up the deed and who directs the course of history.

There are no easy answers to difficult questions. The question of violence or non-violence has to be settled in the light of what is *the necessary deed*. Not what is right or good, but what is *necessary*.

Can we have a bloodless revolution? That remains to be seen. Whatever kind we have, it is certain that revolution is inevitable. We will have to decide which it shall be.

LEON WATTS

War for Our Cities

"America has already become the dangerous society. The Nation's major cities are becoming police states. There are only two roads open to it. Either wholesale extermination of the black population through mass massacre or forced migrations onto reservations as with the Indians . . . Or self-government of the major cities by the black majority, mobilized behind leaders and organizations of its own creation and prepared to reorganize the structure of city government and city life from top to bottom. . . .

"But the war is not only in America's cities; it is for these cities. It is a civil war between black power and white power, the first major battle of which was fought . . . between 18,000 soldiers and the black people of Watts."

JAMES BOGGS, Detroit
(*The Washington Post*,
September 25, 1967)

"There's going to be a lot more violence until whites accept us as equals. That report on the riots—that's just more talk."

PHYLLIS ALLEN, Long Beach, California

If I Were Running Things

If I were trying to run things my way, I would do everything that I could to teach everybody that they were not able to run things like me. I would teach that to build something else meant that whoever wanted to do it would have to become like me. I would finally teach that I was the only person who knew enough to make other people like me. If I could manage all that, I wouldn't have to let people know that they were slaves. It would be very important that the slavery I imposed be couched in my definition of freedom, and remain unseen in order that rebellion remained stifled, and my control intact.

CHARLIE COBB, Atlanta, SNCC
(*The New Republic,* December 18, 1965)

Futility of Black Self-Segregation

The troubles are those of white liberalism or, more accurately, of the skin-deep liberalism which now seizes so happily upon the black extremists' rejection. After all, this does make things easier, doesn't it?

If the road to equal, nonracist enjoyment of the fruits of democracy is hard, demanding and sacrificial, aren't we better off if the Negroes don't really want those things? No longer will we be constrained to defend concepts and values of racial equality in an integrated society which (in all honesty) we didn't wholly believe in to begin with.

How fascinating to learn that "they," too, now recognize that their exposure to "our" civilization has been only superficial; that, among other things, they should be moved into a brand-new kind of housing, especially adapted for the tribal type of living for which they still yearn. And how logical that only black architects should design black housing for black people.

Just as only black physicians are capable of diagnosing and

treating the black diseases of black people. Or, as black mathematicians alone can properly understand and teach black mathematics to—naturally—black students. The absurdity of this position would be overwhelming if its entertainment by otherwise rational people were not such a thoroughgoing tragedy.

Majority's Voice

Granted that a confrontation with some of the bright, articulate and angry young Negroes of the day can be heady medicine for the person who has not really had much conversation with Negro peers before. Such a person has no perspective against which to judge what he now hears. He is quite likely to think that he has been listening to the authentic voice of the Negro majority.

But there is still merit in knowing how to pronounce "Negro," and ten years from now it will still be important. Segregated white churches will be disgraceful in 1978, just as they are now. And the best hope for genuine educational equality will still be the integrated school, ten or fifteen or twenty years from now.

Above all, racism will always be a deadly social cancer, whether it is the Ku Klux Klan or the delusions of despairing and embittered Negroes. In a sense, it will be even worse than that, for the black self-segregation which so intrigued Mr. Wicker is without prospect of attainment in this country.

And, as everyone knows, you can sometimes get away with bad principles, but futility is an unforgivable sin.

JOHN A. MORSELL, NAACP
(*The New York Times,* March 2, 1968)

"We can't live without white persons yet. We have to work with or for them. Why create so much animosity talking about getting guns and shooting people.

"If the time comes when we have to do that it's time enough to talk about it."

A WIDOW ON SOCIAL SECURITY

I Love Stokely Carmichael

My name is Russ Meek. I am a writer, a musician, a poet. And I live in the black ghetto on Chicago's West Side. This somewhat imposing building, the Chatfield Apartments, is my daily abode. I am one of those who loves Stokely Carmichael. I am one of those who believe that non-violence is the philosophy of the fool, and that we are a new breed, a class of black men and women who would rather die on our feet than live on our knees.

RUSS MEEK, Chicago

Russ Meek in an interview (November 5, 1967) recorded by Public Broadcast Laboratories. Reprinted by permission.

"Whether we know it or admit it or not, white people believe that Negroes as Negroes are inherently inferior. We are all products of a culture which transmits stereotyped racial myths. . . . Who dares to pretend that he transcends centuries and generations of cultural conditioning? Since the time when slavery justified the economic traffic in human beings by rationalizing a myth of racial superiority, we are all tainted by the belief in white supremacy."

DR. EUGENE S. CALLENDER, New York City
(*Fortune* magazine, January, 1968)

"Honkie, whatcha come to the ghetto for? You come to look at us animals, us criminals, mother? You just write that we're gonna tear down this country."

A YOUNG MAN IN BEDFORD-STUYVESANT, BROOKLYN

The Criminal Element of Blacks

Generally speaking, it is the inferior and criminal element of blacks upon whom so much space, time, and money has been squandered. The "Liberal" news media and the popular magazines have emphasized the less fortunate, less resourceful, less ambitious, and less intelligent Negro as typical. Such racism is astounding. One would never know from them that there are streets, sections, and districts in all of our urban Negro centers that are *not* slums; black people who *are* exceptional, decent, honorable, and patriotic.

So long as the young white crusaders could parade and demonstrate in various parts of the much-maligned South, arm-in-arm with their sable peers (notably from Selma to Montgomery, from Memphis to Jackson, and through the streets of our big cities disrupting traffic and making fools of themselves) the show was regarded by them with satisfaction. However, like many before them, they saw this nuisance differently when it came next door—when they were pursued from one suburb to the other, and were mugged or raped by some mop-headed juvenile delinquent shouting Black Power, and upon whom they had wasted maudlin sympathies.

GEORGE SCHUYLER, New York
(*The Review of the News,* December 20, 1967)

Forget Police Brutality

"Forget this police brutality business, and if the cops have to use a little force, look up at the stars, look away."

"[There is] a small but growing spark in the Negro community which may end the community's acceptance of violence by Negro kids, and thus remove the base from which they operate.

"If the community won't stand for it, it will stop."

BERTRAM E. GARDNER, Cleveland
(*The New York Times,* April 24, 1967)

"It is the activities of the police that have given rise to every incident of violence we have had.

"We can live with the rats and the roaches, and the welfare payments, put buckets under the leaks in the roof and stuff up the holes in the plaster, but we cannot tolerate the blows to our dignity inflicted every day on the street by disrespectful cops acting on behalf of white society."

OSCAR N. GASKINS, Philadelphia

"That's why you either see a lot of people on the street or none. If there's a lot of people out, you feel safe because you know there'll be witnesses to what the police do. If there aren't people on the street, you better get off—because they can shoot you or beat you and nobody is going to believe you if there weren't witnesses."

A NEW YORK TEENAGER

Let Us Do It Ourselves

"What is needed is a positive and truly meaningful partnership of the haves and have-nots that will place capable black men side by side with capable white men in an entrepreneur effort that can succeed.

"Every community is going to have to face up to the fact that this generation of angry black Americans will not be willing to stand idly by, hungry, depressed and deprived, while the economic royalists of the construction industry collect fat paychecks week in and week out building an environment for us. This time around they had better let us do it ourselves."

BERKLEY G. BURNELL, Washington, D.C.
(*The New York Times,* April 7, 1968)

"The way they'll do a man is something awful. And right in front of his family, his kids. If they feel like it, they'll make a man feel like nothing right in front of his own kids."

A BLACK TRUCK DRIVER, Chicago

Negro Priests Criticize Church

All seven Negro priests serving in the Roman Catholic Archdiocese of Chicago said this week that the church in the United States had a "suspicious disdain" of militant Negro elements and termed it a "great mistake."

In what they termed a position paper, the priests were critical of the Catholic Church's attitudes toward Negroes and contended it consistently had followed rather than led the demands of Negroes for fulfillment of legitimate aspirations.

They outlined what they termed minimum steps that should be taken to erase the church's image among Negroes of "being unrelated to the needs of the black community for identity and power." . . .

Represented at the conference were a majority of dioceses in the United States.

Grass Roots Cited

"The militants, whether we like it or not, are de facto in touch with grass roots in the black community," the priests wrote. "They are composed of the intellectuals, the students, and the middle class blacks."

The disdain for the militants, the priests continued, means that the militants will remain alienated from the church and will be unable to make "their potentially great contribution" to the church.

The church has failed to realize, they contended, that the power

From *The New York Times,* February 8, 1968. © 1968 by The New York Times Company. Reprinted by permission.

center has moved away from the "docile, agreeable, middle-aged black leaders" with whom the church has preferred to deal.

The development of Negro Americans "will be along lines far more unsettling to white people and to traditional religious leaders," they said.

The priests wrote that the church's work among Negroes had been aimed genuinely at their betterment. But they criticized the church's "assumptions" that Negroes had no genuine contribution to make and would remain merely beneficiaries of the church indefinitely.

Suggested Actions

The clerics recommended that the Catholic Church do these things:

¶Recruit more Negro seminarians, for until there is a significant number of Negro priests the Catholic Church will continue to be a "white church" to Negroes.

¶Select carefully staffs serving in the Negro communities, choosing people who understand the aspirations of Negroes and join in the fight for their achievement.

¶Require that seminarians achieve at least "minimal knowledge" of Negro history, relevant sociology and psychology of race prejudice, and have a fairly broad perspective of the current race problem.

¶Have church leaders, in matters affecting the Negro community, consult not only with old line organizations but ascertain militant sentiments as well.

¶Use its influence to promote economic growth in the Negro community, and particularly development of Negro commercial enterprises.

¶Act to eradicate conditions that breed crime and delinquency among Negro youths, and work toward rehabilitation of those who have been victims of these conditions.

¶Consider the cultural heritage of Negroes in developing liturgical life in the Negro community, especially music and art forms.

The priests also urged that Catholic educational institutions accept militancy of Negro students "as a healthy phenomenon" and refrain from suppressing it.

Stokely, Yes; Rap Brown, Maybe

"There's a place for the Rap Browns and the Stokely Carmichaels. They've instilled a lot of pride and dignity in a lot of Negroes— especially the young Negroes. These guys have given many Negroes the courage to talk back.

"I don't agree with everything Brown says, but I do with almost all Stokely says. The idea is that these are blacks speaking their mind, and this has been very good for the Negro. This way it will wake up a lot of Negroes to think and discern for themselves, not just to follow these guys blindly. It's made whites understand that the Negroes will fight back, will stand up for their opinions—and stand up forcefully."

CARL WASHINGTON, Long Beach, Calif.

Believes in Integration

"There are many, many Negroes who don't share the concept of black power. We have always won our victories with allies from the outside. Seldom have we won anything separately. I believe the separatist movement is a minority of a minority point of view. It will reverse its course when it recognizes the futility of its pursuit. I feel the mainstream of Negro life will move steadily toward integration."

H. H. BROOKINS, Los Angeles

Integration Needs Sunlight

As a Negro, I find it difficult to understand why members of my own race take such antiquated and prejudiced stands. Must we forever incorporate into our own thinking every distorted and hypocritical view of the white power structure? Must every Negro celebrity marry within the race so that other Negroes will approve?

And let me remind my "soul" brothers and sisters who denounce mixed marriages that there are enough of us walking around with fair skins and straight hair to remind us that it's time that the night integration was exposed to the light of the sun.

WILLIAM GOLD, East Orange, N. J.
(*Ebony* magazine, September, 1967)

The Suppressed Premise

The suppressed premise is that there is nothing fundamentally wrong with America and that good black people have been misled by evil outsiders who have penetrated the ghetto Garden of Eden with heady fruit from the tree of good and evil. The strategy here is a strategy of deflection. Most white people don't want to believe that black people are really mad. They don't want to believe that so many people are justly aggrieved against them and their institutions. For if they believed that they would have to look at themselves and their institutions. And it is much easier to look at Stokely Carmichael and other alleged "outside agitators."

But talking about outside agitators is a way of not talking about the rioters; it is a way of not taking them seriously, of not giving them their full stature as men. And in order to stop the riots Americans are going to have to look not only at Stokely Carmichael but at their most cherished institutions. They are going to have to admit that black people are rebelling because they are men and because they live in a society which denies that they are men.

For the riots to end, in short, democracy must begin. And the first step on that road is to see the rioters for what they are: rebels in open revolt against a system which denies their humanity.

The lesson of Newark and Detroit was that a large number of black people are totally alienated from a society which has done everything to bring out the worst in them. They have been remarkably patient over the years, but now they are saying that they would rather die than live the way their fathers and forefathers lived. They are serious, and America cannot meet their challenge unless it becomes serious, too. When a man attacks a Sherman tank with a Coca-Cola bottle, when a man risks his life in order to validate his humanity, you can't offer him less than what he needs and be relevant.

LERONE BENNETT
(*Ebony* magazine, October, 1967)

"A judicious and persistent use of the ballot will solve many of the Negro problems. This must be related to continued improvement in education. And the wise use of buying power—use of the boycott, for example—will force the culture to give Negroes an equitable share. But there will be violence. After centuries of discrimination and oppression, large numbers feel they have no stake in the culture."

THE REVEREND HOMER C. McEWEN,
First Congregational Church, Atlanta
(*Fortune* magazine, January, 1968)

We could argue for years about what Jews have done *to* and *for* Negroes in this country; and whether what has been done has resulted in good or bad for the Negro people. But who in his right mind can argue that that which was done and is being done by Jews in particular, whether good or bad, is part of a gigantic plot to dupe and take advantage of Negroes; a deliberate, agreed-upon "Zionist," "Jewish Community," "Semitic" plot against Negroes?

Where is that proof!

I am not sentimental about Jews, Negroes, or anybody else. And I am not grateful. People should fight for freedom because they believe in freedom. I know Jews who do, and I know Jews who don't; I know Negroes who do, and I know Negroes who don't. A man should fight for what he believes in—and the fact that he fights is his reward. I owe him nothing.

Harlem is a deprived and exploited community, but are Jews the only ones who profit from this exploitation? No! Are Jews the ones who profit *most* by this exploitation? I strongly doubt it.

From *Freedomways* magazine, First Quarter, 1967, p. 78. Reprinted by permission.

Whatever Jews are guilty of exploiting Harlem are not guilty because they are Jews, but because—along with many Catholics, Protestants, Negro and white—they are exploiters. In a war against all exploiters whomsoever I am an ally. But [I am not] for a *war* against Jews.

You see, I consider myself a Black Nationalist, and proud to be one . . . but not a Black racist. And I consider the difference between them too fundamental for compromise.

Black Nationalism is as legitimate and honorable a vehicle of the black man's anguish as Irish nationalism was to the Irish, and Zionism to the Jews. But *Black racism* is no different from any other racism.

OSSIE DAVIS, New York

Jews Should Inspire Blacks

Reference to the Jews, who have used education as the most powerful weapon, should inspire us to put education in the forefront (along with African history, *au naturel,* and the rejection of racial oppression).

Every leader should stump every hillside, valley, and ghetto of this country, arousing and motivating our people to educate themselves to their fullest potential. These leaders would set an example. It ought to be clear to us that we are educating ourselves to liberate our people, and not for self-aggrandizement. The badge of the most fervent black nationalist would be his intellectual and educational achievement for his people, not how loudly he can denounce white people. The true leader will tell our people to exchange their guns, bricks, and Molotov cocktails for slide rules, books and tickets to Fisk, TSU, etc. In this critical period in our history, Mr. Rowan should be joined by Stokely, Dr. King and all people of good will (black and white) not to denounce but show and encourage our people to seek first the Educational Kingdom.

JIMMY DALE LOFTON, San Francisco, Calif.
(*Ebony* magazine, October, 1967)

PART THREE

Is Anybody Listening?

A Day of Grief

BY THE PRESIDENT OF THE UNITED STATES

A Proclamation

To the people of the United States:
The heart of America grieves today. A leader of his people—a teacher of all people—has fallen.

Martin Luther King Jr. has been struck down by the violence against which he preached and worked.

Yet the cause for which he struggled has not fallen. The voice that called for justice and brotherhood had been stilled—but the quest for freedom, to which he gave eloquent expression, continues.

Men of all ages, all religions, all regions must join together in this hour to deny violence its victory—and to fulfill the vision of brotherhood that gave purpose to Martin Luther King's life and works.

NOW, THEREFORE, I, Lyndon B. Johnson, President of the United States, do call upon all Americans to observe Sunday next, the seventh day of April, as a day of national mourning throughout the United States. In our churches, in our homes, and in our private hearts, let us resolve before God to stand against divisiveness in our country and all its consequences.

I direct that until interment the flag of the United States shall be flown at half-staff on all buildings, grounds and naval vessels of the Federal Government in the District of Columbia and throughout the United States and its territories and possessions.

I also direct that the flag shall be flown at half-staff for the same length of time at all United States embassies, legations, consular offices, and other facilities abroad, including all military facilities and naval vessels and stations.

IN WITNESS WHEREOF, I have hereunto set my hand this fifth day of April, in the year of our Lord nineteen hundred and sixty-eight and of the Independence of the United States of America the one hundred and ninety-second.

LYNDON B. JOHNSON.

A Common Commitment to Act

The comfortable American does not enjoy thinking about the human misery festering at the other end of town. He does not enjoy knowing that many of his fellow citizens live in conditions that breed every variety of social evil. It is not easy for him to acknowledge that his own infant, dropped into that ruinous environment, would just as surely fall victim to it. He averts his eyes from the human damage that occurs there. . . .

Poverty is not easy to eliminate, whether the poor are black or white. In the case of the Negro it is made harder by the evil of racism.

But we cannot afford to be discouraged by the difficulty of the problems. If they were easy, we would have solved them long ago. When we formed this free society we did not commit ourselves to solve only the easy ones.

The tough problems are the ones that test our resolve.

I have heard the authentic voices of hatred, and the threats of violence—from white men and black. But those who hate cannot save us; they can only destroy.

What can save us is, first of all, a great effort on the part of white Americans to understand and extend a hand across the gulf of fear and anger. They must make a full commitment to right injustices and build a better future. What is also needed is a recognition on the part of the Negro community that that better future cannot be built instantly. The wrongs of centuries cannot be righted in a day or a year. But a common commitment to act now can create the climate in which solutions are possible. . . .

We cannot have two nations, one white and one black. Every time we salute the flag we pledge allegiance to "one nation indivisible."

One nation indivisible it must remain.

JOHN W. GARDNER,
Former Secretary of Health, Education and Welfare
(*Life* magazine, March 8, 1968)

One Man's Crime

The Negro Americans must decide whether the death of Martin Luther King is the murder of all Negro people, committed by all white people, or if it is another unspeakable crime, in a long history of unspeakable crimes, committed by one man under the compulsion of his own deranged mind.

Many great Americans have died as did Dr. King—John F. Kennedy, William McKinley, and the greatest humanitarian of all, Abraham Lincoln. Both Harry S. Truman and Franklin D. Roosevelt narrowly escaped assassination during their terms in office.

Great men are prepared to die for noble causes, and often do. Martin Luther King is now martyred for all time, and, like other great men, his image will grow as time passes.

Actually, his death has given new meaning to his life, for no cause is so noble as one for which a man has died; the Negro community must recognize his death for what it is, a murder, a crime against all people, but nevertheless the death of a man and not the death of an idea. Millions of white Americans have not committed murder against millions of Negro Americans. One man has killed his fellow man.

JACK BERNHARD, New City, N. Y.
(*The New York Times,* April 8, 1968)

What white Americans have never fully understood—but what the Negro can never forget—is that the white society is deeply implicated in the ghetto. White institutions created it, white institutions maintain it, and white society condones it.

THE KERNER REPORT

Black as Senator Brooke

A conspicuous achiever such as Sen. Brooke has about as much to contribute to a poverty study on Negroes as I would have to contribute to one on Indian poverty—my Dad having inherited one quarter Choctaw blood from both his parents.

I am indisputably white, but if the Negro blood were that close, I would be as "black" as the senator, and from my prosperous middle class tower, just about as equipped to cope with race riots. Roy Wilkins was a better choice, but even he is too far removed from the nitty-gritty.

I don't profess to have any answer to the horrible hypocritical mess but certainly a fact-finding panel of prestigious names is not the answer.

MRS. OPAL JAMES, Chevy Chase, Md.
(*Ebony* magazine, December, 1967)

How Not to Prevent Civil Disorders

The Report of the National Advisory Commission on Civil Disorders is so comprehensive as to be useless: the attempt to include everything makes it unselective, though for this very reason, unobjectionable. Nothing is left out, but there is no distinction between the desirable and the possible, and no priorities are given: all things—from changing personal attitudes to rebuilding cities—are to be done (by spending money) at once; wherefore none will be. . . .

There is not a shred of evidence indicating that the riots were caused by our sins—any more than that epidemics of bubonic plague, or the sack of Rome, were caused by the unquestioned sinfulness of the population. Now, if the Report had mentioned infection, or weakness—but it does not; it cannot, because it is part

From *National Review* (150 East 35th Street, New York, N. Y. 10016), March 26, 1968. Reprinted by permission.

of both—a symptom rather than a diagnosis of the malaise it was to scrutinize. For the riots—the report notwithstanding—were caused less by our sinfulness than by our attempts to repent for it —to repair the harm done—and by the guilty conscience so dramatically manifested by the Commission. . . .

Negroes have certainly been discriminated against, beginning with slavery. They have suffered from deprivation and lack of opportunity, from unfulfilled promises, and, finally, from demoralization. Yet discrimination has diminished, and conditions have rapidly improved since the Second World War. There has been more improvement in the last twenty years than in the previous two hundred. . . .

The riots occurred not despite, but because, of this rapid improvement. . . .

Modern empirical research states these matters less succinctly and elegantly, but confirms them amply. The inevitable is tolerated, the inadequate is not: improvement as a process leads to more dissatisfaction than static misery, for aspiration fueled by the process of improvement pulls ahead of any possible fulfillment. . . .

Not only does the Commission blame the riots on those rioted against—it also proposes to make rioting more rewarding. The equation is: if there are riots, people are dissatisfied; let's satisfy them, for we must be at fault if they were dissatisfied. The conclusion, for anyone dissatisfied or resentful—for good or bad reasons—is obvious: if you riot, you get what you need or want fast; if you don't, you don't, and you may never. It should be obvious that grievances should be remedied according to their merits, but never so as to reward the aggrieved for expressing their resentment by injurious actions. However, it was not obvious to the Commission. . . .

Indulgence Is Not the Remedy

Nothing is more pitiful therefore, and sillier, than the stance of the "white liberal": "I know we are at fault; I'll help you, I'll give you anything, just tell me what you want." Negroes are embarrassed. For what they—particularly young Negroes—feel they want, but cannot consciously articulate—though they certainly act it out—might be paraphrased: "We don't want to be given a damn thing by you. Stand up like a man, so we can fight you; we want to beat you up, to express our anger, not to bargain it away for any concessions. Whatever you offer we will ask for more—until you are ready to fight. For the benefits you offer cannot possibly match our fantasies, or make us feel powerful." Such a psychological condition requires specific remedies; indulgence is not among them. (Incidentally, the white liberal attitude is most apparent to Negroes in Jews—and it is a major cause of their antisemitism.) . . .

People commit crimes or riot because, given their condition, the desire for the satisfaction felt, or sought, prevails over the desire to avoid the risk of penalties. They refrain if the desire to avoid the cost prevails. Riots will increase if the penalties are reduced, or the desire is raised. Riots can be decreased by raising the cost, or by reducing the desire. The cost of riots to the rioters is more easily and swiftly changed than the conditions producing the inclination to riot. Costs are within the power of the government to change immediately, whereas the conditions producing the propensity to riot will necessarily take a long time to change; some may be altogether beyond the control of the government. The Commission's one-sided emphasis on these conditions, and its undue neglect of costs, will contribute to more riots. . . .

Can anything be done about the whole mess? A great deal, I think. Some things can be done easily with immediate results. Others will take time and are difficult; still others require more research. I have had space only to suggest a few problems and solutions. However, one thing is clear; if we are to make progress we must look at the actual problems and forget about the pathetic handwringing, the pompous threats and reassurances, and the silly clichés the President's Commission has produced.

ERNEST VAN DEN HAAG, Sociologist

Most Americans Are Decent

So let us acknowledge the tragedy, but let us not exaggerate it.

Most Americans—Negro and white—are leading decent, responsible and productive lives.

Most Americans—Negro and white—seek safety in their neighborhoods and harmony with their neighbors. Nothing can destroy good will more than a period of needless strife and suspicion between the races.

Let us condemn the violent few, but let us remember that it is law-abiding Negro families who have really suffered most at the hands of the rioters.

It is responsible Negro citizens who hope most fervently and need most urgently to share in America's growth and in America's prosperity.

LYNDON B. JOHNSON

The Unhealed Wound

Riots in the cities of America are the portents of civil disaster, which may be postponed by repression, but cannot now be prevented without massive social reconstruction.

We cannot meet this crisis on the basis of "business as usual." The crisis is a national emergency necessitating a commitment of national resources and a personal sacrifice commensurate with the gravity of the emergency.

The present threat to our nation is closer than the coastline; it is in our midst—and has been for generations. Our enemy is the persistent and pervasive *racism* of the white majority of our land, against which the riots are an anguished and self-wounding protest.

Riots are the symptoms of a schism in our society which may prove fatal. Men do not risk pain and death by violence except in desperation. They cannot be explained away or blamed on "outside agitators." The real "outside agitators" are the white masters who have long dominated the ghetto in the North as they have the plantation in the South, by overt means or subtle.

Whatever else in our Nation's agenda may come second, the elimination of injustice in all its forms comes first.

No other interest or commitment of our nation can take precedence over the cure of this malignancy and the repair of its ravages

—not primarily the repair of property but the repair of human spirits which have been stifled and stunted over the years by prejudice, discrimination, repression and exploitation.

Too many of us have congratulated ourselves on having solved the crisis in our society by legislation, but the riots have demonstrated that we have not found an adequate solution. A prophet could say of us, "They have healed the wound of my people lightly, saying peace, peace when there is no peace." (Jeremiah 8:11) Now the unhealed wound is broken open, and it will not be closed again except at great cost.

A RESOLUTION OF THE GENERAL BOARD
OF THE NATIONAL COUNCIL OF CHURCHES
(September 14, 1967)

Assassin Glorified

Fire bombs in Washington, murder in Chicago, tear gas used in Raleigh, Federal troops in Baltimore, looting in New York, and a state of emergency in Detroit and so many other American cities. Are we not viewing in this the glorification of the assassin and the dishonor of the assassinated?

For what more could Martin Luther King's assassin ask?

HENRY V. S. HALL, Stamford, Conn.
(*The New York Times,* April 7, 1968)

The white middle class can afford the luxury of being titillated by the derring-do of its children in the New Left. But it is the Negro masses that must pay the price for the damage done by the ideologues of "Black Power."

PAUL FELDMAN

From *Dissent,* January–February, 1967, p. 79. Reprinted by permission.

"Somebody's got to give the people jobs. When you're 18 or 20 and don't have a job, you're going to get into trouble, no matter what."

DAN A. KIMBALL,
Chairman of Aerojet General's Executive Committee
(*Newsweek* magazine, November 20, 1967)

"I always thought I was in business to make money. Why the hell should I get involved in the race problem?"

A NEW YORK BUSINESSMAN
(*Newsweek* magazine, November 20, 1967)

The Uses of Violence—and Its Future

Looking back upon this summer and trying to figure out what, if anything, we have learned from the riots, I feel rather like Charles Dickens when he wrote the opening lines of *A Tale of Two Cities*. This may not be the best of times or the worst of times, but every event of the summer and every theory about those events seems to have both a good and a bad aspect. Integration versus "black power," violence vs. non-violence, and Negro progress vs. Negro defeat are all susceptible of dual interpretations.

Was the violence only the latest crest of a wave of Negro revolution that has been moving for a dozen years? Or was it an outburst of "slave despair"? Did the violence and the "hate whitey" slogans damage the cause of integration? Or did they wake up white society as to how much farther the nation has to travel toward equality? Is "black power" a viable concept for Negro progress? Or is it merely the psychological expression of impotence?

A case can be made that, despite the useless destruction of property and the lost lives, the violence is a sign of movement and of growing self-confidence on the part of Negroes. It shows that

William V. Shannon, in *Commonweal*, September 29, 1967. Reprinted by permission.

Negroes are no longer afraid of white police, white landlords, white businessmen, and all the rest of the white world. No man can be liberated by others; every man has to emancipate himself. Perhaps the Negro is finally stretching toward his full manhood in America.

White immigrants from Europe who suffered no worse indignities than the Negro newcomers to cities today were far less patient in bearing their misfortunes. The Irish rioted in New York, Philadelphia and Baltimore in the 1840's and '50's, and in 1863 the Irish-dominated draft riots tore New York City apart for three days running. The Jewish immigrants from Eastern Europe had not been in this country 20 years before they were organizing unions in the garment industry and staging monster protest demonstrations against the sweatshops and other iniquities. Passivity has never been prized as an American virtue.

But although we can see some psychological uses for violence, it would be misleading and dangerous to romanticize violence. The highly-civilized editors of *The New York Review of Books* published on their cover in August a diagram for the making of a Molotov cocktail; this was, as they say in the television industry, a "grabber." But aside from grabbing hold of the reader's attention, it did not speak very well for the editors' commitment to liberal, humane values. That review also carried articles deriding the Rev. Martin Luther King Jr. as no longer "with it" among real, swinging Negroes and reporting on the Newark riot in apocalyptic terms as if it were the opening engagement of a proletarian revolution.

Even the therapeutic value of violence is arguable since it provides at best only a temporary release, but psychology aside, violence is morally indiscriminate and politically self-destructive. A society that is 90 percent white is not going to allow its cities to be wrecked by guerrilla warfare and its streets terrorized by Negro commandos. Violence is much more likely to evoke counter-violence and severe repression than it is to produce constructive programs. As if offering a self-fulfilling prophecy, "black power" militants at the Conference for New Politics in Chicago and elsewhere have begun adverting to "genocide" and "concentration camps." Such horrors are not likely to materialize, but it is possible that a whole generation of Negro youths now entering manhood could be brutalized by their futile resort to violence.

Does non-violence still have a future as a tactic for Negroes in the United States? Non-violence and loving thine enemy, in the view of some psychiatrists, is sound Christianity but poor psychology. It leads, they argue, to bottling up rage and aggression that ought to find natural outlets. But for a minority lacking economic and political power, it is a useful tactic. Moral leverage is a much safer technique than violence and much more likely, though not certain, to produce results. It worked dramatically in the South from the student sit-in's in 1960 to the Selma-to-Montgomery march in 1965 because it dramatized for the whole nation the savagery of Southern white power, symbolized by cattle prods and police dogs. Non-violence has not worked so well in the North because the antagonists—the slum landlords, the paper-shuffling school superintendents, the lily white trade unionists—are less easy to dramatize. Another difficulty, paradoxically, is that in the North the Negroes have some economic and, particularly, some political leverage. But the presence of Negro councilmen and congressmen serves to diffuse responsibility and blunt issues rather than make progress easier.

Non-violence continues to commend itself to the great majority of Negroes and to their established organizations such as the NAACP and Dr. King's Southern Christian Leadership Conference. Like other Americans, they rely upon their own individual efforts, on peaceful persuasion, and on politics to advance their interests. But, of course they are not the restless young people who start riots or quickly join them. How to reach these rebels who regard everybody but themselves as "Uncle Toms" is, so far, an unanswered question. Simply giving in to them and accepting their slogans and their programs is no answer as the white radicals who attended the New Politics Conference discovered. It does not help any Negro to scramble the problems of Vietnam and Venezuela or to link Lyndon Johnson with George Lincoln Rockwell. Along with a lot of racist posturing and chauvinism, there is also an ugly strain of anti-Semitism among the black militants which has begun to surface.

Successful capitalist societies traditionally dispose of revolutionary agitation by buying off the agitators. If enough duchesses invite Ramsay MacDonald to dinner, he soon ceases to be a very effective Labor prime minister. If trade union leaders serve on enough civic committees, they soon begin sounding as ponderous as Chamber of Commerce executives. Better jobs, more scholarships, old age pensions, these are means that rich societies use to damp down discontent and buy internal peace.

Sensible economists are already at their desks working out the calculations to dispose of Negro unrest by economic means. When a society is as rich as the United States, generating $700 billions worth of goods and services every year, it is ridiculous to have poor people, whatever their color, rioting in the streets. The wise investment of a trifling two or three percent of the gross national product in public works, family allowances, different kinds of schools, and youth programs would dull the discontent. No investment, however, would bring about the ideal racial integration, the renewed sense of neighborliness, and the human fulfillment that Christians and secular dreamers alike seek but which is beyond government's powers to attain.

The summer is over. The study commissions have been appointed. Congress remains conservative, and the Administration remains war-preoccupied. Neither the shouts of the rioters nor the empirical reasonings of the economists find an answering echo. The nation, leaderless, torpid, and distracted, shrinks nervously back within itself. The National Guard improves its riot-control training, and Ronald Reagan makes political headway.

WILLIAM V. SHANNON

Not Against Negroes

"I don't think this is a good idea, busing the children. I've given a lot of thought to this, and I'm as fair-minded as anyone, I believe. I'm not against the Negroes. They're Americans, and they're entitled to get their rights. I think it's terrible the way they treat them down there in Alabama and Mississippi. That's why we're having all our trouble up here; the Negroes were abused down there.

"But we're not in the South, and up here it's up to every person to be himself and live where he wants and do what he wants. I don't want any special favors, and I don't think the Negro should get any. He's one type of person, and so are we all. No one is perfect, and no race is perfect—I believe that. In the Depression years we all had a bad time, and some of us are still struggling, and we're white. Now my husband is doing well, and I think we're as comfortable as we could want to be. Frankly, I believe a Negro has to work hard just like us, and he's entitled to what he can get —just like us. Not one cent more, though—he's not entitled to one cent more.

"So, if Negroes want to move out here, that's one thing; but, to bus them in—that's unheard-of. It's against all our traditions, and I think it's bad for the Negro child and bad for ours."

A WHITE SUBURBAN WOMAN
(quoted in *Saturday Review,* December 16, 1967)

"They're no good. They've never done anything for this country but cause it trouble. You have to tell them everything twice. But they're doing a good job over there in Vietnam, and some of them can be real reliable. We recently hired three in our accounting division—we had to. Actually, they turned out better than I ever thought. One of them is very smart, and I'd trust him even with higher responsibilities.

"The way I see it, they have to prove themselves. I don't believe most of them can. They're not up to us. But any that are—well, I'm for them. If a man can work his way up this system, without government handouts and free-loading, then I'm ready to shake his hand. That doesn't mean I want him around me all the time, but that goes for whites, too; there are a lot of white people I respect, but don't like."

A WHITE FATHER
(quoted in *Saturday Review,* December 16, 1967)

"I'm against bigots, white or Negro. I believe in fair play, and in an even break for everyone. We need more dialogue, more communication between the races. But the extremists—they're the ones who are pushing things, and making it hard to move along. The way I see it, you have to go slow, and get people used to changes. You can't just force new ideas, new programs on them. I believe you need a lot of discussion, and time—that's the most important thing, time. That's why we've got to punish the extremists and stop and think this whole thing over. We can't be destroyed by violence and hasty moves."

A WHITE FATHER
(quoted in *Saturday Review,* December 16, 1967)

"Business has shown a lot of willingness. But business has been so long removed from the level of the disorders, from the public process, that it cannot respond. It will be marked by failure to deliver."

AN URBAN PLANNER
(*Newsweek* magazine, November 20, 1967)

Claims, Rights, and Prospects

I. Legitimate and Illegitimate Claims Distinguished

Negroes want something—and find something wanting—in American society. Not all their many wants arise from their status as Negroes. Taxes may be too high or wages too low for the poor of any color; but a racial inequity exists only if a hardship is suffered by Negroes because they are Negroes. However, not all disadvantages suffered by Negroes as such can be corrected by public means; only those which can be so corrected justify a demand for public action. Legitimate Negro claims thus must:

Ernest Van Den Haag, in *Modern Age,* Fall, 1965, pp. 354–355. Reprinted by permission.

1) be directed against an actual hardship;

2) rest on inequity, on rights granted to other Americans and withheld from Negroes because they are Negroes;

3) be satisfiable, or enforceable, by public social means, such as laws, payments, or institutional arrangements which

4) must be effective and rational—likely to help achieve the legitimate ends sought without unreasonably impairing rights granted all citizens as such; the effective means which cost (i. e. impair or diminish other rights) least, are the most rational.

Thus, Negro claims are not legitimate as such (whether they be legitimate citizen's claims or not) if the rights claimed are not withheld from Negroes because they are Negroes; or if, although withheld from Negroes as such, the rights claimed cannot be granted by public social means, either because these could not be materially effective, or because the use of these means would unreasonably impair other, no less important, rights or, the rights of others.

At present confusion between illegitimate and legitimate claims prevails among Negroes and whites alike; it is manifest in Congress, in the courts, and among educational authorities and tends to weaken legitimate Negro claims as well as the social fabric as a whole. The tests offered neither exhaust the distinction between legitimate and illegitimate Negro claims, nor clarify it in all instances. They may be useful, however, by drawing attention to such a distinction and indicating the criteria that must be applied.

II. Warranted and Unwarranted Discrimination

All legitimate Negro claims arise from unwarranted discrimination. Discrimination by law, or in public institutions, or by public officials, or even by private persons and means in situations strongly affected with the public interest, is unwarranted if it is irrelevant to the situation or activity at issue, and places a person or group at a material disadvantage. Both elements are necessary: neither a material disadvantage nor an irrelevant distinction alone suffices; the combination does.

Unwarranted discrimination ("discrimination against") can be distinguished from warranted discrimination in the following illustration. If a teacher grades his students according to their scholastic performance, he discriminates among them (and distributes advantages and disadvantages that may ensue) by using a criterion of distinction relevant to the (scholastic) situation or activity. However, if he grades students according to parental wealth, physical attractiveness, race, size, sex, or religion, the students who get low grades would suffer *unwarranted* disadvantages: the criterion of discrimination is not relevant to their activity and to the teacher's task. However, the casting director of a musical would be warranted in discriminating according to sex, beauty, size, or race where this may influence the visual, aesthetic, amusement, or erotic appeal of his show. The criterion irrelevant to one situation is relevant to another. Discrimination according to religion would be relevant in selecting missionaries, but not in casting chorus girls. Discrimination thus gives rise to legitimate claims only (but not always: a claim for public action must also meet tests 3 and 4 noted above) when a person or group is placed at a disadvantage not warranted by his actual task, situation, or activities.

Purely social discriminations by definition cannot be irrelevant, since selectivity in terms of personal preference is the essence of the social, and is displayed in discriminations. To put it paradoxically, the irrelevance (to anything but one's own arbitrary and capricious preference) of social discriminations, being of the essence of the social situation, is that which is relevant to it by definition. Whether social discriminations rest on misjudgments and prejudices, or on correct assessment of one's preferences and of those likely to meet them, the individual has a clear right to discriminate socially in however foolish a manner he wishes—though he might be wiser, and serve his interests better, by not exercising it.

ERNEST VAN DEN HAAG, Sociologist

The President's Posture

The President, by constitutional arrangement and political tradition, is the molder of the national will, the educator of the people, the guardian of its interests, and the protagonist of its ideals. The President is the incarnation of the nation-in-action; when the nation wants to know what it is about, it looks to the President to find out. When the country looks to Lyndon Johnson these days, it gains the inescapable impression that Vietnam is America's top priority. Mr. Johnson uses the bully pulpit of the Presidency (not to mention the Rose Garden) time and again to tell a painfully divided nation why it is fighting and must continue to fight in Southeast Asia. No amount of resistance—and it is growing—can blunt his resolve. Few question his personal resolve on the Negro problem (he is, after all, the President who proclaimed "We Shall Overcome!" in a speech three years ago). But his public posture here projects none of the sense of urgency that marks his Vietnam crusading.

HANS MORGENTHAU, University of Chicago
(*Newsweek* magazine, November 20, 1967)

I wish I were an Alabama trooper,
That is what I really want to be,
'Cause if I were an Alabama trooper,
I could kill a nigger le-gal-lee.

DOGGEREL SONG POPULAR
IN A CHICAGO HIGH SCHOOL

What Chance for Black Power?

If there is a lesson in America's pluralistic history, it is that the ability of an outcaste minority to advance in the face of majority prejudices partly depends on its ability to develop countervailing power. It is extraordinary that so conventional an idea has evoked so bitter a controversy in the civil rights community. For, stripped of rhetoric, the idea of "black power" merely emphasizes the need to augment Negro influence by developing separatist institutions, ranging from economic enterprise to political organization.

Frances Fox Piven and Richard A. Cloward, in *The New Republic,* March 30, 1968. © 1968 by Harrison-Blaine of New Jersey, Inc. Reprinted by permission.

Older civil rights organizations take umbrage at the separatist impulse because it appears to repudiate the principle of integration. Considering that ethnic labor unions, ethnic political machines and other ethnic institutions have been essential to the rise of various minorities, it is puzzling to hear it said that Negroes must restrain themselves from following the same course. Indeed, those institutions in the black community which are "integrated"—whether political organizations, the rackets, or social welfare agencies— actually contribute to black impotence, for they are integrated only in the sense that they are dominated by whites and serve white interests.

Those who are dismayed by the separatist position also fear that it will alienate liberal and labor allies. Blacks are a minority, to be sure, and cannot go it alone. But neither will they ever be more than a nominal participant in coalitions unless they are better organized; rather, their leaders will serve mostly to legitimize programs from which others benefit. An organized group need not sit about debating the pros and cons of seeking allies; it will be sought out by others, and offered genuine concessions because it has strength to bring to any alliance. Those who now urge color-blind coalition are unable to show why the black poor would have more effective leverage in future alliances than they have had in the past.

FRANCES FOX PIVEN AND RICHARD A. CLOWARD,
Columbia University School of Social Work

The Basic Emotion Is Hatred

The American Negro may not yet be ready to compete on equal terms with the white man, but he is far more advanced than most of the darker peoples who have won their independence since World War II, and taken seats, in all their exotic splendor, in the United Nations. Neither in Africa nor in the Caribbean nor in Latin America is there any group of Negroes so prepared for self-

I. F. Stone, in *The New York Review of Books*, August 18, 1966, p. 8.

government as our 20 million American Negroes. No other Negro group has so high a level of literacy, so wide an educated stratum, so large an elite, so much experience with politics, as the American Negro. But he alone of all these Negro or mulatto nations has no territory of his own.

Such cries as "Freedom Now" or "Black Power" reflect the repressed recognition of this bitter anomaly. As slogans or political programs they may make little sense in a country where he is little more than a tenth of the population, and where he is fenced off by taboo as racially untouchable in marriage. What does "Freedom Now" mean? Freedom from what? It really means freedom from the white man's presence, just as "Black Power" really means need of white man's power. If America's 20 million Negroes were concentrated in an African territory under white rule, or even concentrated in a Black Belt here, these cries clearly would make political sense. They would mean the end of white rule and the beginning of black rule. It might be less competent, and even more corrupt, but it would restore racial self-respect, as the need of white domination has done in Africa. This is the deep string these phrases pluck in black American hearts. This is what they cannot achieve in a white man's country and this is why you have leaders floundering around in despair, one day fighting segregation and the next day fighting integration. The basic emotion is hatred of "Whitey" and this is why Black Nationalism of one variety or another strikes so deeply into the apathetic, disillusioned, and despairing black masses. Of the conventional leaders only Martin Luther King sways them, and he does so for reasons that have little to do with the creed he preaches. They see him as a Moses, but they have no Promised Land.

I. F. STONE

Why? And for What?

The only slaves my ancestors had were their durable wives. I have never been able to afford even once-a-week household help, white or black.

There isn't a slumlord, or a price-gouging merchant, or a loan shark in my family. I didn't have to be re-educated to use the word "Negro." "Nigger" was never in my vocabulary.

For the multitudes of Negroes who have raised themselves to the solid middle class, the question, as it is for whites like me, must be not only WHY? but FOR WHAT?

The people who jeered and threw stones at firemen in Detroit have no more regard for the lives of these "Uncle Toms" than they have for "Whitey," so why fan the flames by citing a crook who charges $1 for a loaf of bread or a half gallon of milk?

If that kind of journalism is the answer, then what was the question? Again, please?

Mrs. Maribeth Hanna, Washington, D. C.
(*Ebony* magazine, December, 1967)

The Plight of a White Picket

I became a member of ACCESS (Action Coordinating Committee to End Segregation in the Suburbs) about two years ago. At that time and since, they mainly picketed segregated buildings in Maryland and Virginia suburbs, and pressured political leaders.

I marched with this group various Saturday and Sunday afternoons. One particular day made a rather large impression on me (although my behavior at the time may seem like pettiness).

There were ten of us picketing, 9 white and 1 Negro. I was marching right behind the Negro. He had washed neither himself nor his clothing for seemingly a month or more and it was in the dead of summer. He was singing and smoking a huge cigar. After about a half hour of picketing behind him, I stepped out of line for a breather (literally). Aside from thinking that I would never want this man for a neighbor, I began to wonder why we picketers were 90% white. Why was I giving up weekends to fight for a cause which apparently the Negroes were not?

Now, two years older, and I hope a good bit more compassionate, I think I can imagine the answers to these questions. However, that summer I dropped out of ACCESS, became involved in my own life, and have been ever since. Whether or not I will ever again become more than a passive supporter of this cause remains a confused question.

JOAN NICHOLS,
Arlington, Virginia

White Progress?

In your essay, you wrote: "Whether he likes to be reminded of it or not, the Negro has made spectacular progress in the past decade." Is it possible that it is the white man who has made the progress? For two centuries we have enslaved and discriminated against the Negro, exploited his labor, shunted him into inferior schools and housing, denied him his civil rights, prejudged and hated him. Yet for 99 44/100% of that time, he has done a minimum of hating and rebelling. Now that the legal and cultural evidences of our hate and prejudice are being exposed and we are being forced by the conscience of the world to begin rectifying the situation, it seems patronizing to remind the Negro of how far *he* has come.

DOYNE E. MICHIE, Associate Pastor
First Presbyterian Church, Decatur, Ill.
(*Time* magazine, September 3, 1965)

Recommendation for Change

Education: *The over-all goal is quality integrated education.*
Employment: *The long-term goal must be a full-employment economy.*
Health: *A national effort must be made to raise health standards among Negroes to the levels enjoyed by whites.*
Housing: *National policy should promote the dispersal of Ne-*

groes from the ghetto into integrated city and suburban neighborhoods.

Welfare: *The goal of national policy should be a humane and
radically simplified system that guarantees that no American will
go without the minimum necessities of life.*

Southern Development: *To reduce the pressure on Negroes to
move into the ghettos, national policy should be consciously directed at developing jobs and decent living conditions in the rural
South.*

NEWSWEEK MAGAZINE
(November 20, 1967)

Dr. King and the Law

In this period of corporate quiet and massive backlash, let us not
ignore three facts.

Dr. Martin Luther King Jr. had no more right to inject his personality into the Memphis garbage strike than he would have had
in the New York fiasco.

After the initial demonstration deteriorated into bloodshed and
riot, Dr. King vowed to repeat his march, even in violation of a
Federal injunction. Had he not been insistent upon flouting the
law, this man would be alive today.

No man has the inherent right to place himself above and beyond the law, even though he may personally consider that law to
be onerous.

STANLEY BARNARD, New York
(*The New York Times,* April 8, 1968)

Keep the Contacts

What I would like to say is this: as a Southerner, I am aware that
much of our racial problem has lain in the fact that there has been

simply no, or very little, contact between the races, naive as this may sound. No contact leads to the state that a member of neither race really knows one of the other as a person. He rather knows the other as a White (or Negro, or White Conservative, or Uncle Tom, or White Liberal or Negro Radical, etc.). Mr. Carmichael urged Whites to organize and work in White Communities if they wish to "do something." And rightly so. But I feel that it is vitally important that all meaningful contacts between races be maintained. I think it is also important (and it will become more so in the future) that Negroes meet Whites who aren't racists or grudging moderates. It is just as important that Negroes see Whites as human beings as it is that Whites see Negroes as human beings. Surely Mr. Carmichael and SNCC have nothing to fear from that.

Just as SNCC and others feel that it is vital for the Negro self-image, his personal and collective psychology, to be able to respond to Negro leaders and politicians (not just White liberal-leaders), I feel that it is just as vital for the collective mental health of Negroes and Whites to know and trust each others as individuals, as teachers, as organizers, or even as political leaders. Otherwise we'll have more of the same old thing.

Don't cut off the contacts completely.

RICHARD KING, Charlottesville, Virginia
(*New York Review of Books*, December 1, 1966)

Need Black Militance Be White Hatred?

But what of today, when one American city after another explodes in racial violence and radical change has come about in the civil rights movement? The link between militancy and tolerance may not hold for black power advocates as it did for the followers of Dr. King. Indeed, reading the mass media might lead one to assume an inverse relationship between the two. A great many observers have been quick to label black power as "racism in reverse."

To be sure, anti-white sentiment exists within the black power

Gary T. Marx, in *The Nation*, February 12, 1968. Reprinted by permission.

segments of the civil rights struggle, just as it exists within the Negro community at large. For some black radicals any tolerance for whites smacks of Uncle Tom. Yet this is peripheral to the emergence of the black power movement. Anti-white prejudice is not something suddenly created by the black power movement and is not what the movement is about. The tie so often made between black militancy and hatred of whites stems more from the sensation-seeking bias of the mass media and the incipient racism of white society (which recognizes the legitimacy of white ethnic interest groups only) than it does from a careful consideration of the facts.

The emergence of something like the black power movement was to be anticipated; it is only surprising that it did not occur earlier. The dream Martin Luther King spoke of in his March on Washington speech and the idyllic vision held by early civil rights workers of a just interracial society have not materialized; in some respects things have gotten worse and continue to deteriorate. The relevant statistics are all too well known and need not be repeated.

As was the case with the Jews in Europe, the type of orientation dominant within an ethnic minority group at any one time is to an important extent dependent on the receptiveness of the dominant group. When the dominant group seems approachable, emphasis is placed on inclusion and assimilation. When the dominant group is not receptive, or its supposed receptiveness proves illusory, the minority group may increasingly turn inward and in a separatist direction. Other periods in American history show Negro protest movements going toward or away from the dominant society. For example, the hopes raised by the Civil War and World War I led to an initial emphasis on inclusion; the shattering of those hopes led to the predominance of separatist leaders such as Booker T. Washington and Marcus Garvey. Other leaders, for example Paul Cuffee and Martin Robinson Delaney, like many of today's black power leaders, began strongly in favor of integration and then, overwhelmed by futility, took up separatist positions.

GARY T. MARX, Department of Social Relations, Harvard University

We Made Jobs

The rabble-rousers have been shouting about jobs. We made jobs available just by meeting with businessmen. No shouting and no marching and no hate. We are working with men that King had declared were bigots and would never hire a Negro. Who would want to hire someone sent by King or Carmichael?

> REV. HENRY MITCHELL, Chicago,
> President of North Star United Missionary Workers of America

From *American Opinion*, March, 1968, p. 31. Quoted by permission.

"No hen has the right to cackle who hasn't laid an egg. Black Power folk, many with no soap and no bath tubs, are cackling about their power. They need to *do* something first."

> DR. J. H. JACKSON, Chicago, President,
> National Baptist Convention

Quoted in *American Opinion*, March, 1968, p. 28. Reprinted by permission.

Double Impatience

"Why are the good people on both sides drifting so far apart? One of the troubles is that the nation is suffering from what might be called a severe case of 'double impatience.' The white man is impatient because he feels the Negro is trying to cram two centuries of reform into this decade; the Negro is impatient because he believes the white man does not comprehend the urgent reasons for equality now. An impasse in impatience, you might call it."

> JUDD ARNETT
> (*Detroit Free Press,* July 27, 1967)

You Can't Help a Jackass

The negro male does not look for responsibility, he hides from it, he loves women and laziness, you can't help a jackass who won't get up & pull his own load. Furthermore, the gov't. by legislation forced the majority into the mainstream of life when they are not ready for it. Those with money like LBJ and others shoot off their mouths as they do not have to rub elbows with those who do not know how to live. It is like someone placing a dish of very distasteful food in front of you or I, and telling us it is delicious, to go ahead and eat it, even if you know you can't. Why is the poor image the negro portrays kept hush, hush? Why are not the deficiencies aired in the open and if they want a better life, then they should be told to get moving, but is this done? Why not? Why all the pussey footing around with no worthwhile results forthcoming? No one dares to speak out.

A New York Resident
(From a letter to C. Eric Lincoln)

It Ought to Be Possible . . .

This nation was founded by men of many nations and backgrounds. It was founded on the principle that all men are created equal, and that the rights of every man are diminished when the rights of one man are threatened.

Today we are committed to a worldwide struggle to promote and protect the rights of all who wish to be free. And when Americans are sent to Vietnam or West Berlin we do not ask for whites only.

It ought to be possible, therefore, for American students of any color to attend any public institution they select without having to be backed by troops. It ought to be possible for American con-

---

From the late President's address (1964) declaring civil rights "a moral issue."

sumers of any color to receive equal service in places of public accommodation, such as hotels and restaurants, and theaters and retail stores without being forced to resort to demonstrations in the street.

And it ought to be possible for American citizens of any color to register and to vote in a free election without interference or fear of reprisal.

It ought to be possible, in short, for every American to enjoy the privileges of being American without regard to his race or his color.

In short, every American ought to have the right to be treated as he would wish to be treated, as one would wish his children to be treated. But this is not the case.

JOHN F. KENNEDY

Negro Has No Sense of Family

I disagree with [the] thesis that the negro enjoys an inferior status in contemporary America because of reasons dating back to slavery. [They] say the white man destroyed the negro family, but the negro has had very little sense of family. He is not unlike the male animal who impregnates the female and then abandons her to impregnate another female. The negress attends to her children without her mate as does the female animal.

Western Civilization had its roots in Europe where the white man was inculcated with the teachings of Christianity. He developed a sense, first of family, then of community and then of nation. European man was transplanted to America and in the South, he instituted slavery to help his agricultural economy. Slaves were imported from Africa and treated as chattel property, to be bought and sold at the slaveowner's caprice.

The Emancipation Proclamation freed the negro from his ignominious condition and negroes fled the South in large numbers to inhabit Northern cities. No longer protected by his white masters on the plantation, he had to fend for himself in his ghetto surroundings. Because of his proclivity to crime and illegitimacy, he has become a burden to the white dwellers of the cities who must support his victims. Because of his lesser intellectual abilities, he has secured but marginal employment where he has been employed at all.

The negroes, however, have been sensing a community among themselves and this accounts for the rise of black movements. They blame the white man for their inferior status and the more extreme among them advocate violent revolution to right this injustice. This is a dangerous situation and I believe it will become more dangerous with time.

I believe our approach to the negro problem must be an economic and not a legislative one. I believe the means of production should be nationalized, profits reduced and used to pay for welfare services, provided on a national basis. All Americans, regardless of race, would thereby share equally in education, medicine and insurance. An American would not only have a political birthright, but an economic one as well.

The white man cannot be blamed for the negro's moral and intellectual deficiencies, but he can be accused of not creating a society in which the negro can better himself and thereby mitigate his deficiencies.

STANLEY SINGER, New York

"Americanization Job" Not Desired

"We don't want to do an Americanization job on the Negro so as to fit them neatly into middle-class pockets of society. Still, if the objective of a college is to train a fair number of leaders, then they should be leaders who can work well with the white majority as well as with their own kind."

DEAN DAVID B. TRUMAN, Columbia University
(*The New York Times,* May 1, 1967)

National Renaissance Bulletin

How come everytime a police officer attempts to protect people by arresting, or if necessary, shooting a negro criminal, we suddenly witness an uproar among liberal action groups, the slanted newspapers and black agitators demanding an "investigation" and the establishment of a "Civilian Review Board"?

If a policeman has to shoot a black criminal, he is called a "murderer" by these same black agitation groups. The newspapers with their pro-negro attitude, make it look like the negro criminal shot by the police was some kind of innocent victim of "police brutality". Just what is a policeman supposed to do in order to stop the rising black crime rate? Is he supposed to look the other way everytime a white woman is raped? Is he supposed to turn his head and walk away while white men, women and children are robbed, assaulted, stabbed and murdered on the streets and in the subways? The answer is YES, according to the civil rights agitation groups!

WHAT IS A "CIVILIAN REVIEW BOARD"?

The real motive behind all the shouts of so-called "police brutality" by civil rights groups is to establish "Civilian Review Boards" which will investigate the police and discipline any policeman whom the board feels is guilty of "police brutality" and discrimination against negroes and other "minorities". The purpose of the "Review Boards" is to place a group of liberal, pro-negro agitators over the heads of the police that will dictate and control police policy.

In order to control the streets and be free to do as they please, the black agitation groups must first remove the major obstacle in their path. . . . THE POLICE! The "civil rights" groups are out to CONTROL THE POLICE Departments with the establishment of the "Civilian Review Board". If you think things are bad now, just wait until your police DO NOT DARE PROTECT YOU or your women and children for fear of losing their jobs or of being accused of "discrimination" by the "Civilian Review Board".

POLITICIANS DON'T CARE!

The politicians do not care about the white people, who are the majority, because the politicians depend on the minority vote to keep them in office. White people divide themselves up as "republicans" and "democrats." The negroes and Jews do not divide themselves up. They vote together (united) as a solid bloc vote. When all the votes have been cast, the republican votes and the democratic votes just about come up EVEN . . . AND with whomever the negroes and Jews cast their vote, that person is going to WIN THE ELECTION! That is why the politicians do as the negroes want! That is why politicians don't care about the white people. Politicians are greedy opportunists who want to stay in office and in order to do so they must kiss the foot of every negro they can find!

WHITE PEOPLE! UNITE AND FIGHT BACK!
PROTECT OUR WOMEN!
For further information write:

NATIONAL RENAISSANCE PARTY
10 West 90th Street   New York 24, N.Y.

Concentration Camps for Blacks?

Talk of repression in one form or another is widespread today. Radicals mutter about black rebels being shunted into concentration camps—and their conversation reflects a real element of fear, not just agitators' hokum. There are advocates of garrisoning the ghettos and of limiting freedom of speech in the face of a clear and present danger. "What is remarkable," says political scientist James Q. Wilson, "is that there has not yet emerged a McCarthy of race: a figure with a mass audience . . . who would say boldly and demagogically what millions of people are already thinking."

Clearly, many Northern whites today are thinking of repression —much as Southern segregationists always have. Whether their thoughts will ever be translated into political reality is anybody's guess. But American politics is already reflecting their mood—or, at least, the politicians are telling themselves that they are reflecting the public temper. They are probably right. Every public man feels obliged at some point or another to deliver a homily about the innate kindness or the conscience of the American people, but nearly all shake their heads when they ponder the application of those virtues to the current racial situation.

NEWSWEEK MAGAZINE
(November 20, 1967)

Uncle Toms and Mahyofesnicks

"Black Power" says that black is good and that black men must stand proudly to shape their own destiny. It says that the ballot is an instrument for freedom, that political self-reliance and economic self-reliance go hand in hand. It says that the Negro masses must no longer be content to rely on the beneficence of friendly whites or on the mediation of those few Negroes who have "made it" into the middle class. It says that too much civil-rights legislation has been of present benefit only to the middle-class Negro and has not touched the needs of the Negro still locked in Northern ghettos and in Southern rural degradation.

No analogies are complete but there are instructive correspondences in Jewish experience that should help us understand this thrust of the Negro revolution. The American Jewish Congress came into being a century after the political emancipation of the European Jew. It was founded upon a rejection of the mediation of the wealthy who had "made it" or the friendliness of influential Gentiles. It was built upon the determination that the Jewish masses would have a share in the shaping of their destiny and that Jewish self-respect and Jewish militancy would use the ballot and the forces of law for the achievement of human rights. It rejected the Uncle Toms (we called them "shtadlonim") and the "yassah-yas-sah" response of those whom we called "mahyofesnicks". It fought against Jewish self-hatred and taught our young that "Jewish" means "good".

More than others, we should be able to understand the frustration and disappointment that grow out of the fact that in many respects the Negro situation has grown worse rather than better: the income gap has widened, unemployment has increased, so-called "urban renewal" has frequently herded Negroes into ever more crowded slums, school segregation and educational inadequacy continue. We are called upon to respond with special vigor to every Negro initiative for auto-emancipation, to be alert to the

From an address by Rabbi Arthur J. Lelyveld, President of the American Jewish Congress.

possibilities of shared labor in concrete projects, to educate our own people to the demands of our tradition for the warm reception of and the proper respect due our fellowmen.

RABBI ARTHUR J. LELYVELD

It is interesting, too, to see how liberals of all colors choke on the word "black," brought up as they were on the notion that color is irrelevant and that the proper approach is to pretend it doesn't exist.

Concern
(October 1, 1967)

Negroes are just as guilty as the rest of us of wanting the best of two worlds. They want to be obnoxious as hell, but still beloved. Negro maids want $1.75 per hour *and* their carfare. I make about that and I don't get carfare.

And in a larger, psychological realm, I think we are all afraid of freedom. Freedom, or, if you prefer, "success", carries with it a frightening "what now" quality, a "where do we go from here" feeling. This fear is a stumbling block for all of us individually, and perhaps for the Negroes as a group. How many of us have sheepishly admitted that, without "such and such" to gripe about, we would feel quite lost. It *is* easier to sit around and blame someone else for our woes. As one Jewish friend of mine said, "Why not, instead of burning down their rent-controlled houses, take buckets and soap and scrub them. After all, a landlord is not going to pour $100 a month into a place that the Government allows him to charge only $40 for."

A WOMAN IN CIVIL SERVICE,
Arlington, Virginia

Education, the Best Hope

So far our discussion of educational quality has been solely in terms of standardized achievement tests. But there are those in Harlem and other ghetto communities who are speaking out against this single criterion. Their argument is that standardized achievement tests are "culturally biased" in favor of middle-class norms and values; and since, in their view, middle-class American life is corrupt, Negroes should set their own goals and develop a curriculum which will build upon the strengths of their own culture.

We are sympathetic with such feelings, but they raise a major practical difficulty. For all their inadequacies, standardized tests do tend to measure the kinds of abilities that are rewarded in the job market. It is all very well for those who have made it into the middle class to reject the kinds of achievement measured on these tests, but the ghetto Negro simply cannot afford to, for such achievement is his ticket out of the ghetto. We may not like this, but until the United States is willing to undertake some form of substantial income redistribution, "standard" educational attainment remains the Negro's best hope for breaking out of poverty.

We believe that there *is* a case to be made for decentralization and more community participation in the running of the schools, just as there is a strong argument for compensatory education, but only as these policies *accompany* the drive for integration rather than substitute for it. There is no question that school systems in large cities are overly bureaucratic and inflexible, and that they should become more responsive to local needs. We support the notion of strengthening the authority of school principals and their faculties, and we share the hope that increased participation by parents in the life of the school will have a salutary effect on the motivation of the children.

But if these ideas make sense for segregated schools, they should make even more sense for integrated ones. Similarly, if teaching techniques are developed in compensatory programs to capitalize on reduced pupil ratios, these techniques should prove effective in

From *The New Republic,* January 6, 1968. © 1968 by Harrison-Blaine of New Jersey, Inc. Reprinted by permission.

an integrated setting. Integration *by itself* is not going to be enough to close the achievement gap. If experiments in decentralization prove to have a positive impact on achievement, these findings should influence our planning for *all* schools.

ROBERT SCHWARTZ,
THOMAS PETTIGREW,
MARSHALL SMITH

Education? For Whom?

We need to turn around our pulpits and preach to ourselves. *We* are in need of the Gospel, not they. We are the ones who need to be changed, not just others. We have thought for too long that we could hand out the Christian faith, stretching our long arms to the place of need, converting others to our way of seeing things at the same time. This is no longer possible.

We have tossed about the cliche that race progress in this country will take "education—a lot of education." We have meant by this that the Negro was going to have to be educated to the place where he would be like we are, whatever we are. Now we must say that *we* need to be educated.

JOHN P. ADAMS, Director,
Department of Public Affairs,
General Board of Christian Social Concerns
of the Methodist Church

Middle-Class Mythology

Whites brought up on the middle-class mythology of social darwinism, the protestant ethic, and American success stories find it difficult to sympathize with the Negroes' lack of opportunities. And because they themselves are the products and carriers of white supremacy, whites find it impossible to comprehend that Negroes are frustrated to the point of explosion by the secondary status assigned them by the whole social system.

> RICHARD NEWMAN, Department of
> Human Relations, Boston University
> (*Concern*, October 1, 1967)

Assumption of Guilt in a Segregated School

Eliciting the confession of lies out of children who didn't lie and hadn't lied can easily become one of the most highly developed practices within a segregated school. An assumption of prior guilt is often so overwhelming and so absorbing that even a new teacher with strong affiliations to the Negro community, and sometimes even a teacher who is Negro, will be surprised to discover the extent to which he shares it. It seems at moments to require an almost muscular effort of the imagination to consider the possibility in a particular case that the Negro child might actually *not* have done it, that he might *not* be telling any lie. I remember several incidents of this kind when a pupil whom I knew for certain to be innocent was actually brought around to the point of saying, "Yes I did it" or "Yes I was lying," simply from the force of a white adult's accusation.

> JONATHAN KOZOL

Jonathan Kozol, *Death at an Early Age* (Boston: Houghton Mifflin, 1967), p. 55. Reprinted by permission.

The vital needs of the nation must be met; hard choices must be made, and, if necessary, new taxes enacted.

> THE KERNER REPORT

No Integrated Education Without Genuine Desegregation

What are the long-term prospects for desegregated schools?

I do not think we will ever have genuinely integrated education until we have a genuinely desegregated society. And such a society —one in which every man is free to succeed or fail on his merits, to qualify for a job on the basis of his ability alone, to live where he chooses as long as he can pay the rent or make the mortgage payment—seems a long way off. We have made progress in every one of these areas during the 1960's, but we have far to go. The question that confronts us is whether we can move fast enough in the years immediately ahead to keep the hopes our small progress has generated from turning into bitter frustration and hate.

It is a curious thing that a little progress often brings a disproportionate amount of frustration, anger, and violence. Every white person knows other whites who—reacting to the riots in our cities and to the continual demands of our deprived minorities— ask, "What more do *they* want?" And every black person, I suppose, knows at least one Negro who proclaims his willingness to blow the country up tomorrow if Whitey does not come across today.

Such white reactions—in the case of persons who felt at least an initial sympathy with the civil rights movement—stem partially from a defective sense of our nation's history. Resenting a riot, of course, does not require any historical sense; a riot is just plain wrong. But whites who ask, "Why don't they *work* their way up the way we did?" might be chagrined to discover that American Negroes *are* "working their way up" in a fashion not dissimilar to that previously engaged in by a number of white minorities: through a combination of strenuous toil, political pressure, and outbreaks of violence.

HAROLD HOWE II, Commissioner,
U.S. Office of Education

From *The Urban Review*, February, 1968, p. 23. Reprinted by permission.

"I was disappointed in the Kerner report . . . [it] more or less points out what other reports before it have pointed out. It is time to stop reporting [on the subject] and start solving the problem.

"Are the Negroes moving too fast? Perhaps the question should be put this way: 'Are the whites doing enough to solve the problems and grievances of the Negro people?' We should be doing so much more. All the suppression of violence may be necessary, I guess. But it only points out a sickness. It's not the answer. . . . what we need is the application of more energy and resources to the righting of wrongs.

"Carmichael is too hostile, I think. He said Negroes should arm and take to the streets. It's going against everything King stood for. This man (King) has given his life. As Roy Wilkins said, I believe it was Wilkins, King was the best friend the white man had. It's too bad the white man found it out too late.

"Let's hope there's no more violence. Let's hope the slaying of Dr. King brings America to its senses.

"Naturally, the approach of the extremists is not right. It's wrong, but it also points up the sickness (of American society) and we must be aware that the rhetoric of violence is a symptom of what's wrong in America.

"Our greatest answer is to help the situation. Many of my friends feel it's already too late.

"The moderates have been too late with not enough. I believe that. But I also believe it's not too late to effect a reconciliation of the races. We must bring good out of the horribleness of our world. We must be aware of the violent nature of society and try to change it."

REV. DWIGHT HOELSCHER,
First Congregational Church
Long Beach, California

"It's unfortunate that the (Kerner) report doesn't give us a true perspective—unfortunate in the regard that the people on the commission were liberal, and therefore we got a liberal report. What we got in the commission's report, you can get from the Communist Worker. It's common knowledge.

"The (black) militants in this country are sincere, but sincerely wrong. Theirs is the wrong approach. It's common knowledge where most of their money is coming from. It's coming from the Communist countries. The riots are being financed by the Communist countries. It's been proven by the FBI and other federal sources."

REV. BOB RAYBURN, Associate Pastor,
Central Baptist Church,
Anaheim, California

The Golden Rule Was White

I grew up just 19 miles from Appomattox. The teaching I received both in school and from my parents was hard-core South, with no chance of insight into the thinking and ways of other peoples. I was taught to look down upon Negroes, tolerate Jews (because we had to do business with them) and ignore Catholics.

We celebrated Jefferson Davis's birthday, but ignored Lincoln's; the name Robert E. Lee was spoken with reverence and Appomattox was a shrine. The Golden Rule only applied to others who were either Methodist or Baptist, white and without a foreign-sounding name. . . .

A FORMER SOUTHERNER

We pray to Almighty God, the Author of our liberty, for the hearts free from hate, so that our nation can be free from bitterness.

We pray for strength to build together so that disorder may cease, progress steadily continue, and justice prosper.

LYNDON B. JOHNSON

The Racists

In the wake of Dr. King's tragic death, there is once more exposed the curious alliance between the purveyors of racist hatred, both white and black. The twisted mind of the white criminal who murdered Dr. King is matched by the psychotic reaction of Stokely Carmichael who publicly urges murder in the streets.

The extremists of both sides seek to take advantage of the hatreds, suspicions and fears that are this nation's troubled legacy from the complex past. The white racists pander to the insecurities of those who feel threatened by the Negro push for equality; the Carmichaels and Rap Browns seek to capitalize on the resentments born of the discrimination, poverty and humiliation which have been the common tragic experience of millions of Negroes.

Fortunately, however, the overwhelming majority of American whites and American Negroes know each other as individuals, and value each other as individuals. This country has still far too much segregation, but it has an enormous amount of integration as well. In thousands of factories, mines, stores, schools, hospitals throughout this country, Negroes and whites know each other as colleagues, as fellow workers, as friends. In Vietnam these past three years hundreds of thousands of Americans of all shades have fought together, and all too often died together.

In the United States today, the fate of whites and of blacks is inextricably intertwined. To the extent that this nation is powerful and prosperous, it is because of the contributions of all of its citizens. The promise of an even better America with more justice than in the past and with its riches more widely distributed can only be realized with progressive cooperation of white and black.

Those who would set the two groups against each other will, if successful, only bring disaster to all. Martin Luther King understood this and his life was an unceasing effort to preserve that brotherhood and extend the American dream to all Americans. The senseless criminal who shot Dr. King ended his physical being; the Carmichaels seek to repudiate the whole concept of brotherhood that gave to Dr. King's life meaning, inspiration and significance for tomorrow as well as today.

THE NEW YORK TIMES (from an editorial, April 6, 1968)

Hatred and "Special Feelings"

We have it on the authority of James Baldwin that all Negroes hate whites. I am trying to suggest that on their side all whites— all American whites, that is—are sick in their feelings about Negroes. There are Negroes, no doubt, who would say that Baldwin is wrong, but I suspect them of being less honest than he is, just as I suspect whites of self-deception who tell me they have no special feeling toward Negroes. Special feelings about color are a contagion to which white Americans seem susceptible even when there is nothing in their background to account for the susceptibility. Thus everywhere we look today in the North, we find the curious phenomenon of white middle-class liberals with no previous personal experience of Negroes—people to whom Negroes have always been faceless in virtue rather than faceless in vice— discovering that their abstract commitment to the cause of Negro rights will not stand the test of a direct confrontation. We find such people fleeing in droves to the suburbs as the Negro population in the inner city grows; and when they stay in the city we find them sending their children to private school rather than to the "integrated" public school in the neighborhood. We find them resisting the demand that gerrymandered school districts be rezoned for the purpose of overcoming de facto segregation; we find them judiciously considering whether the Negroes (for their own good, of course) are not perhaps pushing too hard; we find them clucking their tongues over Negro militancy; we find them speculating on the question of whether there may not, after all, be something in the theory that the races are biologically different; we find them saying that it will take a very long time for Negroes to achieve full equality, no matter what anyone does; we find them deploring the rise of black nationalism and expressing the solemn hope that the leaders of the Negro community will discover ways of containing the impatience and incipient violence within the Negro ghettos.

NORMAN PODHORETZ

From Norman Podhoretz, *Doings and Undoings* (New York: Farrar, Straus & Giroux, 1964). Copyright © 1964 by the publisher. Reprinted by permission of the author.

The Self-Fulfilling Prophecy

The role of "Negro" is again a critical factor. Put simply, the Negro is not expected to be bright. To reveal high intelligence is to risk seeming "uppity" to a white supremacist. And once more the self-fulfilling prophecy begins to operate, for the Negro who assumes a façade of stupidity as a defense mechanism against oppression is very likely to grow into the role. He will not be eager to learn, and he will not strive to do well in the testing situation. After all, an intelligence test is a middle-class white man's instrument; it is a device whites use to prove their capacities and get ahead in the white world. Achieving a high test score does not have the same meaning for a lower-status Negro child, and it may even carry a definite connotation of personal threat. In this sense, scoring low on intelligence measures may for some talented Negro children be a rational response to perceived danger.

THOMAS F. PETTIGREW

From *A Profile of the Negro American* (Princeton: Van Nostrand, 1964), p. 115. Reprinted by permission.

Property Rights vs. Individuals' Welfare

The quelling of the recent riot in the Washington area has produced some interesting results which other cities across the nation will want to examine.

For the first time in the recent wave of urban riots, law-enforcement officials—the metropolitan police force, the D.C. National Guard and the Federal troops—apparently exercised a great deal of restraint in their efforts to end the disturbance.

These law-enforcement officials relied much more on the technique of arresting looters rather than on threatening them or shooting at every person suspected of committing a felony.

These actions will undoubtedly create mixed feelings in the Washington metropolitan area. By using these new riot procedures the city probably experienced a greater loss in merchandise than would have occurred under a system which relies upon force alone. However, if one looks back at last year's riots in Detroit and Newark, where "force and threat" were employed, it becomes evident that what Washington may have lost in merchandise it probably saved in lives.

In addition, we may also be experiencing one of the first times in American history when the rights of private property were subordinated to the welfare of the individual. If this concept could be applied to our major urban problems, it might have a positive effect on American political, social and economic life.

> BERNARD H. ROSS, Assistant Professor of Government,
> The American University, Bethesda, Maryland
> (*The New York Times,* April 9, 1968)

The Specter of Conflict

But why should the white American, particularly the segregationist, help the Negro to achieve greater equality when inequality is one of the major bulwarks against integration? Here the American Creed and the dream of government by consensus, not by force, become relevant. It has become painfully evident in the past few years that, unless the nation begins to take longer strides on the first mile of the long road to equality and integration, the Negro revolt will change from a nonviolent to a violent one. The white community will have to fight those Negroes who have too much spirit to submit any longer, and it will have to support with its charity those who are too apathetic to fight. The only other alternative will be increasingly repressive measures which would change the nature of the Republic and destroy the image of American democracy in the eyes of the world. There is no easy way out. The battle has been joined. The question is whether the conflict will rend

From *Racial Crisis in America: Leadership in Conflict* (Englewood Cliffs, N.J.: Prentice-Hall, 1964), pp. 143–144. Copyright © 1964. Reprinted by permission of the publisher.

American society irreparably or draw its racially separated parts together in some yet unforeseeable future.

LEWIS KILLIAN AND CHARLES GRIGG

We White Folks Brought Them Here

Herein lies the importance of whether the urban disturbances are called "riots" or "rebellions." The difference between a "riot" and a "rebellion" is that a rebellion is assumed to have goals. The physical incidents of riot and rebellion are very similar. An eyewitness would perceive much the same events in either case: people running through the streets; orators haranguing spontaneous assemblages; the precinct police station stoned or the home of the distributor of stamps sacked; tea dumped into the harbor or TV sets taken from certain stores; finally shooting, mostly by uniformed representatives of constituted authority, and bodies on the sidewalks.

Yet one such occurrence will be called a "riot," defined by the dictionary as "disorderly behavior," because the eyewitness fails to see an ordering of action by intended goals. A similar happening, no different in its externals, may go into history as a "rebellion"—"open renunciation of the authority of the government to which one owes obedience"—if those who write the history empathize with the motives of the protagonists.

This is why black radicals insist on the term "rebellion" or "revolt" ("a casting off of allegiance; . . . a movement or expression of vigorous dissent or refusal to accept") rather than the term "riot." They perceive order in the disorders. As Tom Hayden, staff member of the Newark Community Union Project and a founder of Students for a Democratic Society, has observed, those who rioted in Newark regarded what they did as a more rational relating of means to ends than anything available from the channels of decision-making customary in quiet times.

It may help us to approach an understanding of the political philosophy of the American resistance to existing authority if we

Staughton Lynd, in *The New York Times Magazine*, September 10, 1967. © 1967 by The New York Times Company. Reprinted by permission.

attempt to relate it to the theory of revolution found in Locke, the Declaration of Independence and Abraham Lincoln's first Inaugural Address.

"This country," President Lincoln said when he took over a government on the eve of dissolution, "belongs to the people who inhabit it. Whenever they shall grow weary of the existing government, they can exercise their constitutional right of amending it, or their revolutionary right to dismember or overthrow it."

The harshest critic of Stokely Carmichael will have to recognize some kinship between Lincoln's affirmation and Carmichael's statement, reported last October by the United Press, that "there is a higher law than the law of government. That's the law of conscience." Clearly President and peripatetic agitator agree that government cannot be the ultimate arbiter of right and wrong. And well they might: for that way, surely we would all concur, lies Eichmann.

Nor can anyone deny that in his statement on the occasion of his arrest, July 26, 1967, H. Rap Brown employed precisely the logic of the preamble to the Declaration of Independence.

"I am charged with inciting black people to commit an offense by way of protest against the law, a law which neither I nor any of my people have any say in preparing. . . .

"I consider myself neither morally nor legally bound to obey laws made by a body in which I have no representation. That the will of the people is the basis of the authority of government is a principle universally acknowledged as sacred throughout the civilized world and constitutes the basic foundation of this country. It should be equally understandable that we, as black people, should adopt the attitude that we are neither morally nor legally bound to obey laws which were not made with our consent and which seek to oppress us."

This dignified statement was made the same day that Martin Luther King, Roy Wilkins, A. Philip Randolph and Whitney Young issued a joint public declaration so far abandoning the First Amendment that it urged advocacy of riot or arson be punished as equivalent to the commission of those acts themselves.

There is one important difference between the political philosophy of the Declaration and that of Carmichael and Brown. In classical democratic theory the right of revolution belonged only to majorities. This was one of the reasons that a bourgeois gentleman like Locke could justify revolution with such confidence.

"Nor let anyone say," he wrote, "that mischief can arise . . . as often as it shall please a busy head or turbulent spirit to desire the alteration of the government. It is true such men may stir whenever they please, but it will be only to their own just ruin and perdition; for till the mischief be grown general, and the ill designs of the rulers become visible, or their attempts sensible to the greater part, the people who are more disposed to suffer than right themselves by resistance are not apt to stir." Locke's majoritarian theory of revolution might appear to cut the theoretical ground from under the activists of the New Left in general, and of S.N.C.C.

Yet a dispassionate observer might rebut as follows: In the first place, S.N.C.C. is not, for the moment at least, attempting to overthrow the Government of the United States. The rioters have not gone downtown. What they want is control of those neighborhoods in which they constitute a majority. They ask, not that City Hall move over and make room for them, but that City Hall and especially City Hall's policemen stay out of where they are. Rap Brown's argument that men cannot be bound by laws to which they have not given their consent would fit this situation perfectly, provided it could be shown that such consent had not, in fact, been forthcoming. In the Deep South the prima facie case that whites have imposed on blacks a "law and order" expressive only of the wants of whites is overwhelming.

In the second place, it is hardly the fault of Afro-Americans that they constitute a minority in the United States. We white folks brought them here, and one of the persistent considerations in the minds of those who did the importing was to get enough black laborers to do their work for them but not so many that the laborers might successfully revolt. What is the Afro-American supposed to do? It seems to him that his oppression is of that pervasiveness and degree which Locke said justified revolution on the part of those oppressed. Should he then not rebel because his numbers are few? That counsel hardly fits with the tradition of white revolutionaries who sought liberty or death. Whether or not he would concede the kinship, that is the tradition to which Rap Brown belongs.

STAUGHTON LYND

Read and Pass On

How would you like it if your exquisitely formed White child was no longer White? Pink cheeks no longer pink? Blue eyes no longer blue, lovely hair no longer lovely?

It's sensitive mind no longer sensitive but ape like? It's beautiful body no longer beautiful but black and evil smelling?

A few drops of negro blood in your child's veins and it could have a coal black negro baby.

The blood in your White child is the most precious thing on earth (civilizations are built upon it) and many evil minded men know this to be a fact. They have organized into groups to "get" this blood away from you.

Some foolish Christians tell you it is God's will—as if God who aims at the beautiful, the good, and intelligent, would want to destroy and dirty his loveliest gifts.

These evil men have organized child movements and camps to further their evil designs. Some of these camps are Jewish, some Christian, some political, some union. All pose as democracy in action and the object of all is to get your White child's blood.

People only go after what is better than they have and never hunt something inferior to what they possess.

Remember it is always grown people "adults" who operate these camps. Adults with a queer bent who could never prey upon a grown person but must have the tender, innocent, unsuspecting mind of your child with which to do their evil work.

Scientists claim that such adults who are unduly attracted to White children and wish to mix them with negroes are suffering from a Freudian Complex that gives them a sex thrill at the very thought of mating your lovely child with the evil ape like body of the negro.

This act of mating is not done at the camps but your child's mind is poisoned with false social and religious ideas at its most susceptible stage so that the act of marriage can be accomplished later. They must steal your child's mind before they can steal its body.

This should be warning enough. You know where your treasure is. Protect it. To keep your child from negroes it will be necessary to keep it away from all youth movements—with especial emphasis on those that pose as religious or political or democratic.

Don't let the devil with the angle's wings carry away your Lovely. It is only the lovely they want and what a howl these hyenas can make of race discrimination when they can't get your lamb in their fangs.

Remember all youth movements have for their special feature the mixing of negroes with your White child and if it were not for the beauty of the White child none of these camps would be in existence.

Boy camps condition your boy to bring home a negro buddy for your little daughter. Girl camps condition your daughter to bring home a negro pal for your White boy. Don't let them get by with it.

Here is just a few with sweet sounding names. The spider's web to catch the unsuspecting fly—in this case your pretty White cherub.

YMCA, YWCA, Labor Union Camp, Chicago Community Conference, Youth Congress, Young Adult Councils, Youth For Christ, Young Civic Councils, Political Action Volunteers, Youth For Democracy, Jewish Welfare Group, Scout Camps For Boys, Scout Camps For Girls.

These are just a few. A lot of these camps change their names when they are found out, but they continue to operate under new names and their object is to destroy the civilized world for Communism by mating your White Innocent with the loathsome negro.

Negro Blood Destroyed the Civilization of Egypt, India, Phoenicia, Carthage, Greece and Rome. It will Destroy America!

National Renaissance Party
10 West 90th Street
New York 24, N.Y.

The American Problem

For the cries of pain and the hymns and protests of oppressed people have summoned into convocation all the majesty of this great government of the greatest nation on earth.

Our mission is at once the oldest and most basic of this country: to right wrong, to do justice, to serve man.

In our time we have come to live with moments of great crisis. Our lives have been marked with debate about great issues; issues of war and peace, of prosperity and depression. But rarely in any time does an issue lay bare the secret heart of America itself. Rarely are we met with a challenge, not to our growth or abundance, our welfare or our security, but rather to the values and the purposes and the meaning of our beloved nation.

The issue of equal rights for American Negroes is such an issue. And should we defeat every enemy, should we double our wealth

From President Johnson's remarks to a joint session of the Congress, March 15, 1965.

and conquer the stars, and still be unequal to this issue, then we will have failed as a people and as a nation.

For with a country as with a person, "What is a man profited, if he shall gain the whole world, and lose his own soul?" There is no Negro problem. There is no Southern problem. There is no Northern problem. There is only an American problem. And we are met here tonight as Americans to solve that problem.

LYNDON B. JOHNSON

The Right to Brick

"I don't know that a nonviolent revolution is, in fact, realistic in the United States. But then it has never been tried except for isolated situations. We are either successful here in Milwaukee or it goes over to violence. Rap Brown was right when he said violence was as American as cherry pie. We've all thrilled in American history classes to the spectacle of an oppressed people rising up against their oppressors with violence. I believe, with Malcolm X, in the absolute necessity of self-defense. I believe in what you might call 'the right to brick.' "

FATHER GROPPI, Milwaukee (*Ramparts,* November, 1967)

Thinking Black

Thinking black today remains more style than substance, more mood than program—but it commands white America's attention simply because it is so pervasively there. Whether or not it is the majority view is neither measurable nor relevant: it is the operative mood of both the alienated ghetto young who make riots and the new Negro leaders who increasingly shape the public discourse about what is to be done.

NEWSWEEK MAGAZINE
(November 20, 1967)

A Segregated Christ

If charity begins at home, let it begin there. Picket every church in the land until every clergyman stopped fulminating against others when those same evils are officially condoned by his own organization. To avoid rowdiness and unfairness I would suggest that members of each church picket their own edifice. If students and others have the courage to do that, then when the nationwide job of integrating the churches is accomplished I should join the picket line in front of the holdout stores. If I am any judge of human or ecclesiastical nature, I would say that the stores, individual and chain, will have integrated everywhere long before the churches have half succeeded. The armed forces were first to achieve what the spiritual forces deem unwise, inexpedient, and infeasible. If I were a student I would feel shamefaced as a picket in front of Kress when my church maintained a segregated Christ.

RALPH L. MOELLERING

Ralph L. Moellering, *Christian Conscience and Negro Emancipation* (Philadelphia: Fortress Press, 1965), p. 101. Reprinted by permission.

A White Christ

"We're not trying to tell these people that Jesus was a Negro. Historically, this is not true. We are trying to establish an ethnic identity with Christ.

"The Negroes have been deprived of so much by the white people and they have been presented with a white Christ. Some day, I hope, it won't make any difference to them that Christ is white.

"But now they are beginning to develop a dignity and pride in being black and they can relate to the black Christ."

FATHER RALPH CAMPBELL, North Philadelphia
(*The Philadelphia Inquirer*, March 9, 1968)

"Anyway, the whole problem of racism boils down to this: if the Church was really doing its job, the phenomenon of racism would have disappeared a long time ago."

FATHER GROPPI, Milwaukee
(*Ramparts,* November, 1967)

Who Would Be Black?

If an American, because his skin is dark, cannot eat lunch in a restaurant open to the public, if he cannot send his children to the best public school available, if he cannot vote for the public officials who represent him, if, in short, he cannot enjoy the full and free life which all of us want, then who among us would be content to have the color of his skin changed and stand in his place? Who among us would then be content with the counsels of patience and delay?

JOHN F. KENNEDY

From a nationwide televised address by the late President in June of 1963.

Superior Uncle Toms

Poor Uncle Tom: his posthumous destiny has been even more cruel and unjust than his fictional one. Over the years his very name has become a synonym for servility and cowardice, so that for any Negro now to be branded "an Uncle Tom" is to suffer a public humiliation of the most devastating kind. In fact, this process has gone so far—and the new orthodoxy is now so firmly established—that no one any longer seems aware of the enormous irony of it all. . . .

Something tells me that I had better make it clear, at this point, that I believe the Negro's struggle for civic equality to be absolutely just, and the use of militant methods in this struggle

Irving Kristol, in *Harper's Magazine,* February, 1965, pp. 95–96. Copyright © by Harper's Magazine, Inc. Reprinted by permission of the author.

to be perfectly legitimate. What does worry me is the kind of self-defeating fanaticism that this kind of struggle almost inevitably generates. It is right that the Negro should wish to be equal, in all respects, to the white man. But something has gone wrong if Negroes—and their white liberal allies—seem unable to realize that the Uncle Toms and Booker T. Washingtons were not equal to their white contemporaries only because they were superior to them.

No man can achieve an authentic equality—no man can even achieve an authentic identity—if, in the effort to do so, he denies his forefathers. That there were Negroes who, in some degree or another, approximated Uncle Tom, strikes me as something that could be a source of immense pride to Negroes—and of continual envy to whites. That today's "Negro liberation movement," in its single-minded emphasis on militant action, fails to perceive this, represents a grave weakness of that movement. It is denying to itself a historical and psychological dimension that is essential for Negro self-understanding—and for Negro self-respect.

IRVING KRISTOL, Senior Editor,
Basic Books, Inc., New York

The Cause of the Crisis

Let no one be fooled: the crisis of our cities is not caused by agitators or irresponsible malcontents. It is caused by suburbanites —good people who wish no man ill. It is caused by a social system that has created an American form of apartheid that is every bit as vicious, albeit uncodified, as that in South Africa. It is caused by us good white folk who refuse to accept anyone who looks and acts differently from the way we do—or who lives in a life-style foreign to ours. It is caused by our fear of the unknown. In other words, the crisis of our cities is caused by our failure to trust, have faith in, the God who meets us at the limit of our own understanding.

ALLAN R. BROCKWAY
(*Concern,* October 1, 1967)

Black Racism

Recently, a cross section of citizens came together under the auspices of educational television to consider the problem of race relations. What was mainly significant about the meeting was the rapidity with which the moderates were forced into virtual paralysis by black racists. The argument of the racists ran along these general lines:

"White people understand only one language—the language of violence. They are not going to let go of anything unless they are hit over the head and it is taken away from them. For more than 400 years the white man has raped our women, flogged us, forced us into slavery. We will be slaves no longer. We want what is ours in the world and we know there is only one way to get it— by force, the way the white man got it from us. We don't want the white man's help, we don't need his help. We know what we can expect from him. If we're going to make it, we've got to make it on our own. We will run the world. So, white man, get out of the way. We're on the move and we won't be stopped."

It was heady stuff and it fixed the mood of the meeting. Most of the young people cheered; they had heard a call to arms and they were manning the battle stations. But what was most significant and disquieting was the effect on the moderates, black and white. It was almost as though they feared they would be regarded as spineless backsliders if they were to challenge the racists. The few blacks who tried to raise questions were hooted down as pathetic Uncle Toms. The whites, mostly women, all seemed to feel the need to precede anything they said by declarations of commitment to the cause of civil rights; they clearly reflected an inability to be relevant to what was happening.

This recent experience is not unique. More and more, leadership in the struggle for civil rights is gravitating to the racist, violence-prone extremists. The effect on some moderates is to cause them to abandon their own position, lest they be cast aside altogether or made to seem supine. Responsible Negro leaders like

Norman Cousins's editorial in *Saturday Review*, September 30, 1967. Reprinted by permission.

Martin Luther King, Roy Wilkins, Whitney Young, and Edward Brooke are being denounced as temporizers. Men of this character and stature are not going to abandon their convictions, but they are being thrown increasingly on the defensive. Young white activists who have gone into the Negro ghettos to-tutor or teach or attempt to upgrade living conditions are being reviled.

Civil rights supporters in general are reluctant to stand up to the black racists because they do not wish to be aligned, however vaguely or unfairly, with the opponents of full economic and political rights for the Negro. But it is important nonetheless to recognize today that black racists are among the main enemies of basic progress in the field of civil rights. When Negroes act like Ku Klux Klanners, they must be treated like Ku Klux Klanners.

There is no contradiction between militant support of civil rights and saying no to the black racists. Indeed, reluctance to confront the black racists serves to retard, not advance, progress in the field of civil rights. It is absurd for whites to withdraw or retire from the field out of confusion or intimidation. For the moderates have not run out of options, at least not yet. There is much that can be done. The men mentioned earlier—Martin Luther King, Roy Wilkins, Whitney Young, and Edward Brooke—need far more support from the white community than they are now receiving. Men on the firing line, like President Frank Rose of the University of Alabama, who are accepting the challenge of integration, should be encouraged.

It is a mistake to take the view that the positions and policies of black racists must be condoned because of the long history of abuse of the American Negro. Sustained, massive social injustice produces revolutionists. This is a truism made luminous by men like Thomas Jefferson and Thomas Paine. But just proclaiming himself a revolutionary doesn't win a man immunity from the consequences of violent nonsense.

Much has to be done. A vast upgrading is needed and needed soon in housing, education, health care, and job opportunities. The American business community has yet to put as much of its resources and facilities as are available into the strengthening of American society. Too many labor unions are feudal and bigoted in their attitudes about universal membership. In the community at large, there is still inadequate comprehension of the basic requirements of respect and dignity that are natural to human life.

One thing is certain, however: dangerous fools are not competent to lead the fight for civil rights in the United States. That fight will be won—not because of the racists, but despite them.

NORMAN COUSINS

After the Lost Weekend

Not since the Civil War has this country experienced an epidemic of domestic violence so widespread as it was this weekend. The looters and arsonists who rampaged through the streets of Washington, Chicago and other cities disgraced the memory of Dr. Martin Luther King and mocked the principles for which he stood. These criminals burned down their neighbors' homes and ransacked the stores serving the black ghettos, thus victimizing thousands of Negroes who were left homeless or deprived of normal facilities for obtaining food and other necessities.

But it is important for all Americans to understand that it was only an infinitesimal minority of this nation's Negroes who participated in this mindless debauch. For every Stokely Carmichael seeking to fan the flames of destruction, there were hundreds of thousands of Negroes who worked hard and effectively to cool passions and to prevent or to end violence. Grim as was this lost weekend, it would have been unimaginably more dreadful if it had not been for the massive contribution of responsible Negroes— acting in the spirit of Dr. King's life work—to the maintenance of law and order.

The great majority of this country's black people stood aloof from or actively resisted the forces of anarchy that sought to capture the American Negro community these past few days. This is eloquent testimony that, despite past setbacks and disappointments, the majority still believes America's democratic institutions can and will satisfy the justified demands of the Negro people.

An editorial in *The New York Times,* April 6, 1968. © 1968 by The New York Times Company. Reprinted by permission.

In the wake of Dr. King's martyrdom and its painful immediate consequences, the imperative task is to make these hopes reality. The need is for quick passage of legislation which will insure full civil rights, including open housing, for American Negroes. There must also be legislation appropriating the large sums required for a realistic attack on the unemployment, bad housing, semi-literacy and other ills afflicting millions in the ghettos. Congress bears the heaviest share of the responsibility and opportunity, but the legislatures of the states—from New York to California— whose cities are caught in today's great urban crisis must also act rapidly. No one who has lived through the past few days can have any doubts about the alternative if the surviving hope and faith are betrayed once again.

Black Power and White Liberalism

One of the primary troubles with black power is white liberalism. Black power doctrine challenges and in some cases refutes every tenet of the faith in which most whites have fought the so-called "civil rights" or "integration" battles of the last fifteen years, and that is one of the major reasons why so many of these whites have muted or abandoned their efforts.

Are you a Southerner who risked livelihood and community status to advocate integrated schools? Black separatists will tell you that "separate but equal" schools are what they want, assuming that they truly are equal. Merely to state this idea obviously refutes point-by-point the contention of the Supreme Court of 1954 that separate schools for the two races are inherently unequal.

The Old Beliefs

Are you careful how you pronounce "Negro"? Better say "black people," anyway. And don't worry any more about suggesting that black people have more rhythm than whites; they are proud of it. Do you think segregated white churches are shameful on the face

Tom Wicker, in *The New York Times,* February 15, 1968. © 1968 by The New York Times Company. Reprinted by permission.

of it? Black power theorists believe that the black church, which has been let alone to thrive and grow in its own way, is as a result the strongest of all black institutions. . . .

In fact, it may be the flat assertion of black identity, and the uncompromising demand for white recognition of it and respect for it, that offer something like a racial *modus vivendi* in America. If so, that would be more than the integration movement could achieve, and better than anything else now in view.

TOM WICKER

"Guerrillas are arming themselves around the country. While they're not Communist, they're lining up with Communists—using their methods, training and techniques.

"I've talked to black nationalist leaders, and they admit they're lining up."

GEORGE ROMNEY, Governor of Michigan
(*The New York Times,* February 17, 1968)

What Freedom Means

As in many revolutions, *freedom* has assumed a definition special to the situation. Freedom for protesting Negro Americans means a complete casting off of the inferior role of "Negro"; it means the cessation of all of the disabilities traditionally placed upon black skin by American society. It means the stilling of self-hatred. Freedom also means an end to claims of white superiority, to dire poverty, to the social conditions permitting inflated rates of disease and inadequate medical care, low intelligence test scores, and heightened crime rates. Freedom means, in short, the right to participate fully in American society with the dollars and dignity of other Americans.

THOMAS F. PETTIGREW

Forty Years More

"It's [the situation in Memphis] not bad at all. If the Negro ministers would tend to their ministering instead of trying to stir things up, we wouldn't have had this trouble.

"Nothing can be done about this situation. It's going to take maybe 40 years before we make any real progress. You can't take these people and make the kind of citizens out of them you'd like."

THOMAS W. FAIRES, President,
Memphis Chamber of Commerce

Psycho Niggers

WHY DO YOU NIGGER EDUCATORED (MISFITS) KEEP YAPPING ABOUT WHAT THE PSYCHO NIGGERS ARE GOING TO DO TO WHITEY IF WHITEY DOESN'T GIVE THESE PSYCHO NIGGERS THE COUNTRY WITH A FENCE AROUND IT? DO YOU REALLY BELIEVE THAT 22 MILLION LAZY GOOD-FOR-NOTHING PSYCHO NIGGERS COULD KILL 180 MILLION WHITE AMERICAN? OR, IS THIS THREAT O VIOLENCE THE BIGGEST BLACKMAIL SCHEME EVER FOIST UPON (WHAT YOU NIGGERS BELIEVE) A NAIVE PEOPLE. WHEN YOU PSYCHO NIGGERS START BURNING WHITEY'S HOMES—RAPING WHITEY'S WOMEN AND KILLING WHITEY YOU PSYCHO NIGGERS WILL FIND OUT THAT WHITEY IS NOT THE WHITEY THAT YOU PSYCHO NIGGERS THINK THAT HE IS.

YOU PSYCHO NIGGERS WOULD WISH THAT YOUR ANCESTORS NEVER LEFT AFRICA. BY THWAY WHY DON'T YOUR PSYCHO NIGGERS GO BACK TO AFRICA? IS IT BECAUSE IN AFRICA YOU WILL BE JUST ANOTHER NIGGER? THE NIGGERS WILL NEVER INTEGRATE WITH THE WHITE PEOPLE IN THIS COUNTRY, BECAUSE 99% OF THE WHITE PEOPLE DON'T BELIEVE IN MISCEGENATION. THEY DON'T WANT THEIR DESCENDANTS NIGGERIZED—FOREVE TAKEN OUT OF THE WHITE RACE.

IN CONCLUSION—I WOULD SAY TO YOU STUPID PSYCHO NIGGERS
—YOU HAVE BEEN BRAINWASHED WITH YOUR OWN PROPAGANDA
—22 MILLION LAZY GOOD-FOR-NOTHING NIGGERS PSYCHO NIGGERS
KILLING 180 MILLION WHITE AMERICAN.
HOW SICK CAN YOU PSYCHO NIGGERS GET?

Anonymous Letter Addressed to C. Eric Lincoln

What White America Must Do

On the whole, the massive report by the National Advisory Commission on Civil Disorders is a brave and basic document—far better than progressive Americans, white or black, had expected. It even drew a hopeful response from Black Power spokesmen. Yet the aftereffect of reading the commission's historic indictment of white racism as the "fundamental" cause of Negro rioting, and its detailed (too familiar) description and (bigger but still familiar) prescriptions for steps to alter ghetto conditions, is a terrible letdown. Where do we go from here?

The crucial question remains unanswered: What can be done to prevent recurrent rioting and even open rebellion? The commission's proposals provide a blueprint for comprehensive action on causes. But they do not tell us what should be done *now* to reduce the possibilities of bloodshed in the cities this summer. Nor does the report detail the causes of or prescribe cures for the underlying erosive factor of racism.

A timebomb is ticking in the cities. Tensions, resentment, and militancy grow among Negroes who are cynical about a national government that has cut back such essential programs as the youth Job Corps and training, and about local governments that have done nothing since last summer except beef up their police arsenals. The commission has handed the country a laundry list of unexceptionable programs so massive and manifold that action on all but a few before summertime is clearly impossible.

Jeanne R. Lowe, in *Saturday Review*, March 16, 1968, pp. 26–27. Reprinted by permission.

We can do virtually nothing between now and June to win the war on poverty, or to undo the multiple burdens of discrimination and segregation detailed by the commission. What is possible, and what must be done, is to buy a little time by giving substance to the faith that the majority of Negroes still have in this country through a major demonstration of our commitment to new national priorities and full equality.

We must take immediate dramatic steps, backed up by the most effective legislative programs, to close the credibility gap that steadily pushes black America further away from white America and breeds violence.

Whitney Young of the Urban League is right in declaring that the Negro problem has been studied to death and that the time has come, instead, to study the problems of white America. For as Swedish social economist Gunnar Myrdal found so clearly some twenty years ago in his study of the Negro in America, "the Negro problem is predominantly the white man's problem," and, "All our attempts to reach scientific explanations of why the Negroes are what they are and why they live as they do regularly led to determinants on the white side of the race line."

For generations, Myrdal wrote in *An American Dilemma,* the majority of Negroes, although subordinated and suffering the consequences of the failure of America to live up to its creed of equality, justice for all, and the essential dignity of man, were "under the spell of the national suggestion." The summertime riots indicate that the new, young, urbanized and more educated Negro has fallen out of the spell; he has lost faith.

What can America do *now*—between now and June? To begin with, we can certainly stop debating spending priorities between Vietnam versus the cities, and a tax increase versus inflation, as though these were the only alternatives. Doubtless a tax increase will be needed, but within the proposed current federal budget the Administration and Congress can cut back major nonessential, nondefense spending and divert billions into crash programs for cities. This shifting of funds and priorities will demonstrate to black America that this country means what it says. Money can be available if we:

Cut back a good part of the several billions that are paid annually to farmers and growers for keeping land out of cultivation and for price supports. As it is, little of this farm payments program fights rural poverty.

Shelve plans to build the SST. The prospect of flying Americans from New York to London in an hour and a half is of far less importance than moving Negroes into the mainstream of American life.

Divert large sums from the moonshot. By postponing this effort in order to repay a long overdue debt to the American Negro, we will do far more to enhance our world prestige.

Slow down the crash program for urban highway construction. The temporarily unfinished highways can serve as visible monuments at the entrances to cities of our nation's unfinished business. As it is, proposed routes only threaten to wipe out the homes of poor Negroes who have no place else to go. And these "freeways" are a mocking reminder of the Negro's immobility in metropolis, while the white suburbanite moves freely.

With money thus saved, Congress should enact and fund several major programs that will do the most the soonest for the people living in ghettos:

A major rent supplement program to allow hundreds of thousands of slum dwellers to move into existing standard private housing at decent occupancy standards. It seems impossible—based on past performance—to build any part of 600,000 new publicly assisted units this coming year; only a fraction of 6,000,000 are possible in five years.

A massive work-study-training program for at least half a million youths, tied in to urban and rural rehabilitation projects, to direct their frustrated energies and hopes into constructive, meaningful work that will give a stake, as well as a part, in improving their environment.

Give Negro youth hope of a fair chance in the job market if they study and train by putting major federal funds into staffing the Equal Employment Opportunity Commission and making our civil rights laws a reality.

Let a Negro's dollar buy housing wherever he can afford it, and without the "color tax," by enactment of a strong federal open housing law with full enforcement power and staff to back it up. (The commission soft-pedaled the severe effect of the discriminatory housing market on the whole complex of forces affecting the Negro's chances.)

Enact an emergency summer-school program to pay the salaries of teachers, for operation of schools and even busing of children, to give remedial instruction to youngsters who are falling behind in class.

What can we do—indeed, what must we do—to cure the "fundamental cause" of our so-called Negro problem: white racism?

Unless each white American can honestly examine himself and admit his blame for racist behavior patterns and come to see that the current crisis is the product of a failure in human relations and the practice of democracy—unless we can recognize these things and start doing something to change them—we will never root out the basic illness that corrodes our society.

We must listen to the militant Negro American's critique of American society and of individual white Americans' conduct toward blacks; see how he perceives our practice of "democracy," "equality," and "human dignity." Read books that explain the false basis of race pride and prejudice and white superiority. We must be willing to reexamine, rewrite, and start teaching correctly to both adults and children the history of the Negro in America as it really is, and of white conduct toward the Negro. We must come to see that the reason the Negro American has less than his share of the goods of America is because white America has systematically (if sometimes unconsciously) excluded him, and then alter this system. We must make an effort to expose ourselves to the actual conditions of life for ghettoized Americans, and endeavor to help them help themselves to change things. White Americans must learn to know black Americans as fellow men and women.

Unless we also do these things that cost not money but human effort, no amount of money will help. If we begin, we may win the wars that we are now losing both at home and abroad.

JEANNE R. LOWE

It is time now to turn with all the purpose at our command to the major unfinished business of this nation. It is time to adopt strategies for action that will produce quick and visible progress. It is time to make good the promises of American democracy to all citizens—urban and rural, white and black, Spanish-surname, American Indian, and every minority group.

THE KERNER REPORT

Beliefs We Did Not Practice

One of the causes, we must now see, as if for the first time, is that we as a nation and as a society, have not taken seriously the things we say we believe. We have enshrined the Declaration of Independence, the Constitution, and the Bill of Rights in the National Archives, but we have continued to ignore their grand principles in all of the practical ways. We have talked about our religious commitments and then exploited them for our own interest.

JOHN P. ADAMS
(Concern, October 1, 1967)

Who Wants Integration?

The belief that "integration" is the solution to "the racial question" has been dominant in American opinion outside the South, especially among intellectuals and publicists, for a generation, and official doctrine since 1954. Mainstream dialogue concerning racial issues assumes the ideal of integration and debates only subsidiary questions of timing and method. But surely events compel us to

From *National Review* (150 East 35th Street, New York, N.Y. 10016), August 22, 1967, p. 887. Reprinted by permission.

re-examine the root concept itself. The facts seem to prove that the mass of the population, black as well as white, does not want integration in practice, whatever some may say in theory. They do not want it, and they find ways to evade or avoid it. . . .

Nor is it whites only who reject integration. We are learning . . . if we had not known it before, that many Negroes reject integration even more wholly than any whites. "Black Power" is not an integrationist slogan.

This country is not exceptional. In truth, though there are a few countries without racial troubles—mostly those composed of one race only—there is no country with genuine racial integration. Moreover, as Daniel Moynihan and Nathan Glazer showed in *Beyond the Melting Pot,* in the United States there has not taken place a full integration even of the diverse ethnic strains among the whites.

The American idea of integration, conceptually at any rate, is the opposite of the South African idea of apartheid. Both concepts are interpreted as *total* and *coercive.* For South Africa, the races are to be required by law and force to operate along separate lines in all dimensions: to live, eat, love, vote, play, learn, work separately (though in practice this last provision cannot be strictly maintained). For the United States, law and force will require that there shall be *no* separateness, *no* discrimination or distinction between the races in any dimension: not in housing, schooling, voting, eating, marrying, holding office, playing, traveling. Surely these opposite extremes—mirror images, really—do not exhaust the alternatives.

"We have demonstrated that we, as a church, are part of the problem. We are part of the sickness . . . We are now in a moment of passing grace that God has given to us. We must use it quickly."

THE RIGHT REVEREND JOHN E. HINES,
Presiding Bishop, The Episcopal Church

Civil Rights and a UN Police Force

The place of the "civil rights" movement in the Communist drive to take over the United States has been clear since 1928. All of the present developments were projected in Communist pamphlets of instruction issued in 1928 and 1934, and reaffirmed by numerous official meetings and publications since. The Negroes were to be considered as an *oppressed colonial* people. They were to be agitated, propagandized, frightened, and coerced into an increasing appearance of at least tacit support for the riots created and conducted by professional revolutionaries—and for the still more "revolutionary" developments which were then to follow. . . .

As a more comprehensive aspect of this development, the Communists will demand that their rioting gangs be given the status of an "army of national liberation," with some "provisional government" of a Negro Soviet Republic soon demanding "recognition" and "negotiations." Whether or not they will actually follow through, in trying to set up such a "liberated" separate nation within the present boundaries of the United States, or will merely use that uncompleted drive for its help in taking over the whole country, we have no idea, because the Communists themselves have wavered back and forth on that point since the middle 1950's. But in the meantime the pretense of a "revolution" for "freedom" on the part of the Negroes—even though ninety percent of the American Negroes want no more to do with it than did ninety percent of the Moslem Arabs in Algeria—will have served many vital Communist purposes.

It will be an excuse for the establishment of a *national* police force, responsible only to the central government in Washington. This national gendarmerie will be so handled as to allow the riots plenty of time to get well under way before proper measures are taken to stop them. And if this "police force" consists primarily, in actual practice, of army detachments, the procedure will greatly aid the claim of the agitators that they are not engaged in rioting, but in fighting a *war* against an *army*.

Robert Welch, "This Is It," in *American Opinion*, March, 1968, pp. 10–11. Reprinted by permission.

There will follow an increasingly widespread destruction of property; a constant repetition of more numerous murders; the breakdown of civil law and of normal police protection; the recurrent establishment of curfews and of martial law; the constant fear of attacks and of vandalism; the confusing maze of hatreds engendered; the gradual realization that our government is actually on the side of the "revolutionaries"; and the planted but growing demands that a United Nations police force be "requested" and brought in to restore peace on American soil.

> ROBERT WELCH, John Birch Society

I'll Be Damned and Hanged

I am not an advocator of violence. I am not an advocator of overthrowing our government, or the Constitution of the United States. But I'll be damned and hanged if I'll stand by and watch our city get burned, looted, and robbed, and whatnot, while the politicians and the Supreme Court are passing laws making it more and more possible for these black radical animals to exist, and to let the Communists into this country.

> ANTHONY IMPERIALE, President,
> North Ward Citizens Committee,
> Newark, New Jersey

Carmichael as Robespierre

When the Negro movement has completely superseded the old coalition, the Thermidorian reaction will have arrived. In the meantime, we must go through a (hopefully) short Jacobin period with Stokely Carmichael apparently playing the role of Robespierre.

From "Letters to the Editor," in *Commentary,* January, 1967, p. 8. Reprinted by permission.

Perhaps liberals (both black and white) should not be overly sad that the open, creative, Girondist stage of the Negro revolution is over. Had we had history in mind, we would have known that the spirit of the early 60's could not last.

But of course we were hoping for much more from the Negro revolution, a transformation of the whole American way of life. Unfortunately, Negroes will not bring this regeneration about. Contrary to the unspoken but implicit hopes of liberals, Negroes are no better than white men, and no different.

Those who want this redemptive transformation will have to look for a new revolution. Where? Perhaps Stokely Carmichael has indicated the answer when he suggested that liberals concentrate on changing the white community.

Martin Luther King's open housing marches in Chicago have laid bare the depths of hatred prevalent among certain white ethnic groups. These people have rioted, but nobody seems to care why. . . . Perhaps liberals should find out what these second-generation ethnic groups are afraid of, what they want. Perhaps if we did something about their fears and their needs, we could accomplish some real victories in open housing. . . .

In the present, Jacobin phase of the Negro revolution, white liberals should not feel intimidated by Negro leaders who tell them to get out. We should speak our minds, but preferably *to* Negroes, rather than *about* them in publications of mass white circulation.

PETER B. DENISON
Somerset, Massachusetts

The Strangled Cry

The nation is appalled by the murder of Martin Luther King, but it is not appalled by the conditions of his people. It grieves for the man, but not for his cause. This is the curse and tragedy of America.

At least the extremists have kept their promises. The white

James Reston, in *The New York Times,* April 7, 1968. © 1968 by The New York Times Company. Reprinted by permission.

racists said they would kill King, and the black racists said they would burn us to the ground. And we will not hear again that strangled cry or the rolling Biblical cadences of that magnificent voice; and the smoke is drifting this weekend through the cherry blossoms by the Jefferson Memorial, and the rest of us have not kept our promises to the Negro people.

The Real Crime

This is the real crime of which the assassination of Dr. King is but a hideous symbol. It will not be redeemed by the capture of the murderer. It can only be redeemed by the transformation of the lives of the Negro people, and even now America has not faced up to the cost of this historic debt.

When President Johnson's riot commission surveyed the results of the twenty major outbreaks of racial violence recently, it reached the conclusion that, despite all the turmoil and the efforts of many concerned citizens and officials, the main reaction in the ghettos of Los Angeles, Detroit, Cleveland, New York and the other trouble spots was that "nothing much changed—one way or the other."

The Balanced Costs

When Gunnar Myrdal, the Swedish social philosopher who has followed the Negro problem in America for forty years, came back here recently, he felt that a great deal had changed for the better, but concluded that we had greatly underestimated the scope of the Negro problem. It would take a revolution in white attitudes, and twenty years, and "trillions of dollars" to deal with it, he felt, and the cost of not dealing with it would in the long run be much more.

The revolution in the white attitudes is probably the main thing. Neither the Congress nor the Court will solve it. President Johnson may appeal to the conscience of the nation and get another civil rights bill passed, and that may help some, but it is not the answer.

For the problem is not that the Congress is unrepresentative of the American people on the question of jobs and open housing for Negroes, but that it is representative. It may even be ahead of the people. Even if the war in Vietnam ended this month, the chances of getting Congress in its present mood to transfer the war appropriations to the ghettos would be extremely remote, and the reasons are fairly clear.

Despite the progress of the last decade in Negro education, jobs and housing, the evidence is that a majority of the people are opposed to open housing and many other Negro demands for an equal and integrated society; and while Negro violence may produce concessions, it is rapidly reaching the point where it will produce fear and counterviolence that could reverse the trend toward a more compassionate society.

One of the many tragedies of Dr. King's death is that it has silenced the most eloquent Negro voice for nonviolent protest and tipped the balance toward the black nationalists who call for war and guns. Here the need is for the transformation of the attitudes of the young Negro militants and their hoodlum gangs. For there is a violent strain in the American people, and if the black arsonists carry the torch from the ghettos to the white communities, it will take more than troops to quell the bloody reaction.

At this critical point, therefore, the leaders of every community —all of them, black and white, labor and management, educational and religious—will have to mobilize to deal with their local situation, whatever it is. The revolution will not be contained by Federal or state officials and appropriations alone, or even by local mayors, and fortunately we now have the beginnings of a structure for doing just this through the Urban Coalition led by John Gardner, the former Secretary of Health, Education and Welfare.

Further Polarization

For this is not a problem of government alone, but of American attitudes and assumptions. There was an outcry from some quarters when the President's riot commission suggested that we were moving toward two separate nations, one white and the other black. But the fact is that for most white and black people in the North, this is already a fact, and violence on both sides will merely hasten the process.

The evidence is plain before our eyes. For violence, while it can destroy indifference, which is the curse of the moderate middle class, cannot choose. It destroys good as well as evil. Brute coercion and savage intolerance of the Negro must be destroyed, but they cannot be burned away by raging demons intoxicated with illusion.

JAMES RESTON

Opposed but Respected

I am a Southerner from Baltimore and a segregationist, who many times marched for freedom of choice. I once marched against the tactics of the late Dr. King.

I have seen much as far as civil rights marches are concerned, and I have seen hate on both sides. I disliked Martin Luther King Jr. for his ideas—ideas such as his proposed "Poor Peoples' March on Washington" and his forced "open housing" tactics. I never really believed he was all he seemed to be, yet when I heard about his murder I couldn't believe it.

Whoever killed him was blind to the fact that murder solves nothing. And with a leader such as Dr. King, his killing could do harm to nonviolence. I deplore assassins. They are sick people. I did not like Dr. King, but even as a segregationist I must pay respect to his memory. He was brave, and even if I disagreed with him I believe that he thought his way of life—integration—was best. I respected his right of choice and of thought.

RAYMOND RICK NIELSEN, New York
(*The New York Times,* April 8, 1968)

Society's Laws

I sat for hours, stunned and horrified, as I watched and listened to the reports and reactions to the murder of Martin Luther King.

The horror that overwhelmed and sickened me came as essentially platitudinous, irrelevant expressions of regret rolled through my living room from the mouths of politicians and the other national "leaders."

And then this morning a neighbor summed it all up neatly for me. "Act of a madman," he said as he set out to perform his rituals for the day with his customary complacency.

This was not a madman's act. It was the controlled, deliberate, premeditated action of each and every one of us who like the "good Germans" have sat by day after day, week after week, year after year, until the shot was fired.

It is not men's hearts that need change. It is society's laws which need change and society's money which must be voted at once to begin to bring to an end the racist conditions under which we all live.

Not eulogies, not memorials, but serious legislation tied to appropriations in whatever sums necessary, whatever taxes necessary to make clear, unmistakably clear, to all that we are determined to rebuild our country and provide the conditions of life in which all men can be truly free.

To rebuild America would be truly for the good of all, white and black alike, for in solving our "racial" problems we solve all the great problems confronting our country. We rebuild our cities, clean our rivers and air, untangle our congested streets and roads, provide the health and educational services so desperately short of manpower and adequate funds.

To do less is truly to consign our country and our lives to unmitigated chaos and destruction.

MARC STONE, New York
(*The New York Times,* April 8, 1968)

"It's too bad [Dr. King was murdered]. It should have been Rap Brown."

A YOUNG GIRL, Long Beach, California

Parity, Not Preferment

Unfortunately there are, in the ranks of men and women genuinely committed to racial justice, some who insist that unanimity of purpose requires uniformity of plan. They insist that whites and

Kyle Haselden, in *The New York Times Magazine*, October 6, 1963. © 1963 by The New York Times Company. Reprinted by permission.

Negroes who share their objective also adopt their methods—however unruly, eccentric and impractical those methods—or accept vilification for Uncle Tomism. This absolutist, autocratic spirit believes that justice for the Negro is the ultimate criterion of all human action and that this end validates any means, whatever practicality or religious principle may dictate to the contrary.

This is a dangerous mood. It divides those who seek justice for Negroes; it alienates influential moderates unnecessarily; and, most serious, this authoritarian spirit lures the Negro into activities which corrupt his purpose and defeat his ultimate hope.

In the struggle for racial justice a technique is not valid simply because it annoys the white man or because it promises some temporary advantage to the Negro. It is valid only if it honors the moral ground on which the Negro makes his claim for justice, respects the right of all men to the same justice, preserves in the human relationship values which are equivalents of justice, and promotes rather than prevents the Negro's progress.

The idea of compensation, which has been suggested as a device to equalize competition between whites and Negroes, fails these crucial tests. By compensation—in the passive rather than the active sense—is meant compensation *for* the Negro rather than *by* the Negro. It has been proposed that the Negro cannot succeed in his search for freedom and equality unless there is an arbitrary—in fact, artificial—removal of the academic, cultural and professional lag forced upon him by over two centuries of slavery and by another of exploitation. It is argued further that the Negro's years of involuntary, payless servitude established a collectible claim against the descendants of those who enslaved and exploited him.

How can this debt be paid? The proposal is that the Negro be given preference in employment wherever a vacancy occurs, a premium in salary, and a quota system guaranteeing that one-tenth of all people hired by firms, professional enterprises and industries be Negroes. Even though this proposal is obviously un-feasible, what shall we say of it as a theory?

Compensation must be rejected as an equalizer of competition between Negroes and whites for several reasons, all of which rest on the grounds to which the Negro appeals in his demand for freedom and equality.

First, compensation for Negroes is a subtle but pernicious form of racism. It requires that men be dealt with by society on the basis of race and color rather than on the basis of their humanity. It would therefore as a public policy legalize, deepen and perpetuate the abominable racial cleavage which has ostracized and crippled the American Negro. Racism, whoever may be its temporary beneficiary, should be eliminated from the social order, not confirmed by it.

Second, preferential economic status for Negroes would penalize the living in a futile attempt to collect a debt owed by the dead. The 20th-century white man is no more to blame for the fact that his ancestors bought and held slaves than are 20th-century Negroes for the fact that some of their ancestors captured and sold slaves. This is the ironic tragedy of exploitation. It leaves with the descendants of the exploiters a guilt they cannot cancel and with the descendants of the exploited a debt they cannot collect.

Third, a scheme which gives Negroes preference in employment and a premium in salary would bestow on Negroes the debilitating social status which has for centuries cursed the initiative and enterprise of the white man in the South. Preferred status for the Negro, however much society may owe him a debt, will inevitably destroy in him the initiative and enterprise required of a minority people in a highly competitive society. Slavery corrupts ambition and self-reliance; so, too, does patronizing social status.

Fourth, compensation for Negroes would be unfair to other minorities handicapped by their history or by rapid social and industrial change: Puerto Ricans, Mexican-Americans, migrants of all races, Indians, coal miners and others. Negroes are entirely right in demanding that they be hired, paid and promoted on their merit and in boycotting those enterprises which discriminate on a racial basis. But they are not right in demanding an artificial scheme which is unworkable, racist, destructive of initiative and unfair to other struggling Americans.

Our goal should be parity, not preferment, and there are three things we must do, none of them pleasant, none easy, if we are to attain it.

First, there must be a total, across-the-board desegregation of American society. Wherever the white man will not voluntarily surrender the psychic and material advantages of racial discrimination, the Negro must use the law, his power as a consumer, his increasing political leverage, and coercive nonviolent protests to assail and destroy the color structures of our society. . . .

Our second task . . . is to undertake a nationwide crash program for the education, training and employment of the underprivileged, underdeveloped one-fifth of the nation, a domestic Point Four which would give to the employable a fair chance and to the unemployable qualifying education and training. Such a program would be based not on race but on need. Negroes would of course be the chief beneficiaries of an educational and economic crash program, because of the predominant number of deprived Negroes. But a domestic Point Four program aimed at the needs of *all* the nation's backward peoples would close rather than widen the nation's racial cleavage.

Finally, irritating as it may be, the fact might as well be faced that no immigrant or minority group has ever made its way into the mainstream of American life without studying and working harder and longer than the general population. This is the third task as it now confronts the Negro.

During their long pilgrimage through slavery and semi-slavery, most Negroes did not have an incentive for the kind of active self-compensation by which other minorities have climbed out of humiliating servitude into respected equality with other ethnic groups. Slavery and peonage do not generally encourage ambition. Even now the Negro must divert himself—his native abilities and his acquired skills, his initiative and enterprise, his devotion and endurance, his ablest leadership—from the pursuits followed by free men to the claiming of those dignities and opportunities which are the birthright of every American citizen. Yet the hard historical fact is that self-compensation is essential if he is to escape that social substratum into which a cruel history and an arrogant, avaricious white man have coerced him.

Along with several million Caucasian Americans, most Negroes need a lift from their Government if they are to overcome the handicaps of a tragic history. More than that, however, Negroes need to throw off the white man's domination if they are to discover at last what they can do for themselves unencumbered in an open society.

KYLE HASELDEN, Editor, *The Christian Century*

Black Apartheid and the American Future

Black Apartheid has emerged as a major force in American life for the first time this summer. If it grows stronger, it could even become a threat to the persistence of a united United States.

At one level the challenge is presented by the National Conference on Black Power resolution for "starting a national dialogue on the desirability of partitioning the United States into two separate nations, one white and one black." That conference also adopted other resolutions calling in effect for beginning the organization of a black army and of a separate Negro economy, the latter based on a "buy black" movement.

At a more primitive level the same impulse is represented by the "kill Whitey" shouts of Negro rioters, by the demand of the leader of the so-called Student Non-Violent Coordinating Committee (SNCC) for what amounts to Negro war against white society, and by the words "soul brother" scrawled across Negro-owned establishments in riot-torn Newark and Detroit to protect them from black arsonists and looters.

All this comes as a shock to millions of whites of goodwill who have long believed that the essence of the Negro problem was the need to assure integration against the resistance of white racists. Now the fact must be faced that a significant fraction of American Negroes—including many of the most articulate and politically active—want integration as little as the Governors of Mississippi and Alabama. . . .

Today's Black Apartheid does not look to a return to Africa, is not primarily Communist-inspired, and extends far beyond the few hundred thousand members and sympathizers of Elijah Muhammed's sect. It is a sentiment with a base in both the Negro middle class and the Negro proletariat.

One root is simply mass Negro disillusionment. The high hopes raised by the Supreme Court's 1954 school integration decision and other legal gains have not been realized. As a result, some Negroes now despair that the white community will ever satisfy

Harry Schwartz, in *The New York Times,* July 31, 1967. © 1967 by The New York Times Company. Reprinted by permission.

their aspirations and are receptive to the argument that only in a Negro nation can their condition be fundamentally improved. Meanwhile, as this turbulent summer has shown, many of the frustrated find satisfaction in violence that lets "Whitey" know the depth of their hatred.

But the other root is the wave of victorious nationalism that has swept the world these past two decades, in particular the emergence of numerous black-ruled nations in Africa and elsewhere. If Negroes can rule themselves in Ghana, Uganda or Jamaica, why should American Negroes settle for anything less? Or so, at least some calculate.

For some middle-class Negroes the idea of a black nation carved out of the United States has a special attraction. It would require a new bureaucracy. It would have jobs for Cabinet members, ambassadors, generals, mayors, school superintendents—all jobs for black men. In a black nation, Negro lawyers, doctors, engineers, architects and journalists would be protected from white competition of the type that in many cases now hinders them from achieving their ambitions. Similar sentiments, it may be recalled, made some Negro schoolteachers in the South bewail the prospect of integrated education when the Supreme Court spoke more than a decade ago.

Improving the System

To recognize that a major new political force has been set into motion is not to predict its triumph. There is not the slightest indication that even a sizable part of the Negro minority favors carving up the United States, even were it possible, which of course it is not so long as there is a white majority. And the overwhelming majority of Negroes, including many of the most bitter and the most frustrated, still look to improvement within the existing system rather than to the ordeal of trying to destroy the existing society and build a new one.

Yet the hatreds, fears and animosities unleashed this summer have worked terrible damage on relations between whites and Negroes, making more difficult than ever the integration and reconciliation the moderates on both sides want and work for. That is precisely the first goal of the black racists.

HARRY SCHWARTZ

Integration

INTEGRATION, DEGENERATION, MONGRELIZATION call it what you will is the Deliberately Forced Social Association of White People and Racially Inferior Negroes the purpose of which is Racial Intermarriage and the production of a Race of Simple Minded, Docile Mulattoes who will be obedient to their Jewish Masters.

To further their Diobolical Ends it was decided by the International Jewish Hierarchy that as the White Race would not consciously destroy itself—OUR WHITE CHILDREN WERE TO BE BRAINWASHED. The Forced Transfer of Our Young White Children to 'Schools' in Crime Infested Negro Jungles of Fear is deliberately being done with the Knowledge that these Impressionable Young Childern will pick up the Delinquency, Sexual Promiscuity and Narcotics Addiction Habits which abound where ever the Culturally Inferior Negro Lives.

Thus Brainwashing Our Young White Childern into accepting the Inferior Savage-Like Negro as equal and accelerating the delivery of our Once Great and Proud White Race and Nation to the Pagan Altar of International Jewry.

From a broadside distributed by The National States Rights Party.

Segregation and poverty have created in the racial ghetto a destructive environment totally unknown to most white Americans.

THE KERNER REPORT

The Right to Riot

"Black Power, promoted by the demagogic exhortations of Stokely Carmichael and H. Rap Brown and others of their ilk, has created a climate of unrest and has come to mean to many Negroes the right to riot, burn, loot and kill."

This was the first public statement Mr. Hoover has made on Black Power.

It has long been suspected by various analysts in Washington that the U.S. Communist Party, riddled by internal dissension, found a new rallying cause in the Black Power movement. It is also giving active support to the planning and execution of anti-Vietnam-war demonstrations. Hoover added:

"There is nothing the party leadership would like more than to see a continuation of campus disturbances and the disruption of city life by war protestors and riots in the ghettos."

J. EDGAR HOOVER,
Federal Bureau of Investigation

"Where there is trouble there are always individuals that suspicion is attached to, but I would not want to say that the protests and the demonstrations are inspired by foreign foes."

LYNDON B. JOHNSON

America Has Not Confronted Integration

"Has white America ever confronted the issue of integration?" The answer is no; the black man has been waiting for the confrontation and is beginning to shrug his shoulders in despair that the confrontation will ever take place. Separation, like the population trend discussed above, is a fact, and the black man now has little alternative but to accept it and turn it to his advantage.

The major difference between Black Power's attitude and that of the Commission on Civil Disorders is this: the commission is hopeful that America will heed its warning. If the hope is justified, then we will be able to say that Black Power, as it is expressed now, is unnecessary. But black people are not so sanguine; they tend to look to the past, as did Dr. Kenneth Clark, when he told the commission:

John R. Sullivan, in *America*, March 16, 1968, pp. 345–346. © America Press, Inc. Reprinted by permission.

"I read that report . . . of the 1919 riot in Chicago, and it is as if I were reading the report of the investigating committee on the Harlem riot of 1935, the report of the investigating committee on the Harlem riot of 1943, the report of the McCone commission on the Watts riot . . . the same analysis, the same recommendations and the same inaction." . . .

White America must accept the commission's report and do its bidding; at the same time some of us must attune our thinking to the possibility that white America will not do so, that it will continue its present course of attempting to make the world "safe for democracy" while endangering democracy at home; that it will refuse again to provide the will and the means to rescue its cities, and will leave black people to their own devices.

Those devices will follow the policies of Black Power with which we are familiar. Can white America learn to live with this situation if it will not provide the money to do otherwise? Can white America willingly end the "days of the plantation" and abolish black slavery without abolishing the black man? Can it allow black men to become equal without white "help," as they are determined to do?

If it cannot, Black Power will have been proved a failure. It must also be pointed out that America, too, will be a failure. This is the crucial test of American democracy. Yet it is inaccurate as well as futile to pin upon Black Power and its spokesmen, as some have, the charge of "threatening democracy." On the contrary, it is white America, not black, that has created the threat by limiting the choices available to black people. And it is up to white America to remove it, and to do so without violating this nation's democratic traditions, its law and its constitution, or its citizens' consciences. . . .

I think America deserves better than failure at this task. And the black man, who has given so much to America—and who has asked nothing in return but a chance to share in the fruits of his labor—deserves better than failure. For he is engaged in the ultimate bitter irony of disavowing white help and influence, while literally betting his life that white America will let him do so.

JOHN R. SULLIVAN

Some Form of Black Power

As for me, a long time before Stokely Carmichael made the scene, I concluded that it will take some form of black power, and a temporary acceptance of the separatism it implies, to organize the ghettos to utilize the new kinds and forms of public assistance they must have if the rising generation is to break out of the vicious circle that encompassed and victimized most Negroes in the course of the great migration from the pastoral South to center city.

At the same time the fight must go on to remove the last of the institutional barriers limiting the natural growth of the Negro middle class—a necessity not merely to serve the interests of its own members but to provide the white community with the applied interracial experience that remains the only effective means of eradicating the taint of individual racism.

If we can follow this course and manage to fend off the white-black polarization implied in the rhetoric of *Black Power,* we may yet attain the genuine racial integration that has always seemed to me the minimum goal of any civilized community.

HARRY ASHMORE, Director,
Fund for the Republic

Harry Ashmore, in *Center* magazine, January, 1968. Reprinted by permission of the Center for the Study of Democratic Institutions.

Racism Is Racism

[Negroes] speak with approval of racial pride—a concept which is both ludicrous and vicious. If a man need take pride in the color of his skin, it is obvious that there is nothing else he can take pride in. [They] speak with approval of a list of black activities and organizations, ignoring the fact that if "whites only" student groups are justly condemned, changing the color makes no difference. Racism is racism and consists not of condemning a certain race but of believing that such a concept as "race" has any meaning.

BYRON VON KLOCK, New Haven, Conn.

From "Letters," in *Time* magazine, December 15, 1967. Reprinted by permission.

What Black Power Means

Black Power, to most whites, is an ominous phrase and represents a desire by Negroes to dominate American society through force. Yet Black Power to many Negroes means something quite different. . . .

To them, Black Power symbolizes a desire for recognition of the basic integrity of the black community. In their view, it is not integration, but a necessary preliminary to integration—a form of separation which could set the stage for integration.

Black Power, to these Negro leaders, means more self-government by Negroes in the areas in which they live, black principals in ghetto schools, black police and black ownership of ghetto stores made possible by loans and grants so blacks can buy out the shops of white merchants.

This appears to be the approach a growing number of Negroes favor, but one of which many whites are still not aware. To many whites and even some Negroes, this philosophy may seem to be a rejection of the "integration-now" doctrine on which so much of the civil rights movement was founded. But this view of Black Power appears to be a fact which will seriously affect the future course of race relations in this country.

At a time when the nation may face another summer of civil strife in our cities, it would seem to be vital for all citizens to understand the term Black Power and its meaning for this era.

An editorial in *Newsday,* February 24, 1968. © 1968 by Newsday, Inc. Reprinted by permission.

The Myth of Black Power

Some of you who are Negro would like to excuse yourself from the beastly behavior you see all around you by believing that these are the deeds of the white man, the goddamned—the damned of God—white man; or at the least, the deeds of western man, or capitalist man. I think you can not do that. I think if we have understood aright the thoughts of the prophets and the philosophers, the great religious teachers of both East and West, if we have heard them then we must acknowledge that we—even you and I—were part of the mob that killed Cheney, Goodman, and Schwerner; that you and I helped set the charge at the Birmingham church that September morning just before you entered college; that you and I pulled the trigger on President Kennedy; that all these were the deeds of universal man, just as the Catholic Church has now been wise enough to see was the crucifixion of Jesus, and so has lifted its old curse on the Jews. The Jews did not kill Jesus of Nazareth; all men did. Just so, the Klansmen who brutally dynamited that Birmingham church were, first of all, fellow Southerners, fellow Americans, and then—brothers. It was supreme wisdom to say, there but for the grace of God go I.

For I submit to you that nowhere on earth do you find men who possess power behaving better than other men who possess power. The difference is only that some societies have learned better than others how to restrain power. Power seeks always, however, to break the restraints, and I have already commented on how Presidential power in this country is operating today, in regard to Vietnam, with no recognizable restraint. It is not color or race or economic class that has made oppressors of some human beings, but possession of power.

Those who come today talking a myth of Black Power (which, like a true myth, cannot be defined or otherwise rationally explained) are, at best, offering a kind of primitive retaliatory justice. As such, they give you and me merely another choice among all the many other available varieties of self-interest, violent politics, and irrational boasts.

LESLIE DUNBAR,
The Field Foundation

Leslie Dunbar, in *New South,* Summer, 1967, pp. 63–64. Reprinted by permission.

The Misery of the Frustrated Rat

The Negro violence was and is as predictable as the actions of the frustrated rat. It is not really the fault of these pitiful people that our cities have become jungles and places of filth and terror. The same thing would occur if we opened the zoos and turned the gorillas and tigers loose in the streets, but that would not reflect on the "evilness" of the gorillas, only on the stupidity or wickedness of the fatheads who turned such unlikely "citizens" loose upon a helpless city full of people.

All this we saw years ago, and predicted, as we now predict almost unspeakable years of terror and horror ahead, as almost *all* of the Blacks find themselves caught up in the misery of the frustrated rat, as it dawns on their primitive ganglion-minds that the White men who have so wickedly been preaching "equality" to them for short-sighted *political* reasons, especially the Jews, are *liars* and *hypocrits*.

Already, Stokely Carmichael and Floyd McKissick have seen precisely what a *fraud* the "integration" and "equal rights" movement is, and have realized that the Negro will *never* get "equal" by fiat, when biology is the problem. . . .

When Stokely Carmichael and his mobs holler "Black Power!", what they mean is nothing esoteric and complicated—it's the most primitive and simple thing on the face of the earth; the Blacks want *your* power, *your* force, *your* weapons, and the political power to use them against *you* for *their* benefit!

LINCOLN ROCKWELL
The American Nazi Party

Lincoln Rockwell, in *The Rockwell Report,* September–October, 1966, pp. 3, 5.

And if you choose to tear down what other hands have built, you will not succeed; you will suffer most from your own crimes. You will learn that there are no victors in the aftermath of violence.

LYNDON B. JOHNSON

PATRIOTIC PARTY

ALARM

Black Power Document Calls for Sniper Army   *The Detroit News*

Castro to Build Up U.S. Guerilla Force   *Newspaper headline*

Negro Maoists Plan for the Revolution   *Detroit Free Press*

CAN YOU SURVIVE THE NEXT RIOT? IT HAS ALREADY BEEN PLANNED

Next time, they will destroy all utilities, gas, water, lights, phone, and plan to murder all policemen and their families.

THE PATRIOTIC PARTY HAS PLANS TO SURVIVE, AND WIN OVER THIS INSURRECTION

STEP NO. 1—SURVIVE

When the riot starts, you can expect Martial Law which will confine you to your home for as long as a month or more. Start your survival plans *now*. If you wait for the riot to begin, you will be too late. Everything will shut down.

1. Have a gun, and plenty of ammunition. Nothing wrong with a bow and arrow.
2. At least a 30-day supply of food. You will *not* have refrigeration.
3. A supply of drinking water must be stored in jugs, bottles, barrels, etc.
4. Portable radio & flashlight and extra batteries.
5. Portable stove for heat & cooking. Fire extinguisher.
6. Walkie-talkie for neighborhood communication.
7. First-aid equipment.

WE WILL HELP YOU TO ORGANIZE

For further information, contact the Patriotic Party, 4714 Middlesex, Dearborn, Mich.

HURRY!

Getting Ready for Summer

I recall what, in the spring, one eminent journalist, who had lately worked in Mississippi, told me was on order by the Jackson Police Department: two searchlight trucks with protected lights, two hundred new tear-gas masks, two hundred new shotguns, twenty-nine new motorcycles with shotgun scabbards, three convoy trucks (military surplus) with orange covers to designate anti-riot squadron. I remember the special "nigger truck"—a tractor trailer, with steel cages. I remember the two buildings at the Fair Grounds with hog-wire on the windows. Of the expected army of voter-registration workers, Mayor Allen Thompson said: "I think we can take care of twenty-five thousand."

They were getting ready for summer.

Were they getting ready to "point the way for the whole nation?"

Robert Penn Warren

Robert Penn Warren, *Who Speaks for the Negro?* (New York: Random House, 1965), p. 66. Reprinted by permission.

Black Power and the Communists

Mr. President, the drive for Negro revolution in this country is moving toward a climax.

We have seen the pace of this drive greatly accelerated during the present year. Now we face the prospect that a climax may come in 1968.

The forces which have shaped, moulded, and influenced this drive, and which now to a very substantial extent control it, have plans which involve major racial disturbances, of riot proportions, in some 20 cities of this country next year.

These forces to which I have referred are complex in their power structure. From a tactical standpoint, their plans also are complex. Strategically, their planned objectives are not especially complicated.

The primary objective is acquisition of power by the Communists.

SENATOR JAMES O. EASTLAND,
Democrat, Mississippi

From *Congressional Record—Senate,* October 12, 1967, p. S14754.

Violence cannot build a better society. Disruption and disorder nourish repression, not justice. They strike at the freedom of every citizen. The community cannot—it will not—tolerate coercion and mob rule.

THE KERNER REPORT

People Will Not Live Like Animals

"It is time for government officials to recognize that the National Guard is no answer to the problem of slums."

"People will not live like animals. Nor should they live in some of the filthy rotten housing that makes up the urban ghettoes."

"I'd hate to be stuck on a fourth floor of a tenement with rats nibbling on the kids' toes—and they do; with garbage uncollected —and it is; with streets filthy, and with no swimming pools, with little or no recreation."

"I think you'd have more trouble than you have had already because I've got enough spunk left in me to lead a mighty good revolt under those conditions."

HUBERT H. HUMPHREY
(*The New York Times,* July 19, 1966)

Righting Old Wrongs

We whites could find the will, the know-how and the money for a
million pounds of thrust for a rocket to the moon. . . . Let's start
concentrating on finding the will, the know-how and the money for
a million pounds of thrust in righting the wrongs we have for too
long imposed on the blacks.

KATE WILKINSON, New York
(*The New York Times,* April 8, 1968)

The Prejudiced Christian

The facts are that Christian laymen, as a group, are a rather prejudiced lot. Now it is perfectly obvious that there are large numbers
of people in the churches who are not prejudiced, and for whom
Christian ethics provide an important basis for love, understanding,
and compassion. But our basic guide must be proportions, not
simply numbers, and the compassionate, unprejudiced Christians
are not in the majority. The majority of church members hold
religious and racial prejudices, and furthermore they deny the
right of the churches to challenge their prejudices. . . .

Among white Protestant and Catholic church members in California, nearly half say they would move if several Negro families
moved into their block. A third think Negroes less intelligent;
nearly half blame Communists and other radicals for racial tension.
These data were collected in 1963 before any of the riots. Undoubtedly things are worse today.

This brings us to a final point about the contemporary Christian
church member. Not only does he differ sharply from the official
church and the clergy on the matter of his prejudice, he strongly

Charles Y. Glock and Rodney Stark, in *The New York Times,* March 31,
1968. © 1968 by The New York Times Company. Reprinted by permission.

opposes the role being played by the churches to overcome prejudice. Thus, 70 per cent of the laity in [a] study [by the National Opinion Research Center] denounced clerical involvement in social issues, such as civil rights. Indeed, data from a variety of recent studies indicate that the majority of laymen want the church to stick to tending the private religious needs of its members and to stay out of such questions as peace, justice and human rights. . . .

The official churches have failed to reach those people who ought to be most available to them, the people who are actually in the pews listening to the sermons . . . the new interpretations which seek to accommodate the tension between the belief that Christianity possesses unique and higher truth and the religious status of non-Christians have not been given simple, understandable expression. Until this is accomplished, the present situation is likely to endure.

A free-will image of man lies at the root of Christian prejudice toward Negroes and of their negative attitudes toward the civil rights movement and church and governmental efforts to improve the situation of the Negro minority. The simple fact seems to be that a great many church people, because of their radical free-will image of man, think that Negroes are themselves mainly to blame for their present misery . . . one is almost forced to wonder if these Christians are afraid to have Negroes as neighbors for fear that then they would have to love them.

CHARLES Y. GLOCK
AND RODNEY STARK

The Shape of a New "Confession"

Four hundred white men, women, and teen-agers marched in four predominantly white suburbs west of Chicago today in what was described as a confession of white racism.

The Good Friday march through Oak Park, River Forest, Maywood, and Melrose Park was sponsored by the Lutheran Human Relations Commission here. The commission's director, The Rev. George Hrbek, explained:

"We are simply confessing our white racism. We believe the Kerner [riot] Commission is correct in stating that racism in white communities is the cause of the racial crisis and we hope to dramatize this by our march and stimulate constructive action."

Among marchers were representatives of Protestant, Roman Catholic and Jewish faiths. There were no hecklers, and the march attracted few spectators. . . .

THE NEW YORK TIMES
(April 12, 1968)

Cataclysmic Confrontation

"The white liberal and the middle-class Negro prevent friction between white and black America. This is precisely what the black nationalist does not want. He wants friction. He wants a direct, cataclysmic confrontation."

BERTRAM H. GOLD
(*The New York Times,* December 2, 1967)

Who's Going to Pay for Black Power?

I asked myself how the Black Power advocates plan to pay for their own community. That these people should want their own identity and culture is admirable; that they should be willing to work and plan toward that end is most commendable and I wish them the best.

If, however, their plans include Federal aid for their endeavor, my sentiments would be against them. If the black people of this country want their own community and identity as much as they say they do, they should want no part of Federal funds from white Americans.

W. GARRETT MCDANIEL
Old Greenwich, Conn.
(*The New York Times,* February 24, 1968)

"I don't hate niggers. They love me and I love them, and I've played with them ever since I was young. I just don't like their program."

BILL SCOTT, Fayette, Mississippi
(quoted in *The Harvard Crimson,* October 20, 1967)

White Violence

Now that black people have suffered another great tragedy in the long history of violence against them by whites, all our political leaders have raised pious voices against possible black violence. Again the victims are told that any retaliatory violence or law-breaking would be unjustified.

It certainly would be ill-advised, with the might of America poised to crush them. The police, even when acting with restraint, know that their job is to preserve law and order, no matter what kind of an order our racist country has developed. White people cower in their homes, with visions of "the black hordes" dancing in their heads.

It may be true that Dr. King would not have asked his own people, for whom he lived, to rise up when they could not win—not in this country, where violence has always been a white man's prerogative. Not where nonviolence has been the only weapon the black man could use without a complete onslaught of white power as the response to his rightful grievance.

But he would have understood, and from him words of gentleness and peace would have been for preservation of the people he loved, not a veiled warning. This great man wanted his people to survive, but they will not fear death if that is the only place freedom lies.

So I say to my white brothers and sisters, words of nonviolence to blacks are irrelevant. And I say to our political leaders, that if the law and order they prize are to survive, direct the warnings to the perpetrators of the white violence that has gone unchecked. Ignorance, upbringing, are no excuse for such crimes against our brothers.

The assassin is our system and our mania—it was white violence that killed a man of peace, so let us tell ourselves to follow his example if what he stood for is to survive.

EVA HILL, New York
(*The New York Times,* April 10, 1968)

Nigras Are Savages

Perhaps Los Angeles will serve to convince some Northerners what most Southerners have always known—that the majority of Nigras are unstable, subhuman savages. When the riot scratched the fragile "civilized" crust of the biochemistry graduate of your article, the despoiler and murderer of the Belgian nuns in the Congo was revealed.

W. L. SHAEFER, New Orleans
(*Time* magazine, September 3, 1965)

Black District and White Fear

The awesome shame and guilt that might otherwise overwhelm millions of fair-minded and well-meaning whites in both North and South is held in check by ignorance of the shocking facts or assuaged by pernicious rationalizations. It is comforting, self-absolving, to believe that the Negro's innate shortcomings are responsible for his present condition, and hard to acknowledge that the circumstances we force him to live under may be the very cause of this condition.

From William F. Soskin, "Riots, Ghettos, and the 'Negro Revolt,'" staff paper (1964), Office of Planning, National Institute of Health. Reprinted in Kenneth Clark, *Dark Ghetto* (New York: Harper and Row, 1965), pp. 224–225.

Another fundamental that must be grasped is the magnitude of the present psychological gulf between whites and non-whites. The growing anger of the more vocal Negroes, fanned and fed by a growing impatience, comes as a surprise to whites who live comfortably and peacefully far removed from the major Negro centers. The Negro and *his* problems never impinge on their thinking, their world, their smooth running democracy. For them "sit-ins" and "stall-ins" and "freedom rides" are evidence of irresponsibility, of unreasonableness, of lawlessness, of radicalism that reinforce all the myths they have learned to believe. On the other hand, when such whites do come face to face with the Negro world they discover in themselves an entirely new response: fear. They sense the Negro's envy of the "privileged caste," they sense some of his bitterness. They see sometimes the flaring anger that injustice breeds. They realize for the first time how far most Negroes have been forced into a world apart, a world so unfamiliar to the average white that it could as well be in a foreign land. And in this alien world they discover a complement to the white man's rejection: the Negro's distrust. For the failure of the white man thus far to deal honestly and fairly with his non-white fellow citizens has bred a suspicion so deep that very few whites are ever trusted. And out of this recognition of distrust springs an unreasoned, and often unacknowledged fear. . . .

WILLIAM F. SOSKIN, Psychologist

"It is not too far off. I don't put ovens past white America for a minute. What with technology, there is just no more use for black folks, that's all."

LOU SMITH, Los Angeles
(quoted in *The Washington Post,*
September 28, 1967)

Violence and destruction must be ended—in the streets of the ghetto and in the lives of the people.

THE KERNER REPORT

"I've been waiting all my life for something like this to happen. I'm gonna make mincemeat out of some of those mother ———— while I've got the chance."

A WHITE POLICEMAN, Los Angeles

Prejudice and the State of the Union

Prejudice, apathy, and fear are still the ruling moods in large segments of white America. Congress, dominated by Southern racists and Northern Know-Nothings, has exhibited a callous indifference to the urgent need of coming to grips with the causes of conflict at home. President Johnson, obsessed as always with his war in Vietnam, has allowed his Great Society program to be whittled into a ghostly shadow of its original promise.

Given this estimate of the state of the Union, America seems rotten-ripe for revolutionary change. But there is still a chance that it can be achieved through a peaceful, democratic revolution—a revolution in our thinking, a revolution in our concept of moral values, a revolution in our balancing of national priorities, a revolution achieved through the passage of progressive programs. If we cannot achieve this kind of revolution—and it is later than we think—then we shall surely be confronted with a bloody uprising by black Americans whose pleas for peaceful revolutionary change were spurned by the Bourbons—North and South—who wield white power.

From *The Progressive,* October 1, 1967, p. 5. Reprinted by permission.

Fate of Advocates of Moderation

As we consider the consequences of the death of Martin Luther King in terms of its effect on the future of the civil rights movement, we might do well to take into account the striking similarities that exist between that movement and the working-class movement in Western Europe seventy years ago.

On the eve of World War I the working-class movement was split between those who advocated violence and revolution, refusing to cooperate even with bourgeois elements sympathetic to the workers' cause, and those who, like the great Frenchman Jean Jaurès, strove to reconcile antagonistic social groups in the belief that social justice bound all men together.

The strength and influence of each group within the movement depended upon the response of society as a whole to the depressed condition of the workers. As long as society chose to ignore or do little about this condition, the apostles of violence held the upper hand. But when society responded positively to the plight of the proletariat by means of massive doses of social legislation, such a response increased the influence of Jaurès and his followers.

Theory of Inferiority

There are those who argue that class conflict and racial conflict are very different. They should be reminded that there were many in the nineteenth century who believed that the working classes were biologically inferior. They should be reminded that black Americans have responded to their problems today in very much the same way that the working classes a hundred years ago did by taking over their own cause.

"Black power" is a concept which enables these Americans to take pride in themselves after hundreds of years of degradation as well as to move toward taking their rightful place in society. The problem is how to implement "black power."

Stokely Carmichael borrows arguments used a century ago by revolutionaries to the effect that society must be destroyed in order to be rebuilt. Martin Luther King, following in the footsteps of Jaurès, called for reconciliation between antagonistic groups and constructive but peaceful efforts to destroy prejudice.

How tragic it is that both Jaurès and King were murdered because of their belief in peaceful solutions to social and political problems. But although Jaurès died in 1914, the working classes in Western Europe and America, taking advantage of a favorable climate of opinion after World War I, were able to improve substantially their position.

Is it too much to hope that given a favorable climate of opinion and a desire for social justice shared by all Americans, the doctrine of nonviolence preached by Dr. King will prevail within the civil rights movement, and black Americans will find their rightful place in this land of plenty?

ALEXANDER SEDGWICK
Associate Professor of History, University of Virginia
(*The New York Times,* April 14, 1968)

"I don't agree with the report that it's all the fault of white racism. The people living in the slums have to improve themselves; they have to be educated."

JOE BERNAL, Santa Fe Springs, California

Basically, Black Power is black nationalism. Today, liberals want to play down nationalism, which is a "love that hates." They want instead to strengthen internationalism in sentiment and institutions.

While Black Power has many definitions, it is fair to say that actions speak louder than words. What Stokely Carmichael and S.N.C.C. were trying to do when they first raised that shout for Black Power was to set up all-Negro political parties in the few counties in Alabama where they have influence and where there was a majority of Negro voters. These all-Negro political parties have proved ineffective. They failed to elect anyone. But in the county in Alabama where there was a Negro majority and where the policy of integrating Negroes in the existing political parties —in this case the Democratic party—was followed, a Negro sheriff was elected. All-Negro political parties also are certain to provoke all-white political parties as a reaction. Nothing could be worse politically for Negroes than that.

The opposite program of integrating Negroes into the existing political parties has produced six Negro Congressmen, one Senator, a Negro Supreme Court Justice, and a Negro member of the Cabinet (the latter two a breakthrough), and a growing number of Negro state legislators (154 of them now).

Black Power thus is ineffective politically as well as reactionary, like other forms of nationalism.

They have Black Power in Nigeria, for example; and there in a few weeks more Negroes (Ibos) were lynched by other Negroes (Haussas) than have been lynched in the U.S. in the last 50 years. Power is not good or bad on the basis of the color of who exercises it but on the basis of its purpose.

ALFRED BAKER LEWIS, NAACP, New York
(*The New York Times Magazine,* October 8, 1967)

"Shouts of 'Burn, baby, burn,' 'Get whitey,' and 'Get yourselves some guns' bring on anxiety attacks in the nonwhite 'Anglo-Saxons.' Moderately successful, these people are attached to the values of white society. They are anxious lest their status be affected."

CHARLES E. WILSON,
Writer on black nationalism

"I don't think the report will change anything substantially. I see the police preparing for riots. Talk won't change things. This [report] is an idealistic attempt to solve the problem. The Negro is tired of being studied."

DON EISENBERG, California State College,
Long Beach, California

"They're a bunch of no-good black bastards, all of 'em."

A WHITE POLICEMAN,
Chicago

On Black Militant Rhetoric

The intelligent Negro looks around and he sees that despite all the marches and the demonstrations and the legislation that's been passed, the movement for equality is just inching along. He's up against a blank wall of frustration. His only outlet is stronger language. Actually, he'd be satisfied with a middle-class existence.

"I'm a Jew, and when I hear a person say, 'I'm going to Jew you down,' you can imagine how I feel. When you consider what the Negro has to go through, well, that explains why he's so angry.

"The reaction of an individual Negro can be measured by the depths of his anger, and the conditions he has to face."

SAM WHITMAN, Long Beach, California

Best Friend of Whites

I am a white Southern college student, born in Alabama and now living in Tennessee. The martyrdom of Dr. Martin Luther King Jr. has filled me with shame and fear.

I am ashamed because he was martyred in my state, that my Governor showed so little sympathy by rushing police and the National Guard to "keep order" and that Dr. King even had to come to Tennessee in the first place.

I am afraid because the white man has lost his best friend, the Negro leader who constantly urged nonviolence, trust and faith in the brotherhood of man. Too young to march in Selma and Washington, I am filled with a hopeless dread, because there is nothing I, as a white man, can do now.

The white man had his chance and blew it. May God have mercy on our souls—we certainly cannot expect the black man to.

PAUL E. THOMASON, Knoxville, Tenn.
(*The New York Times*, April 8, 1968)

"You can be certain of one thing—there is an organized effort behind all the defiance that we see in our country. We are naive, ladies and gentlemen, if we think that organized Communism is not involved in it. They are the agitators.

"[One answer people give] is that we had better give the ones who are agitating better social conditions. Now I think you've heard this many times . . . but I'd like to remind you of the teaching of History. History teaches that poverty never brings the defeat of a nation, that being poor never destroys society. Prosperity destroys. Complacency destroys. Defiance of the law will destroy, but poverty does not. . . ."

REV. WILLIAM MIEDEMA,
El Dorado Park Community Church,
Long Beach, California

This is our basic conclusion: Our nation is moving toward two societies, one black, one white—separate and unequal.

THE KERNER REPORT

"I think they should have shot every looter they saw."

INTERNAL REVENUE SERVICE WORKER,
Baltimore, Maryland

"I think it is good that they are burning some of those crappy old buildings down; maybe they'll get something decent now."

OFFICE SECRETARY,
Washington, D.C.

"I was in favor of integrated housing up until all this rioting; now I'm going to write my Senator and tell him I think no such legislation should go through until they prove they are really ready for civilization."

FILE CLERK,
Arlington, Virginia

". . . . the commission report should be read and re-read by the President and every candidate for his office, every governor and every mayor of every city where bigotry and poverty exist.

"Strong national will and leadership are depressingly absent throughout the land. Although spending has increased for programs in the ghetto, they have been largely inadequate and ineffectual.

"Some may react with indifference or even antipathy to the shocking conclusions of the commission report. If so, they are turning their backs on a crisis that could destroy us.

"The cost of saving the nation will be high and require sacrifice.

"But measured against the wreckage of a shattered society, no price is too great to pay for survival."

THE LOS ANGELES TIMES
(from an editorial, March 3, 1968)

They Know I am Dead

In a sense, our nation is going mad, our leaders are becoming vulgar in trampling over each other to get to the funeral of Martin Luther King first. The crudity of this excessiveness, even in churches, three-ring circuses outdoing Barnum and Bailey in honor of this great man.

It's a mass demonstration of pent-up social guilt. We treated him so badly while he was here; some hated him so intensely. Let's be gaudy now, let's send the most expensive flowers, let's dash down to the funeral and release all this guilt. Let's show everybody that we would do everything to enhance the name of the late Martin Luther King.

And I can hear him saying now with his quiet humor, They know I am dead.

THE REVEREND EDWARD O. MILLER,
St. George's Episcopal Church, New York City

That Horrible Niche

It is matter-of-factly simple to settle into a comfortable academic or theological *niche,* never to discern what is ever *really* going on. That problem, which confronts all of us, is explicitly shattered with your presentation. Yet, we know what may happen: nothing. And I fear for humanity what greater brutality and inhumanity we can, as a nation (as a race?), inflict upon the black citizens of this country, our citizens, our country.

The White Niche

Too often I have seen theologically and ethically-oriented professors and students adjust themselves to that horrible *niche,* that white niche. Too often I have seen these same people discuss 'black power' as something that really doesn't amount to much, as something that really doesn't exist or really will not challenge all of us. And nobody seems to give a damn.

It is my thesis that the black man will have to liberate the white man from this racist nation of ours. These are hard words for me, a whitey, a 'cracker', to admit. But, truth is neither white nor black. And the truths I hear being expressed come from the lips of the black militants, in many ways more patriotic and human than white civil rights 'leaders'. It is hard for me to accept the role of racist— but is that not a label for all of us? But, these times are turbulent and perhaps only by the grace of God can we really do something significant.

The Kerner report, so terribly ignored by our president, is but such a small recognition of the depth and depravity of our societal ills. The black revolution is now, was yesterday, and will most certainly be tomorrow. Most certainly. But what can be done this summer?

The Lost Summer

I think that this summer is lost, perhaps most of next year. But what we can do is to begin to create the radical change necessary in our perverted society now and pray that it will effect change next year. I don't believe anything that the government has to offer can stem the frustration and futility that most blacks feel.

What is necessary is a radical re-ordering of national priorities, priorities that are of basic human concern and not just pablumated policies of suppression. Our government presently doesn't know how to deal with poverty at any effective level at all. A completely new and radical change will be necessary.

What Scares Me

And I am scared to death. What scares me is not the thought and reality of riots and death and bloodshed but the eventual development and deployment of a national racist police force. The camps in Georgia and Virginia, where riot 'control' is taught, are but a sign. The detention camps used by the government to detain Japanese-Americans during the second World War are being spruced up—another sign.

I am frightened. It is all too clear what this means—apartheid may not be too far off. This government seems intent upon stopping riots rather than *preventing* them. And the best way to prevent them is to insure the equality of the black man, to make sure that everyone recognizes that all black men are first class citizens and *never* anything less. To insure such equality necessitates that we change our country radically. It is always too little and always too late.

The events of the past few days do not bring cheerfulness and affirmation to me. I am more than shocked. "I am surprised that King lived that long" I heard someone say. And I am at a loss of life when I consider the sociological dimensions of that statement. There really should be no reason why the Kings and Browns and Carmichaels do not live to very old ages. Yet, that is the ideal?

Not Because I Am White

I don't want a white country and I don't want to live in the suburbs. I don't want the country clubs and the martinis, the front of the bus, the clean urinal. Just because I am white. To give me anything 'special' is to deny me of my humanity, of my own uniqueness. Black power is not a black problem but a white problem. There really aren't many black racists but there are too many white racists.

I hear Carmichael and I hear Brown and feel that what they say is the gospel. I hear Johnson and know that he lies. I want to free Huey Newton and imprison Beckwith, the murderer of King and the murderer of those children in the Birmingham church.

In Paul's Letter to the Hebrews, it is said that "The Lord is my helper, I will not be afraid; what can man do to me?" But I am afraid, afraid of what more man can do to man.

Kenneth C. Spence
San Francisco Theological Seminary
(from a letter to C. Eric Lincoln)

Let us pray for the day when mercy and truth are met together, righteousness and peace that kiss each other.

Lyndon B. Johnson

EPILOGUE

Weep for the Living Dead

Do not weep for Martin Luther King. He is dead. Weep for his widow and his children. His struggle was for the poor, the deprived. His hope was that every family could have a husband and a father, as he was a husband and a father; that every man could stand at the head of his family and dignify them with his dignity, and shelter them with his love. Weep for his widow and his children. In his death their deprivation is extreme.

Do not weep for Martin Luther King. He is dead. Weep for his people, the black Americans. He blessed them with his leadership. He stirred them with his courage. He warmed them with his love. He cheered them with his smile. He buoyed them up with his hope. He taught them with his wisdom. He sustained them with his faith. Leader, teacher, believer in the righteousness of God and the goodness of man—he is dead. Weep for his people. Who can fill his place?

Do not weep for Martin Luther King. He is dead. Weep for the dream that was his. He dared to dream that the hills and the valleys of privilege and disprivilege could be leveled through love and nonviolence; that our deserts of intimidation and oppression could be transformed into oases of freedom and justice. His dream was that there could be a generation of Americans who could join hands across the nothingness of color and rejoice in the beauty that is brotherhood. Weep for his dream. Of such dreams are the possibilities of our greatness. Of such dreams are the conditions of our survival. We are running out of dreams . . . and of dreamers.

Do not weep for Martin Luther King. He is dead. Weep for his faith and his religion. He was an exemplar of what Christianity claims to be about. He was an example of what Jesus taught and

C. Eric Lincoln, in *The Christian Century*, May 1, 1968. Copyright © 1968 by The Christian Century Foundation. Reprinted by permission.

lived. Like Socrates, he was a gadfly. Like Micah, he was a troubler of the consciences of men. Like Jesus, he paid the ultimate exaction. He gave his life for the privilege of loving mankind, though men have not learned to love each other. His sacrifice was for all men —Jew and gentile, black and white. Together, men could overcome the hatred and the perfidy which alienate them from God and from each other. Weep for the church he loved and honored. Weep for the Christians in the church who by their silence and inaction consented to his death.

Do not weep for Martin Luther King. He is dead. Weep for America. It is the country that he loved, that gave him birth. It is the country that marked him with a mark that is evil, a sign that is sinister, before he quit the womb. As he was marked, so are all Americans who are black. They are marked for torture and for death. Their torture is of isolation, of the anxiety of powerlessness and dependence. Theirs is the torture of always being pawns and never players in the game. They are marked for the slow death that is accommodation to poverty and the ghetto, or for the sudden death that is resistance to the system that defines them. It is the death that dogs the violent and the nonviolent. It is the death that cornered Martin Luther King. Weep, yes weep for America. Weep for our Jerusalem. It is she that killeth the prophets. It is she that consumes her young. It is America that fouls her nest with the feculence and the filth of the racism that is our sickness. Weep for your country . . . and for mine.

Do not weep for Martin Luther King. He is dead. We will honor him with a requiem. We will glorify him with an epitaph. We will hallow him with a sacred place in an integrated pantheon of heroic Americans. But . . .

When will we give substance to the dream he said he had?

Do not weep for Martin Luther King. He is dead; yet he lives. Weep for us, the living. Weep for ourselves, the dead.

C. ERIC LINCOLN